Stealing Lives

Stealing LIVES

The Globalization of Baseball and
the Tragic Story of Alexis Quiroz

Arturo J. Marcano Guevara
and David P. Fidler

INDIANA
University Press
Bloomington & Indianapolis

This book is a publication of
Indiana University Press
601 North Morton Street
Bloomington, Indiana 47404-3797 USA

http://iupress.indiana.edu

Telephone orders   800-842-6796
Fax orders   812-855-7931
Orders by e-mail   iuporder@indiana.edu

© 2002 by Arturo J. Marcano Guevara and David P. Fidler

The paper used in this publication meets the minimum
requirements of American National Standard for Information
Sciences—Permanence of Paper for Printed Library
Materials, ANSI Z39.48-1984.

MANUFACTURED IN THE UNITED STATES OF AMERICA

Library of Congress Cataloging-in-Publication Data

Marcano Guevara, Arturo J., date
    Stealing lives : the globalization of baseball and the tragic story of
Alexis Quiroz / Arturo J. Marcano Guevara, David P. Fidler.
        p. cm.
Includes bibliographical references (p.   ) and index.
    ISBN 0-253-34191-4 (cloth : alk. paper)
    1. Baseball players—Recruiting—Latin America. 2. Baseball
players—Abuse of—Latin America. 3. Quiroz, Alexis. 4. Major League
Baseball (Organization)—Corrupt practices. 5. Discrimination in
sports—United States. I. Fidler, David P., date II. Title.
    GV880.22 .M37   2002
    796.357'089'68—dc21
                                                    2002005638

1   2   3   4   5   07   06   05   04   03   02

To Alexis Quiroz Castellanos and his family

CONTENTS

The analysis in this book of the globalization of baseball and especially the tragic baseball story of Alexis Quiroz directly implicate many individuals who work for the Chicago Cubs and the Major League Baseball Commissioner's Office. Despite repeated invitations and requests from us for interviews, not a single person at either the Chicago Cubs or the MLB Commissioner's Office would grant us an interview. No one from the Chicago Cubs who is involved in Alexis Quiroz's story ever returned any of the multiple telephone calls we made or letters we sent to them. The only formal response we received from the people involved at the Commissioner's Office was a letter refusing to grant us interviews but claiming how proud the Commissioner's Office is of the way major league teams recruit baseball players in Latin America.

We also spoke or had contact with a number of Latin major league players who agreed that serious problems exist in the way major league teams recruit children and young men in Latin America, but who were unwilling to go on the record with their stories and concerns. We hope this book provides the foundation on which these and other Latin major league players can build an effort to convince major league teams to change the exploitative and abusive system they operate against children and young men in Latin America.

This book attempts to take account of events up to March 8, 2002.

ACKNOWLEDGMENTS

The creation of this book would not have been possible without the help and support of many individuals. Foremost, we thank Alexis (Alexi) Quiroz Castellanos and his family for sharing with us Alexi's tragic experience with the Chicago Cubs and Major League Baseball. Alexi's perseverance in pursuing justice for himself and other young Latin baseball players mistreated and exploited by Major League Baseball teams is one of the most remarkable features of the story we tell in this book. The love and support provided by Alexi's family during his ordeal is a testament to the strength and respect of a remarkable group of individuals. We have dedicated this book to Alexi and his family as a symbol of our appreciation of their struggle and of the trust they placed in us.

We also benefited greatly from the willingness of many other people to be interviewed by us for this book, including the following: Alfonso Carrasquel, Tony Fernández, Carlos Jaragüi, Eleazar Medina, Reinaldo Padilla, Angel Vargas, Juan Escalante, Gerdvan Liendo, Luis Peñalver, Ebenecer López Ruyol, Winston Acosta, William Gutierrez, and a number of people who wished to remain anonymous.

We inflicted earlier drafts of this book on colleagues, friends, and spouses, who proved willing to help us improve the manuscript. We thank the following for their labors in this regard: Fred Cate, Hannah Buxbaum, Don Gjerdingen, Jack Bobo, Mary Ann Torres, Shari L. Rogge-Fidler, Sam Regalado, Roberto González Echevarría, Sam Hill, William Gutierrez, Alba Guevara, William Hanna, and John Morris. John Scanlan, Ken Dau-Schmidt, and Dan Conkle provided us assistance with issues relating to immigration law, sports law, worker's compensation law, and ethical issues involving the research. We also thank Steve Fainaru for the interest he took in our research and the issues it raises. Debbie Eads and Marjorie Young provided vital assistance in producing the manuscript as well as willing ears to listen to the various twists and turns of this project's development. We hope the final product does justice to the time and attention these people gave to us and the project.

A.J.M.G.
Toronto, Canada

D.P.F.
Bloomington, Indiana

Stealing Lives

PART I

Building the Global Ballpark

THE "GOLDEN AGE" OF LATIN AMERICAN TALENT IN MAJOR LEAGUE BASEBALL

SAMMY SOSA. PEDRO MARTÍNEZ. BERNIE WILLIAMS. CARLOS DELGADO. OMAR VIZQUEL. ANDRÉS GALARRAGA. For fans of Major League Baseball (MLB), these names are household names in the year 2002. While Latin Americans* have played in the major leagues for decades, their presence and impact on the United States's "national pastime" have grown in recent years. The prominence of Major League Baseball stars who hail from countries in Latin America is at an all-time high.

As with so much in baseball, the statistics speak for themselves. On opening day in the 2002 season, 26.1 percent of major league players were born outside the United States.[1] (For the breakdown of the foreign countries represented on MLB rosters on opening day of the 2002 season, see Table 1.1.) Players from Latin American countries represented 88 percent of the total number of foreign-born players on major league rosters at the start of the 2002 season.[2] Of the Latin American players, 77 percent came from three countries: the Dominican Republic (74), Puerto Rico (38), and Venezuela (38); and 57 percent came from the Dominican Republic and Venezuela, which are the hotbeds of Latin baseball talent today.

The statistics also demonstrate that foreign players make up a significant chunk of minor league rosters. In June 2000, Peter Gammons of ESPN noted that "international development has become nearly as important as the draft, with more than 40 percent of minor league players now being foreign-born."[3] In June 2001, Steve Fainaru of the *Washington Post* reported that "[o]f 6,916 players under contract to major and minor league teams, 44 percent come

---

*In this book, "Latin America" includes Mexico and countries in the Caribbean, Central America, and South America.

Table 1.1.   Foreign-Born Players on Major League Rosters at the
Start of the 2002 MLB Season

Foreign Country (*Latin American country)	Number of Players on Major League Rosters	Percentage (approx.) of Total Number of Foreign Players on MLB Rosters
Aruba*	2	1%
Australia	3	1%
Canada	10	5%
Colombia*	3	1%
Cuba*	11	5%
Dominican Republic*	74	33%
Japan	11	5%
Korea	2	1%
Mexico*	18	8%
Netherlands Antilles*	2	1%
Nicaragua*	2	1%
Panama*	7	3%
Puerto Rico*	38	17%
Venezuela*	38	17%
U.S. Virgin Islands*	1	0%
TOTALS	222	100%

Source: "Foreign-Born Players on Rise," USA Today, Apr. 4, 2002, sec. C, p. 4.

from outside the United States."[4] At the beginning of the 2002 season, 49.6 percent (2,865) of players signed to minor league contracts were born outside the United States.[5]

The evidence demonstrates that Latin Americans dominate the foreign-born contingent in the minor leagues. Major League Baseball teams target their most extensive scouting and minor league development efforts in Latin America, as indicated by the numbers of major league players that come from the Dominican Republic, Puerto Rico, and Venezuela. All thirty major league teams operate minor league training facilities and Summer League minor league teams in the Dominican Republic, and twenty-eight major league teams do the same in Venezuela.[6] Each year, major league teams sign, train, and evaluate hundreds of young players from Latin America in their facilities in the Dominican Republic and Venezuela. At the beginning of the 2002 baseball season, 80 percent (2,274) of all foreign-born players signed to minor league contracts came from the Dominican Republic and Venezuela,[7] an average of 75.8 Dominican and Venezuelan minor league players per major league team. The vast majority of the Dominicans and Venezuelans under minor league contracts play minor league ball in the Dominican Republic and Venezuela because of the

Table 1.2. Foreign-Born Players under Minor League Contracts at the Start of the 2002 MLB Season

Foreign Country	Number of Players under Minor League Contracts	Percentage (approx.) of Total Number of Foreign Players Under Minor League Contracts
Dominican Republic	1,536	54%
Mexico	91	3%
Puerto Rico	123	4%
Venezuela	738	26%
Other countries	377	13%

Source: "Foreign-Born Players on Rise," USA Today, Apr. 4, 2002, sec. C, p. 4.

limited number of immigration visas available to each major league team to bring foreign players to the United States to play during the major and minor league seasons. Although major league teams evaluate potential minor league talent in such countries as Australia and Japan, the scale of the recruiting and training effort in Latin America dwarfs major league scouting efforts in other regions of the world (see Table 1.2).

Major League Baseball recognized the importance of the Latin contribution to its success in March 2000 and 2001 when it sponsored successive "Months of the Americas."[8] A key feature of these celebrations of Latin participation in the major leagues was the staging of exhibition games in the Dominican Republic, Venezuela, Puerto Rico, and Mexico. Baseball Festivals—events that allow fans to bat, pitch, run bases, and get their own baseball cards made—were also held in conjunction with the exhibition games in the Dominican Republic, Venezuela, Mexico, and Puerto Rico.[9]

Leading Latin major league stars gushed about what was taking place in the "Months of the Americas." The Dominican pitching phenom Pedro Martínez said, "It fills me with joy for people in my country to see Ramón [Martínez—Pedro's brother] and me as well as our whole Red Sox team play in the Dominican."[10] The Venezuelan star Andrés Galarraga commented, "I am very proud that Major League Baseball has decided to play games in my homeland of Venezuela. . . . The impact of these major league games will be very profound for the youth of Venezuela[,] and it will create an example that if you work hard you will achieve results."[11] Major League Baseball Commissioner Bud Selig tipped his hat to the countries of Latin America hosting the MLB exhibition games by saying, "This is an effort by Major League Baseball to salute and acknowledge a region of the world that has given so much to the game of baseball. We are honored to be hosted by these countries."[12]

The "Months of the Americas" were about more than celebrating the Latin contribution to baseball. Major League Baseball saw this effort in Latin America as a central part of its strategy to globalize the game of baseball.[13] Major League Baseball followed the March 2000 "Month of the Americas" with the highly publicized start-of-the-season series between the Chicago Cubs and New York Mets played in Tokyo, Japan, on March 29–30, 2000. The Tokyo series was the second time the major leagues started a season with a game outside Canada or the United States. The major leagues opened the 1999 regular season with a game between the Colorado Rockies and San Diego Padres in Monterrey, Mexico, and in 2001, the Toronto Blue Jays and Texas Rangers opened their regular seasons with a game in San Juan, Puerto Rico.[14] These opening-day games in countries outside Canada and the United States represented high-profile MLB tactics in its strategy to make baseball a global game.

Chapter 2 explores in more detail Major League Baseball's strategy to globalize the game of baseball. Part of this globalization strategy involves reaching out to areas of the world that are the "emerging markets" for MLB products—countries in which there has been very little, if any, professional or amateur baseball. Another, more important, aspect of Major League Baseball's globalization effort involves penetrating more deeply countries with long baseball traditions, especially countries in Latin America and Asia. Baseball's interest in Latin America and Asia involves the desire for both labor (baseball players) and consumers (fans). By tapping into traditional foreign baseball markets and new, virtually untapped countries, Major League Baseball hopes to build a global ballpark for its business in which players and fans from all over the world can experience and enjoy the finest professional baseball played on the planet.

While Major League Baseball is reaching beyond Latin America in building its global ballpark, the statistics cited earlier on the number of Latin Americans in the major and minor leagues demonstrate that Latin America plays an unrivaled role in the major leagues' global ballpark. Many baseball fans see the success of Latin stars such as Pedro Martínez and Sammy Sosa without realizing that these classic rags-to-riches stories also tell a tale of the structural role Latin America plays in the major leagues' global ballpark.

The individual Latin stars and the growing prominence of the Latin presence in the major leagues lead some experts to argue that Latin America has entered a "Golden Age" as a source of baseball talent.[15] As Evan Grant of the *Dallas Morning News* put it, "Latin stars are being recognized as never before, and the future looks just as bright moving into baseball's third century."[16]

This vision of the "Golden Age" contrasts with the history of discrimination and racism Latin players faced in making their way in the major leagues, or "The Show," during the twentieth century.[17] The dawning of *La Era de Oro* must seem sweet to the Latin old-timers who struggled to make Latin players part of the major leagues and their future globalization plans. Such sentiment is present in the confidence expressed by some former Latin players about the Latin role in the major leagues. "I've said for a long time," observed Dominican Tony Peña, a fifteen-year major league veteran,[18] "that Latins are going to control the game. Now we are."[19] Former Montreal Expos' manager Felipe Alou, a seventeen-year major league veteran[20] and one of the first Dominicans to play in the majors, expressed the same feeling: "I think we have taken over the game."[21]

Ask Alexis (Alexi) Quiroz, whose story forms Part II of this book, whether Latins have "taken over the game," and he will burst out laughing. Like baseball-loving boys all over the American hemisphere, Alexi Quiroz dreamed of being a major league ballplayer. His heroes were baseball players. He built his life around baseball. He wanted to become a baseball hero for future generations of baseball-loving boys in his native Venezuela. Such dreams for a Venezuelan boy were not ridiculous when Alexi Quiroz began his ill-fated journey into the global ballpark in 1995. If his dreams had come true, Alexi Quiroz would have become part of the emerging "Golden Age" of Latin American baseball players in *las Grandes Ligas*, the big leagues.

As the reader will see, Alexi has a different perspective on the Latin experience with Major League Baseball. But before we tell Alexi's story, the next two chapters look more closely and critically at the structure and dynamics of the globalization of baseball. Central to this analysis is the exploration of how major league teams recruit baseball talent in Latin America. It is here, when major league teams aggressively hunt for Latin children, that we see who controls whom in *La Era de Oro*. Alexi Quiroz would agree with Shakespeare, who long ago observed that "all that glisters is not gold."[22]

CHAPTER TWO

THE GLOBALIZATION OF
BASEBALL

Our National Pastime is now the world's.

—GENE BUDIG, PRESIDENT OF THE AMERICAN LEAGUE[1]

Globalizing a National Pastime

THE UNITED STATES has long claimed baseball as its national pastime. Once upon a time, baseball ruled as the king of U.S. amateur and professional sports. Baseball defined professional sports in the United States and shaped how popular culture related to sports in general. Baseball was once the maker of heroes and dreams of glory for millions of adolescent American boys. Within the male contingent of certain generations in the United States, the names of Ruth, Gehrig, DiMaggio, Robinson, Musial, Mays, and Mantle are still discussed in reverential tones that must echo how the ancient Greeks spoke of the Olympian gods. "Where have you gone, Joe DiMaggio? A nation turns its lonely eyes to you," sang Simon and Garfunkel.

Today, Major League Baseball (MLB) is not satisfied with one nation turning its eyes toward baseball superstars. In the 1990s, Major League Baseball aggressively turned its attention to globalizing the game it oversees. In this global strategy, Major League Baseball followed in the footsteps of the National Basketball Association (NBA), which under Commissioner David Stern, and with the powerful presence of Michael Jordan, turned the NBA into a global brand name.[2] Some believed that baseball had entered the globalization game late because it lacked the foresight of the NBA or even the National Football League (NFL), which attempted in the 1980s and 1990s to establish a global presence, especially in Europe.

Historically speaking, Major League Baseball was not a laggard in international outreach. The major leagues had franchises in a foreign country, Canada, long before the NBA established teams in Toronto and Vancouver or the NFL had its European league. Further, baseball had been recruiting talent from other countries, principally in Latin America, for most of the twentieth century. By comparison, serious NBA recruiting in foreign countries only began in the 1990s. Baseball had also established itself in the popular cultures of many Latin American and Asian nations decades before Michael Jordan laced up a pair of sneakers. Baseball was global long before the NBA and NFL discovered globalization. What was missing was a conscious strategy by Major League Baseball to exploit and expand the global aspect of baseball. Such a globalization strategy emerged in the 1990s and represents one of the most important features of Major League Baseball's activities in the last decade.

Understanding the "globalization of baseball" requires seeing Major League Baseball as a business. The moniker "national pastime" obscures the degree to which baseball has from its earliest days been a business designed to make money. The National League had its origins in the desire of influential baseball men to organize professional baseball around business principles. Influential figures such as William Hulbert, Harry Wright, and Albert Spalding succeeded in turning baseball from a pastime into big business. Part of this transformation meant that "[t]he managing end of the game was to be separate and distinct from the playing end, thus allowing the players to concentrate on performance and leave business affairs and promotion to the owners."[3] Spalding argued that taking ballplayers out of the management of the game merely reflected:

> [T]he irrepressible conflict between Labor and Capital asserting itself
> under a new guise. . . . Like every other form of business enterprise,
> Base Ball [sic] depends for results on two interdependent divisions, the
> one to have absolute control and direction of the system, and the other
> to engage—always under the executive branch—the actual work of
> production.[4]

These men were clearly thinking about baseball as a business rather than just a pastime.

The American League also came to life through savvy business strategies crafted by Byron Bancroft (Ban) Johnson. Johnson transformed a struggling minor league circuit called the Western League into the American League—a force that eventually challenged the professional baseball monopoly of the National League.[5] Johnson hired talent away from the National League by offering higher salaries and advertised the American League's family-friendly atmosphere in the ballpark.[6] The American League brought competition to professional baseball for both baseball consumers—the fans—and baseball talent. The business success of Johnson's American League forced the once-dominant National League to negotiate an agreement with the challenger in 1902 that would prove to be the foundation for Major League Baseball.[7]

The business-savvy founders of the major leagues would probably be astonished at the growth of the business of baseball during the twentieth century.[8] Baseball revenues and expenses have reached huge amounts. In 2001, major league teams had aggregate revenues of $3.6 billion and aggregate expenses of $3.7 billion.[9] This growth in the business of baseball has not, however, deepened baseball's traditional role as the national pastime of the United States. In fact, whether baseball remains the national pastime in the United States is now a serious topic of discussion. The mere existence of the debate is evidence enough that baseball has fallen from its regal and hegemonic influence into grubby commercial competition among professional sports for consumers' time and money.

The growth in the business of baseball also does not mean that the business is entirely healthy. According to Commissioner Selig, the aggregate "loss for all thirty clubs in 2001 will be approximately $519 million" and "total industry debt is currently over $3 billion."[10] Congressional hearings in November 2000 and December 2001 focused on what many baseball experts perceive as one of the most pernicious features of baseball economics: revenue disparities between so-called "big market" teams, such as the New York Yankees, and "small market" teams, such as the Montreal Expos. The "revenue gap" between the highest-revenue team and lowest-revenue team grew from $74 million in 1995 to $164 million in 1999[11] to $208 million in 2001.[12] As U.S. Senator Mike DeWine put it in November 2000, "There is a direct relationship between the level of revenue teams bring in and their ability to compete on the field. As revenue disparity increases, competition decreases. High revenue teams can simply outspend the others."[13] The revenue gap has produced competitive imbalance in the major leagues, with big market teams winning pennants and World Series and small market teams struggling to field competitive teams. Commissioner Selig argued in December 2001 that "[o]nly teams that are able and willing to spend enormous sums on player salaries have any chance to win the World Series."[14] The Commissioner's Office and independent baseball experts believe this competitive imbalance threatens the game's future. Commissioner Selig issued a dire warning in November 2000: "If Baseball does not correct the competitive balance problem, the game's current renaissance could be destroyed."[15]

One of the main economic problems behind the revenue gap involves disparities between gate and local broadcasting revenues generated by big and small market teams. According to Major League Baseball, in 2001, the New York Yankees had gate and local broadcasting revenues of $154.75 million compared to $12.94 million for the Montreal Expos.[16] Although the major leagues adopted a local revenue sharing plan in 1996, under which approximately $155 million of local revenue was transferred from big market to small market teams in 2000,[17] this effort to bring equilibrium to local revenue disparities failed to affect the competitive imbalance Major League Baseball suffers today.[18]

The continued escalation of players' salaries through salary arbitration and free agency (the average salary for a major league player is now more than $2 million)[19] underscores the nightmare that the revenue gap has produced in the major leagues. Each new off-season brings more astonishing contracts for free agent superstars. In 2001, Alex Rodríguez's $252 million, ten-year contract with the Texas Rangers[20] and Derek Jeter's $189 million, ten-year deal with the New York Yankees[21] provided the latest eye-popping free agent signings, and more are anticipated before the 2002 season begins. The market price for the best baseball players has simply left small market teams unable to compete in the free agent contest.

In the December 2001 congressional hearings, Commissioner Selig argued that Major League Baseball's economic problems need multiple answers, including revenue sharing, contraction of the number of teams, and restraint on players' salaries.[22] While revenue sharing already occurs, the potential answers of contraction and salary restraint are very controversial. Major League Baseball's announced plan to eliminate two teams, widely believed to be the Montreal Expos and the Minnesota Twins, before the 2002 season provoked great outcry and congressional bills that would strip baseball of its antitrust exemption.[23] Representative John Conyers of Michigan argued that one reason Congress should take away baseball's antitrust exemption was "its shoddy treatment of the Minnesota Twins and its fans" in the contraction proposal.[24] Any restraints on players' salaries remain anathema to the Major League Baseball Players Association, and the "salary cap" issue looms as one of the most contentious issues of the next round of collective bargaining between the teams and the players' union.[25]

Globalizing the game of baseball is not a panacea for the major leagues' current economic travails. Yet economics drives the plans for globalization of baseball that the major leagues pursued in the 1990s. Like any business, major league teams need to increase revenues and control costs in order to make profits. These needs translate into finding new consumer markets to boost revenues and cheaper sources of labor to control costs. For the major leagues, accessing new consumer markets overseas and continuing to have cheap sources of foreign labor are critical strategies in globalizing baseball.

The chief executive officer of any multinational enterprise knows exactly what Major League Baseball is trying to do in this era of globalization. Faced with maturing or stagnating demand in home markets, companies often seek revenue increases by selling more of their products in new foreign markets. Foreign competition at home and abroad stimulates companies to reduce production costs by relocating manufacturing facilities to countries that have lower labor costs. Companies that pursue these revenue-boosting and cost-controlling strategies globalize their activities and become integrated into global markets for goods and services.

Creating and Tapping New Consumer Markets

Major League Baseball's strategy for increasing revenue by creating and tapping new consumer markets in foreign countries involves a number of different activities, namely (1) playing more major league games in foreign countries; (2) global game development; (3) international broadcasting of major league games; and (4) global sales of MLB-licensed merchandise. Each of these activities is briefly described in the following paragraphs.

PLAYING MAJOR LEAGUE GAMES IN FOREIGN COUNTRIES

In 1999, the major leagues sponsored exhibition games in Cuba. In 2000, exhibition games were played in the Dominican Republic and Venezuela. In 2001, exhibition games took place in Puerto Rico and Mexico. Major League Baseball held opening-day games in Mexico (1999), Japan (2000), and Puerto Rico (2001). Clearly, MLB believes that one way to market its product is to provide potential foreign consumers with a taste of the game.

Although some people believe major league franchises can be established in Mexico or Japan, the strategic rationale for holding major league games on foreign soil was not to test the waters for new foreign franchises. Baseball's economics do not point in this direction. Hall of Fame sportswriter Leonard Koppett argued:

> Today, MLB is already overextended with too many teams. MLB currently has thirty teams, which is too many. Fans cannot really follow thirty teams. So many MLB teams fragment the fan market, and each team gets a smaller level of media attention and fan interest. To believe that MLB could add more franchises in Tokyo, Paris, or Mexico City simply is not realistic, because it would badly overextend the money-making processes of the game of baseball.[26]

Events at the end of the 2001 baseball season suggest that Koppett's analysis is correct. Commissioner Selig announced MLB's intention to eliminate two teams through contraction, including potentially the foreign franchise of the Montreal Expos.

The business strategy behind playing major league exhibition and opening-day games in foreign countries is to build sufficient interest in Major League Baseball that baseball fans in those foreign countries will purchase more MLB products delivered through international broadcasting of major league games and licensed major league merchandise. The overseas games are marketing efforts to get foreign consumers to buy the products that will increase Major League Baseball's revenues.[27]

This commercialization of the game formed part of the controversy behind the Cubs-Mets season-opening series in Tokyo in March 2000. Baseball traditionalists mumbled disapproving comments about the national pastime opening its season in Japan, perhaps fearing what the search for increased revenues will do to age-old traditions. Baseball internationalists hailed the Tokyo series as the beginning of a new age for Major League Baseball, a global era for a global game.

Fueling the dueling commentators was the opinion of one of baseball's towering figures, Mark McGwire. The Japanese wanted to see the then home-run king play in Tokyo against the Mets. But McGwire took the lead among St. Louis Cardinal players in rejecting the offer to play their opening series in Japan. In March 2000, McGwire said:

> What it comes down to is someone in Japan paid Major League Baseball a lot of money. . . . I know Major League Baseball wants to do more internationally, but there's no purpose in it. I don't agree with it. . . . Our game is too international as it is.[28]

Baseball traditionalists also took note of the fact that the major leagues allowed corporate advertisers to "rent" space on the players' uniforms during the Tokyo series.

The commercialization of foreign games also got under the skin of Pedro Martínez in connection with an exhibition game the Boston Red Sox played in the Dominican Republic in 2000. We quoted in chapter 1 Martínez's enthusiasm for playing the exhibition game in his native Dominican Republic, but his perspective changed when he saw what was going on in the stands:

> I was very upset when I heard a seat [at the exhibition game] was $35 U.S. We are a poor country. Not all of us are Pedro Martinez. . . . I don't agree at all, not at all with the prices they have. I think it's extremely abusive for our community. I'm not surprised those seats were empty.[29]

The Tokyo series and the Dominican exhibition game are also interesting to compare when considering Major League Baseball's strategic interest in playing games outside the United States and Canada. As Pedro Martínez noted, the Dominican Republic is a poor country, one of the poorest countries in the world. As such, it does not hold much promise for Major League Baseball's desire to raise revenues in foreign markets.

On the other hand, Japan is a very rich country, with millions of baseball fans with disposable income. These are the kind of foreign consumers Major League Baseball needs to tap in order to boost revenue growth. Affluent people can afford to watch baseball games live or via broadcasts and buy MLB-licensed products. These are also the kind of consumers companies that advertise at stadiums and during broadcasts want to reach, creating a synergy between Major League Baseball's revenue needs and those of willing advertisers.

GLOBAL GAME DEVELOPMENT

The traditional marketing strategy of finding consumers with disposable income also drives Major League Baseball's efforts at global game development. Major League Baseball sponsors a variety of programs designed to develop interest in baseball in other countries. These programs are strategically aimed at children in order to increase the likelihood that they will become lifelong consumers of MLB products. Major League Baseball apparently subscribes to Leonard Koppett's views on sports marketing: "Sports consumers are made during childhood. Very few people become fascinated by sports as adults. You have to get them when they are young."[30] Baseball's efforts at global game development center on its Envoy program; Pitch, Hit, and Run competitions; and Baseball Festivals.

Major League Baseball's Envoy program sends amateur baseball coaches overseas to teach baseball fundamentals to foreign players. The Envoy program began in 1991 when two coaches visited the Netherlands, and it "has expanded to include 40 coaches traveling to 29 countries . . . to spread the gospel of baseball."[31]

Major League Baseball's Pitch, Hit, and Run (PHR) competitions overseas seek "to teach boys and girls of ages 9 to 12 the fundamentals of baseball. The program is designed to put balls and bats into the hands of thousands of school kids who have never experienced the thrill of playing baseball or tee-ball."[32] The PHR program began in 1994 in Australia but has now expanded into "the gym class curriculum in more than 2,000 primary schools in England, Germany, South Africa, and Australia" and reaches 500,000 children annually.[33] Major League Baseball has enlisted the marketing assistance of other globalized companies in promoting PHR. For example, Nike sponsored PHR competitions in Japan, Korea, Taiwan, and Australia.[34]

Major League Baseball also began the Play Ball! program in England to give children ages 9–12 "their first taste of organized baseball" through the establishment and league competitions among forty teams.[35] The Play Ball! program gives these English children "a chance to learn not only about the game of baseball but also the Major Leagues too."[36]

One curious feature of the PHR and Play Ball! programs is that they take place (except for South Africa) in developed countries. Why not have PHR competitions and Play Ball! in the Dominican Republic or Venezuela, where baseball is the king of sports? If the objective is to put a baseball into the hands of a child who has never held one, then targeting Germany and England is better than Venezuela and the Dominican Republic. But the real objective of these programs is not to develop the German or English Sammy Sosa but to create a consumer market for MLB products among children in affluent countries.

Major League Baseball also sponsors Baseball Festivals in various countries. According to Major League Baseball, "[b]aseball festivals are interactive fan events designed . . . to introduce baseball to new audiences. The festivals recreate the sights, sounds and smells of the game—visitors are able to take their turn at bat, clock their pitching speed, run the bases, or have their own baseball cards made."[37] In 1997, Major League Baseball held Baseball Festivals in England, Germany, Taiwan, Australia, and Japan, with attendance of more than 500,000. In 1998, Baseball Festivals were scheduled for Venezuela, England, Germany, and Taiwan and attracted 700,000 participants. In 1999, the major leagues scheduled Baseball Festivals for Venezuela, Mexico, Puerto Rico, Canada, England, Germany, and Australia. A miniature version of the Baseball Festival, called the MLB Road Show, traveled in the summer of 1999 through England, the Netherlands, and Australia.[38] Baseball Festivals were also held in conjunction with the exhibition games played in March 2000 in the Dominican Republic and Venezuela and in March 2001 in Mexico and Puerto Rico.

Again, Major League Baseball held the majority of these Baseball Festivals in developed countries. The motivation, again, is not to develop shortstops from London. Baseball Festivals and the MLB Road Show track traditional marketing strategies of targeting consumers with disposable income. Children in affluent countries hooked on baseball through global game development efforts will be more likely to consume MLB products through international broadcast of major league games and sales of MLB-licensed merchandise, thus offering the major leagues better prospects for boosting their global revenue.

INTERNATIONAL BROADCASTING OF MAJOR LEAGUE BASEBALL GAMES

In 2000, Major League Baseball listed 215 countries and territories in which major league games were broadcast, by either American-based media companies, such as ESPN, or foreign-media enterprises.[39] Major League Baseball overhypes its world broadcasting because many countries listed, including such baseball havens as Bangladesh, Eritrea, Mongolia, and Myanmar, are simply served by ESPN, most likely only at four- and five-star international hotels catering to Western business executives. Even discounting this puffery, the importance and growth of world broadcasting to Major League Baseball are clear. Broadcasters willing to pay Major League Baseball for rights to broadcast games internationally increase Major League Baseball's revenue stream.

Major League Baseball harnesses in its global strategies the synergy developing between the presence of foreign baseball players in the major leagues and foreign baseball consumers. It is easier to sell major league broadcasting rights in Japan when Ichiro Suzuki, Hideki Irabu, Hideo Nomo, and other Japanese players provide a powerful connection between Japanese baseball fans and the major leagues. Tim Brosnan, MLB's Senior Vice President for Domestic and International Properties, said that Major League Baseball "now wants to exploit the game's popularity in Asia and Latin America by showcasing foreign-born players like Dodger pitchers Hideo Nomo of Japan and Chan Ho Park of Korea."[40]

During the 1997 season, for example, each game pitched by South Korean Chan Ho Park for the Los Angeles Dodgers was broadcast live in South Korea.[41] In 1998, Korean baseball fans could tune in to more than 100 games, including live telecasts of Park's games, the All-Star Game, and the World Series.[42] Japanese interest in the success of Ichiro Suzuki of the Seattle Mariners in 2001 illustrates powerfully the connection between MLB international broadcasting and foreign players in the major leagues.[43] This interest can be seen in the hundreds of thousands of All-Star ballots cast in Japan for Suzuki, helping him receive the most votes of any player in balloting for the 2001 All-Star Game.[44] The same synergy holds true for Major League Baseball broadcasts in Latin America.

Some of the push for world broadcasting of Major League Baseball arises from perceptions that the U.S. domestic market for baseball broadcasts has matured, and that broadcasting revenue growth has to be sought overseas. Major League Baseball, as well as the NBA and NFL, are following in the footsteps of manufacturing and service industries in developing export strategies as revenues from domestic markets reach a plateau. Some stagnation in the U.S. domestic baseball market has been caused by Major League Baseball's self-inflicted wounds. Repeated labor controversies, such as the players' strike of 1994, have soured fans on the nation's pastime. Baseball consumers in other countries, particularly in Asia and Latin America, are easier targets than jaded Americans.

GLOBAL SALES OF LICENSED MERCHANDISE

Following in the footsteps of the NBA, Major League Baseball is pursuing a global strategy of selling its licensed merchandise overseas. Major League Baseball licenses to domestic and foreign enterprises the right to use insignias of Major League Baseball and major league teams. These enterprises include baseball card companies, clothing manufacturers, electronic game makers, and others, and Major League Baseball earns big money from such licensing agreements.[45] Major League Baseball Properties (MLBP) was established in 1987 to handle the growing licensing business. In 1998, MLBP signed agreements with federations, teams, clubs, scouts, companies, and stores in 109 different countries for the sale of licensed MLB merchandise.[46] In 2000, Major League Baseball itself had merchandise distribution outlets in nineteen countries outside the United States and Canada.[47] Retail sales of licensed MLB products are projected to grow 200 percent in the next five years under this new global marketing strategy.[48]

The global broadcasting and global licensing strategies are, of course, intertwined. Broadcasting of major league games in foreign countries is designed to increase the likelihood that fans in those countries will purchase MLB merchandise. Through broadcasting and merchandise sales, Major League Baseball deepens its penetration of the sports culture of the foreign countries. In countries such as Japan or Venezuela, where baseball is already part of the respective national cultures, Major League Baseball exploits emerging markets for baseball consumers.

Of course, some of these emerging markets are more lucrative than others. Even though the Dominican Republic has sent more players to the major leagues than Japan has, Japan is more appealing as a market for MLB products because it has a developed, modern economy that produces consumers with disposable income. Despite Venezuela's being a hotbed of baseball talent, Major League Baseball has foreign offices devoted to market development not in Caracas but in London, Sydney, and Toronto[49]—all major cities in rich countries that produce little baseball talent.

Development of Global Markets for Baseball Talent

While accessing "emerging markets" overseas for new consumers of Major League Baseball's products constitutes a fundamental part of the globalization of baseball, equally important is Major League Baseball's efforts to develop global markets for baseball talent. The international search for baseball talent by North American clubs was, in fact, the first step the major leagues took toward the globalization of the sport in the twentieth century. The key area of talent development historically was, and is still today, Latin America, but Major League Baseball has become more serious and organized about how talent from Asia joins major league teams. The steady growth in Major League Baseball's interest in foreign baseball talent can be analyzed by exploring four themes that arise in looking at this aspect of the globalization of baseball: (1) the synergy created by having foreign players in the major leagues and Major League Baseball's efforts to market international broadcast rights and licensed merchandise; (2) the perceived decline in North American baseball talent; (3) the expansion of the number of major league teams in the 1990s; and (4) the cheapness of Latin American baseball players.

SYNERGY BETWEEN FOREIGN PLAYERS ON MAJOR LEAGUE TEAMS AND GLOBAL MARKETING OF MAJOR LEAGUE BASEBALL PRODUCTS

This chapter noted earlier that the presence of foreign players on major league teams helps Major League Baseball market international broadcasts of major league games and global sales of MLB licensed merchandise. Baseball fans in foreign nations, such as Japan and Korea, want to see their native sons play in the big leagues in North America via television. Such fans are also much more likely to buy MLB-licensed merchandise as they follow the wins and losses of the teams on which their favorite national stars play. Major League Baseball can also tap into and deepen such foreign fan interest by playing exhibition and regular season games in foreign countries. Important to the success of these global marketing stratagems is the presence on major league teams of talented foreign baseball players who help the teams win, which is another reason why Major League Baseball has moved aggressively to have foreign stars play in The Show.

The synergy is, however, potentially more profitable in affluent countries rather than in developing countries, which is why the presence of Japanese and Korean baseball players on major league teams may be more lucrative to Major League Baseball's globalization strategy than the presence of Latin players. Chapter 3 explores in more detail how Major League Baseball has arranged to access talent in Japan and Korea, which contrasts dramatically with the approach Major League Baseball teams take in Latin America.

THE PERCEIVED DECLINE IN NORTH AMERICAN BASEBALL TALENT

Baseball experts perceive that Major League Baseball teams hunt so competitively in Latin America not only because Latin players are good, but also because the quality of American baseball talent is declining. Dick Williams, a scout for the New York Yankees, argued that "[t]he American talent has diminished."[50] While American Little Leagues continue to introduce large numbers of American children to baseball, some experts feel that the passion for the game has been lost in the United States. Sports agent Joe Kehoskie noted that, compared to youngsters in Latin America, "the American kids are wealthier, they've got a lot of opportunities, a lot of choices of what to do with their time."[51] Baseball expert G. Edward White put the new scenario this way:

> As fewer young Americans play baseball because of competition from
> other sports, and fewer American families are financially able to attend
> games regularly, the time-honored customs of parents playing catch
> with their children or taking them to the park to watch their heroes
> may give way to other rituals, such as fathers or mothers coaching
> youth soccer for their sons and daughters.[52]

The perceived decline in North American talent has led baseball experts and officials to compare the situation in the United States with baseball-crazy Latin American countries. Joe McIlvaine, general manager of the New York Mets, observed:

> You drive around and look at local ballfields in this country and you'll
> find they are empty. . . . That's what I love about going to Latin American
> countries, places like the Dominican Republic. It's like going back
> in time, the way it was here in the 1940s, '50s, and '60s. You see kids
> playing everywhere, with taped-up balls, taped-up bats, whatever

they've got to do to play. That's why the search for talent is expanding world-wide.[53]

These perspectives suggest how tenuous baseball's claim to be the "national pastime" has become in the United States.

This title more appropriately applies to countries such as the Dominican Republic and Venezuela, where baseball dominates sports. "In the Dominican Republic," Thomas Fitzgerald observed, "baseball is like malaria. It's in the blood and hard to purge."[54] This analogy between baseball and malaria is disturbing and offensive because it likens the Dominican love for baseball to a parasitic disease, but Fitzgerald's attempt to communicate the importance of baseball in Dominican life is nevertheless telling.

In Venezuela, no sport, not even soccer, rivals the popularity of baseball. The fanatical devotion of Venezuelans to baseball has sometimes proved politically useful for Venezuelan politicians, who have passed unpopular laws during the height of the Venezuelan professional season because they believed (usually correctly) that few people would notice. In 1995, Rafael Caldera won election to the presidency in Venezuela and addressed the nation on television in the wake of his victory. But Caldera had the political sense to cut his speech short so as not to interfere with a game between Caracas and Magallanes, two bitter Venezuelan baseball rivals.

The current Venezuelan president, Hugo Chávez, is himself a baseball fanatic, and he uses baseball both in his domestic politicking and in his foreign affairs. He and Fidel Castro once squared off as managers of their respective national teams in an exhibition game.[55] Chávez even took the mound to pitch in this game![56]

The Dominican Republic and Venezuela represent the richest veins in efforts to mine foreign baseball talent for Major League Baseball today, as the statistics recorded in chapter 1 demonstrate. Pre-Castro Cuba used to be the main source of foreign baseball players for the major leagues,[57] but the U.S. trade and business embargo on Cuba and Castro's Marxist policies ended the Cuban connection. Many people in the major leagues would like Cuba to again become a major supplier of quality baseball talent. In confronting the perceived dearth of North American talent, major league teams have overwhelmingly focused their hunt for labor in Latin America. Occasional signings of Asian players, such as Hideo Nomo and Ichiro Suzuki, make headlines, but the real action has been and continues to be centered on Latin America.

THE EXPANSION OF THE NUMBER OF MAJOR LEAGUE TEAMS

The realization among baseball scouts that the North American talent pool was shrinking occurred at the same time Major League Baseball undertook a significant expansion effort. In the 1990s, the major leagues added four new

big league teams—the Florida Marlins, Tampa Bay Devil Rays, Arizona Diamondbacks, and Colorado Rockies. The addition of these new teams expanded
not only the demand for talent in The Show but also the need for players in the
farm systems of the new teams. As Steve Fainaru and Ray Sánchez observed, the
dilution of baseball talent caused by expansion

> caused most clubs to expand their scouting departments well beyond
> U.S. borders. . . . Baseball's globalization extended not only to tradi-
> tional hotbeds like the Dominican Republic and Venezuela, but also
> to previously untapped markets like South Africa and Australia, even
> Russia. In many ways, the game was a typical industry seeking out
> cheap foreign labor to help meet expansion needs.[58]

The Cheapness of Latin American Baseball Talent

Behind Major League Baseball's focus on Latin America stands an important
socioeconomic gap. Boys in affluent North America face many opportunities
and choices that may lead them away from baseball when in an earlier era they
would only have dreamed of being Joe DiMaggio. As John Harper put it,
"American kids may spend more time surfing the net these days than choos-
ing up sides in the sandlot."[59] In U.S. communities, such as the inner cities,
where professional sports is sometimes seen, rightly or wrongly, as the only way
to escape poverty, children and their parents see basketball rather than baseball
as the path from rags to riches.[60]

But many children in the developing countries of Latin America face a
present and future far removed from the experience of most children in the
United States. A reporter assigned to do a story on Sammy Sosa's background
captured the uglier side of children playing baseball in the Dominican Republic: "Neighborhoods where giant hills of garbage and puddles of animal excre-
ment were the landscape on which children played 'baseball' with a tree
branch and a bottlecap as a ball. Man, could they hit that bottlecap."[61]

Lurking behind the impressive growth in the numbers of Latin ballplayers
in the major leagues and major league teams' competitive hunt for Latin baseball players are disturbing questions about Major League Baseball's profiting
from baseball talent refined in the squalor and poverty of developing countries
in Latin America. As Steve Fainaru asked, "what are the responsibilities of the
U.S.-based teams that conduct business in poor, often corrupt societies and of an
industry that wields enormous power over a vast pool of unsophisticated teenage
ballplayers?"[62] Roberto González Echevarría argued that a serious problem with
the growing prominence of the Latin baseball market is "the widespread use of
Latino youngsters as cheap and, ultimately, disposable talent."[63]

Chapter 3 focuses on this problem in more depth, and Alexi Quiroz's story
in Part II of this book provides disturbing evidence supporting Professor Gon-

zález's concern. But for the moment, let Dick Balderson, formerly an execu-
tive with the Colorado Rockies, describe how major league teams look at Latin
American talent. Balderson referred to the major league approach as the "boat-
load mentality": "The boatload mentality means that instead of signing 4
American guys at $25,000 each, you sign 20 Dominicans for $5,000 each."[64]
Behind the "boatload mentality" are basic economics. Sportswriter Thomas
Fitzgerald explains:

> It costs a major league team an average of $1.3 million to sign a first-
> round pick in the U.S. amateur draft. Dominican players are exempt
> from the draft and eligible to be signed at 16, when they're still young
> enough to mold. Players and their families leap at the average signing
> bonuses of $5,000 to $8,000, a pittance for the teams. They can sign
> dozens of kids—and if one or two make the majors, the investment has
> more than paid off.[65]

The "boatload mentality" does not sit well with some people in Latin
America who are involved in professional baseball. Reflecting on Balderson's
description of major league teams' attitudes toward Latin players, Angel Vargas,
president of the Venezuelan Baseball Players Association, critically observed:

> Balderson's statement communicates that he and other MLB execu-
> tives see Latino children and young men as commodities—a boatload
> of cheap Dominicans, as if these human beings were pieces of ex-
> ported fruit. I hope the reader can appreciate how demeaning this
> attitude is toward Latinos, but this is the attitude that MLB displays in
> the globalization of baseball.[66]

While the Latin presence on major league teams in North America may reflect a "Golden Age" for Latin baseball players, the approach of major league
teams to Latin talent in the Dominican Republic and Venezuela represents a
"Golden Arches" approach to Latin children and young men: the mass con-
sumption of cheap commodities.

Gene Budig's assertion that baseball, the American "national pastime," has now
become the world's pastime exaggerates the impact of the globalization of baseball around the world. Such hyperbole also obscures the extent to which baseball may no longer deserve to be called America's national pastime. What
Budig's rhetoric, however shallow, conveys is that Major League Baseball's future
is a global rather than a national one. Most large businesses confront the same
global future today, so it should not be surprising that the business of baseball is
traveling the global path trod many times before by other businesses. Major
League Baseball seeks what other globalizing companies seek: greater profit
achieved by increasing revenue through the development of new consumer

markets abroad and lowering production costs by accessing cheaper sources of labor in foreign countries.

The pursuit of global strategies means that the "national pastime" has become "denationalized" in the interests of growing the game. Whether the globalization of baseball will significantly contribute to the resolution of Major League Baseball's current economic problems is doubtful, but that crisis may exacerbate some of the less attractive features of Major League Baseball's globalizing efforts, especially the need major league teams have for access to cheap labor in Latin America. The Blue Ribbon Task Force on Baseball Economics, appointed by Commissioner Selig to study baseball's economic situation, made the connection between baseball's economic travails and its globalization when it recommended in 2000 the adoption of an international draft for *all* foreign players.[67,*] Such a move would pose significant problems for the "boatload mentality" that is so central to the current major league approach to Latin American baseball talent.

---

*Chapter 14 addresses the proposal for an international draft.

THE STRUCTURE AND DYNAMICS OF MAJOR LEAGUE BASEBALL'S RECRUITMENT OF FOREIGN BASEBALL TALENT

MANY BASEBALL FANS enjoy the skills and excitement that foreign players bring to the game, but most baseball fans do not understand how these foreign ballplayers end up playing for their favorite teams. Most fans are familiar with the annual amateur draft, but beyond some understanding about the draft, the average fan has little idea how Latin American or Asian players end up on major or minor league rosters. This chapter describes the structure and dynamics of Major League Baseball's recruitment of foreign baseball talent.

Three Paths to The Show

Currently, foreign players (defined as persons not citizens of or resident in the United States) find their way to major league teams in one of three basic ways:

- First, Canadian and Puerto Rican amateurs are subject to Major League Baseball's annual draft. Major League Baseball also makes Cuban defectors to the United States subject to the draft on the theory that they become U.S. residents. The draft also applies to amateur baseball talent in the United States.

- Second, foreign players join major league teams through arrangements or agreements between (1) major league teams and foreign professional teams, or (2) Major League Baseball and foreign professional baseball leagues. Mexican players under contract to Mexican professional teams cannot sign with a major league team unless the major league team has an agreement or arrangement with the Mexican team.[1] Japanese and Korean players under professional contracts can find their way to the major leagues through the processes established in formal agreements entered by the MLB Commissioner and the national baseball commissioners in Japan and Korea. The MLB Commissioner may sign a similar agreement with his Australian counterpart.[2] Controversy has also arisen between a major league team and the baseball association of China concerning a sixteen-year-old pitcher who signed as a free agent with a major league team while under contract to a Chinese team.[3]

- Third, amateur and professional players in Latin America (excluding Puerto Rico and Mexico) are free agents who can sign with any team they wish. Cuban players who defect to countries other than the United States (e.g., Costa Rica) also become free agents.

Because 88 percent of all foreign players on major league opening-day rosters in 2002 were from Latin America, free agency is by far the most important method of recruiting foreign baseball talent into the major leagues.

Free agency has importance beyond the traditional Latin American hotbeds of baseball talent. Free agency also occurs in connection with amateur players in Asia in ways other than through the formal agreements, which apply to players already in Japanese or Korean professional baseball. For example, in 2000, the San Diego Padres signed an eighteen-year-old pitcher, Nobuaki Yoshida, to a minor league contract.[4] This signing did not involve the elaborate procedure negotiated between the Major League Baseball and Japanese baseball commissioners concerning flows of players between their respective leagues because Yoshida was not a player for a Japanese team. (The dynamics of the MLB–Japanese baseball agreement are further discussed below.) Further, many of the current Japanese major league players entered as free agents because their contracts with Japanese teams had expired.

In addition, free agency works differently for Cuban players than it does for players who hail from other countries in Latin America. Cuban players who flee Cuba and seek residency in the United States are subject to the annual Major League Baseball draft and cannot sign with any team as a free agent.[5] Cuban players who flee Cuba and seek residency in another country, such as Costa Rica, become free agents and can sign with any team they please.[6] Major League Baseball's rules on Cuban defectors produce a loophole that sports agents, such as Joe Cubas, exploit for Cuban baseball players.[7]

The importance of the draft in terms of foreign talent mainly rests on its application to Puerto Rico. Opening-day 2002 MLB rosters had thirty-eight Puerto Ricans and ten Canadians, which indicates that the draft is far more important in bringing Puerto Rican talent into the major leagues than Canadian talent. Puerto Ricans used to be brought into the major leagues through free agency like all other players from Latin America (excluding Mexico). But in the 1980s, Major League Baseball extended the draft to amateur players in

Puerto Rico. Not all baseball experts thought moving Puerto Rican players into the draft was a good idea. Omar Minaya, who helps develop Latin talent for the New York Mets, laments the demise of free agency for Puerto Rican amateurs: "You used to be able to sign players when they were sixteen. . . . Now you have to wait two years before you can draft them, and they lose two years of important development time with the team."[8]

Because free agency is the most important recruitment channel for bringing foreign talent into the major leagues, understanding how free agency works in Latin America is critical to assessing the current "Golden Age" of Latin talent in the major leagues. Thus, after brief descriptions of how the draft and the Asian agreements operate, this chapter devotes most of its analysis to the recruitment system in Latin America (excluding Puerto Rico, Cuba, and Mexico).

The Draft

The annual amateur baseball draft controls how baseball players from the amateur ranks in the United States, Canada, and Puerto Rico are brought into the professional game.[9] When a prospect is drafted, the major league team that drafted him has exclusive negotiating rights.[10] This prevents major league teams from engaging in bidding wars for North American and Puerto Rican talent. Not only does the draft provide a transparent and open process for North American and Puerto Rican baseball prospects, but it also initially helped "to stop the upward spiral of [signing] bonuses and to distribute talent more evenly."[11]

Prior to the institution of the draft in 1965, American baseball amateur players were free agents and could sign with whatever team made the most attractive offer. This system placed a premium on a major league team's scouting system because the better the scouting the better the prospects of landing the best amateur players. Because extensive scouting systems cost money, the free-agency framework favored richer teams, such as the New York Yankees, which could afford not only the scouts but also the signing bonuses demanded by highly recruited ballplayers. As a general matter, teams with more money had more scouts, and the teams with more scouts tended to find more good ballplayers. Good ballplayers meant winning teams, and winning teams attracted younger players and meant more profits for the owners.[12] Before the draft, scouting was at the heart of the American business of baseball.

This scouting system ultimately proved, however, to be bad for the baseball business. First, competition for baseball talent caused expenses to rise as more scouts were needed and higher signing bonuses and salaries were paid to hotly recruited players. Baseball expert Allan Simpson records that upward pressure on signing bonuses began during World War II, prompting major league team owners in 1946 to make the first attempt to slow down the escalation in signing bonuses by fining teams for exceeding fixed-bonus limits.[13]

Teams discovered, however, ways to get around the fixed-bonus rule.[14] In 1958, Major League Baseball adopted a new rule requiring teams who paid players bonuses over certain fixed amounts to place those players directly on their big league rosters.[15] This rule proved ineffective in preventing signing bonuses from escalating further.[16] Between 1958 and 1963, Major League Baseball teams spent an estimated $45 million in signing bonuses and first-year salaries,[17] and, in 1964, major league teams paid $7 million to amateur players, which was "more than was spent on major league salaries."[18]

Second, because the system favored rich teams over less affluent ones, it threatened to produce competitive disequilibrium in the sport, with more affluent teams winning consistently and less affluent teams losing regularly. Such disequilibrium would be bad for the overall business of baseball because fans would get bored with the same teams always winning pennants and World Series.[19] Bored fans would mean fewer tickets sold and less revenue for team owners.

The draft terminated the economics of the scouting system in professional baseball. It was primarily a business strategy to improve the overall product and lower the cost of producing it. The draft was, thus, an efficiency strategy: produce a better product at a lower cost.[20]

The draft had three general impacts on the way American ballplayers came into the major leagues. First, the draft accorded more protection to baseball players because the process was formal and transparent, so vulnerable teenagers did not have to deal with smooth-talking major league scouts. Second, because the draft determined where a player would play, scouts were largely removed from the process of signing a player. Third, scouts essentially became talent filters for the decision-making process imposed by the draft. While scouting remains important, scouts in the United States, Canada, and Puerto Rico have less power today than they did during the years of amateur free agency.

Major League Baseball rules regulating the draft provide draftees with protections in the process of dealing with major league teams. For example, Major League Rule (MLR) 4(e) mandates that major league teams send to their draftees written notice that they have been drafted, a copy of relevant MLRs that affect the drafting of players, and copies of completed and executed Minor League Uniform Player Contracts.[21] If the MLB Commissioner determines that a major league team violates any of these MLRs, then the player becomes a free agent and can sign with any other major league team.[22] The MLRs ensure that the draftee is fully informed about his status and about the contractual documents that will determine his relationship with the major league team.

The case of Travis Lee illustrates how these rules work to protect drafted players. In 1996, the Minnesota Twins drafted Travis Lee but failed to send him the contract within the time limit specified in MLR 4(e). The Commissioner declared Lee a free agent, and he subsequently signed with the Arizona Diamondbacks.[23]

Other MLRs protect amateur players in the United States, Canada, and Puerto Rico from aggressive recruiting behavior by major league teams. Rule 3(a) generally prohibits major league teams from signing any high school student in the United States, Canada, and Puerto Rico during the period such student is eligible for high school athletics.[24] Rule 3(a) also generally prohibits major league teams from signing a player who is a member of a college baseball team from the date of the first class in the player's freshman year until the graduation of the class with which the player originally entered.[25] American Legion baseball players cannot be signed by a major league team until they are at least seventeen years old.[26] The MLRs also prohibit major league teams and any of their representatives from suggesting, procuring, or influencing a student in the United States, Canada, or Puerto Rico to withdraw from high school or college, or to refrain from playing high school or college baseball, or to transfer from one school to another.[27]

The draft also empowers amateur ballplayers in their dealings with major league teams because it provides opportunities for many ballplayers to retain agents to help them in negotiations with teams that draft them. Agents can help level the economic playing field in contract negotiations between teenagers and savvy business executives. In addition, because most North American baseball prospects and their parents have received formal educations, major league teams cannot systematically dupe them in contract negotiations.

Other protections exist for North American baseball prospects as they prepare for the world of the major leagues. First, baseball prospects typically arrive in the majors through formal and organized systems, from Little League through high school into college. Once upon a time scouts used to find the farm boy with no formal baseball training who was a "natural"; but today, most North American major league players come up through the formal system in place throughout the United States and Canada.

Importantly, much of this system is linked to educational institutions so that baseball prospects also receive formal educations. While high school students used to make up the majority of major league draftees, today college ballplayers constitute the dominant source of talent in the draft.[28] Thus, current North American draftees are older, more mature, and better educated than draftees in the early years of the draft. Further, when major league teams draft North American high school players, the teams often offer them scholarship money so that the players can continue their education in the future.[29]

Second, private and public regulatory regimes protect baseball prospects from unscrupulous agents. The National Collegiate Athletic Association (NCAA) imposes rules on its member universities that regulate student-athlete

contact with agents and with professional teams.[30] Many state legislatures in
the United States have also enacted laws that regulate how agents may deal
with athletes in their jurisdictions.[31] While these private and public regulatory
regimes are not perfect, they offer U.S. baseball amateurs some protection
against the economic forces at work in professional baseball.

This brief overview of the process by which North American and Puerto
Rican baseball prospects become part of Major League Baseball demonstrates
that the process accords many types of protections for these amateurs. The
protections come in a variety of forms: the draft; MLRs; the availability of
agents and the economic incentives fueling agency relationships; organized,
formal training systems linked to secondary and higher education; general
socioeconomic advantages available in the United States and Canada; private
regulatory rules; and public laws. While not perfect, the overall situation gives
North American and Puerto Rican baseball prospects advantages, benefits,
and protections in their dealings with major league teams.

Formal Arrangements or Agreements

Mexico

Mexican professional baseball teams, which play during the North American
summer, do not allow their players to sign contracts with major league teams
unless the major league teams have arrangements or agreements with the
Mexican teams concerning the signing of such players.[32] Major league teams
entered similar arrangements with Japanese teams prior to the agreement between the MLB and Japanese baseball commissioners described below. The
Mexican rules on major league contacts with Mexican players limits major
league access to such players, perhaps explaining the smaller number of Mexican players in the major leagues compared to other Latin American countries.

The Japanese and Korean Agreements

As noted in chapter 2, the MLB Commissioner signed formal agreements with
his counterparts in Japan and Korea that regulate the flow of professional baseball talent between the respective countries. These agreements arose to replace
exclusive working relationships individual major league teams were negotiating
with Asian professional baseball teams. Under these arrangements, the major
league team would have exclusive negotiating rights to players on the Asian professional team should the Asian team agree to release the player to play in the
major leagues. Under one of these arrangements, the San Diego Padres received
exclusive negotiating rights to Hideki Irabu of the Chiba Lotte Marines in Japan.[33] Irabu did not, however, want to play for the Padres but for the New York
Yankees. After interventions by both the Major League Baseball Players Associa-

tion and the MLB Commissioner's Office, San Diego eventually traded Irabu's negotiating rights to the New York Yankees.[34] The formal agreements described below establish a procedure that is open to all teams, which prevents the type of exclusive relationships that led to the Irabu controversy.

Under the MLB–Japanese baseball agreement, a major league club must contact the MLB Commissioner's Office if it wants to engage a Japanese player who is under contract to a Japanese professional baseball team.* The MLB Commissioner contacts the Japanese baseball commissioner to determine the Japanese player's availability. If no approval from the Japanese club is needed, the major league team may contact the player and begin negotiations. If approval from the Japanese team is required, then the MLB Commissioner notifies all major league teams of the Japanese player's potential availability. Interested major league teams bid for the right to negotiate with the Japanese player. The bids can consist of monetary compensation only for the Japanese team that holds the contractual rights to the player in question. Once all bids are in, the MLB Commissioner determines which major league team bid the highest and forwards this bid to the Japanese commissioner. The Japanese commissioner determines whether the bid is acceptable to the Japanese team. If the bid is acceptable to the Japanese club, the MLB Commissioner awards the highest-bidding major league team exclusive and non-assignable rights to negotiate with the Japanese player. If the major league team cannot reach an agreement with the Japanese player within thirty days, then the duty to compensate the Japanese club and the negotiating rights with the player both terminate.[35] The MLB–Korean baseball agreement follows roughly the same procedure.

This type of agreement serves baseball interests on both sides of the Pacific. The procedure makes Asian talent available to all major league teams, and it allows Asian teams to determine whether to release players for major league service, preventing the Asian teams from simply becoming "farm teams" for the major leagues. The process does, however, suffer from the same ailment free agency visits on major league teams — it favors wealthier teams. The bidding war for the rights to negotiate with Japanese outfielder Ichiro Suzuki was eventually won by the Seattle Mariners, which bid over $13 million.[36] Small market teams simply might not be able to compete consistently in such international bidding contests, no matter how structured the bidding procedure is.

The MLB–Asian baseball agreements do not represent the only way Asian talent finds its way into the major leagues. Most Japanese players now on

---

*The process is actually reciprocal in that Japanese teams interested in players under contract with major league teams have to follow the same procedures. Given this chapter's interest in foreign-player flows into the major leagues, we present the process from the major league team's perspective. In addition, while the agreement provides for a reciprocal structure, the agreement will probably most frequently be used to bring Japanese players to the United States rather than sending American players to Japan.

major league teams came as free agents, having satisfied the ten-year Japanese requirement for free agency; and, as noted earlier, major league teams can sign Japanese amateurs as free agents without reference to the MLB–Japanese baseball agreement. The MLB–Asian baseball agreements provide a structured international labor market between Major League Baseball and the Japanese and Korean professional leagues that allows reciprocal player flows while protecting the Asian leagues from "American baseball imperialism."[37]

Free Agency and the Rest of Latin America

The major league draft and the MLB–Asian baseball agreements constitute highly structured, rule-bound processes of bringing foreign talent to the major leagues. By contrast, Major League Baseball's recruitment of baseball talent in Latin America (excluding Puerto Rico, Cuba, and Mexico)—by far the most important way foreign talent enters the major leagues—is often likened to the lawlessness of the American Wild West. In 1985, Ross Newhan of the *Los Angeles Times* described the Dominican Republic as "an open market ungoverned by baseball's amateur draft, a last great hunting ground for eager scouts who are able to sign equally eager prospects for bonuses far below those demanded by already jaded U.S. players."[38] In Latin America, major league teams are not restrained in their recruiting practices by the draft or agreements between the MLB Commissioner's Office and Latin professional leagues. Free agency reigns, giving each major league team the incentive to be the first to sign promising prospects in Latin American countries. Or, as Steve Fainaru put it, the system is "an unregulated, cutthroat business."[39]

Many North American and Puerto Rican draftees might envy the free agency enjoyed by Latin amateurs because the draftees must conform to a system that gives them more limited freedom to negotiate. The term "free agency" also conjures in the average baseball fan a vision of millions of dollars pouring into the pockets of baseball players. But free agency works differently in Latin America than it does with major league superstars or than it would with North American and Puerto Rican draftees.

The free agency process in Latin America has a long history, much longer than either the draft or the recent MLB–Asian baseball agreements. This lengthy record of major league involvement in recruiting Latin American baseball players provides empirical evidence of how major league teams have looked at Latin American talent. Samuel Regalado, a historian and leading expert on the Latin experience with Major League Baseball,[40] has analyzed this historical record and determined that it reflects a deeply rooted major league tradition: "Latin players on the cheap."[41]

Branch Rickey, Cyril "Cy" Slapnicka, Clark Griffith, Joe Cambria, Howie Haak, and others followed the same principle in their efforts to recruit Latin

Americans over the course of most of the twentieth century: quality out of quantity as cheaply as possible.[42] This principle is, of course, exactly the same as the current "boatload mentality" approach of the major leagues described by Dick Balderson (see chapter 2). The "Latin players on the cheap" tradition continues unbroken to this day.

This tradition operates through the combination of opportunity and exploitation. The socioeconomic realities of life in most Latin American countries provide major league scouts with abundant opportunity to offer Latin boys and their parents the chance to escape poverty through professional baseball in North America. Major League Baseball increases the allure of *las Grandes Ligas* for poverty-bound families in Latin American countries through international broadcasts of major league games and by playing exhibition and regular season games in Latin America. René Gayo, director of international scouting for the Cleveland Indians, told the *Washington Post* in October 2001, for example, that he prefers to scout in Latin America because "you can still get bargains down there" given that Latin children are hungrier and desperate to put poverty behind them.[43] The socioeconomic situation in Latin America provides Major League Baseball with scores of boys and young men desperate to escape poverty through baseball.

A second feature of the "Latin players on the cheap" tradition is that major league teams have sought to sign players from Latin America as young as possible. In short, the major league scouting process in Latin America targets *children*.[44] Regalado noted that historically, major league "[s]couts viewed the signing of exceedingly young players as a badge of honor."[45] As Rudy Santin, director of the Tampa Bay Devil Rays' Latin American operation proudly declared in October 2001, the objective is "to get the kid as young as you can."[46] Baseball expert and political scientist Milton Jamail once observed that "[t]here's not a kid in the Caribbean who reaches his 14th birthday without being seen by the major-league teams."[47] In Venezuela, scouts have begun to target even younger boys. Gerdvan Liendo, legal counsel to *Los Criollitos de Venezuela* (Venezuelan Youth League Baseball), told us:

> It used to be that scouts watched kids when they were 14 or 15. Today scouts are evaluating kids at 10, 11, 12, and 13 years old. These scouting practices are hurting *Criollitos* because the scouts encourage these young boys to quit *Criollitos* and not to play international competitions. The situation is out of control.[48]

Prior to the adoption of Major League Baseball's seventeen-year-old rule, major league scouts routinely signed players ranging in ages from fourteen to sixteen. The seventeen-year-old rule provides:

> A player who has not previously contracted with a Major or Minor League Club, who is not a resident of the United States or Canada,

and who is not subject to the High School, College, Junior College or American Legion Rules, may be signed to a contract if the player: (i) is at least 17 years old at the time of signing, or (ii) is 16 at the time of signing, but will attain the age 17 prior to either the end of the effective season for which the player has signed or September 1 of such effective season, whichever is later.[49]

The rule has not, however, deterred major league teams from pursuing and signing Latin children at ages prohibited by the rule. A major league team cannot sign a player who is only sixteen years old unless that player will turn seventeen before the end of the relevant season or September 1, whichever is later. Major league teams behave, however, as if they can sign any player who is sixteen years old. The seventeen-year-old rule does not permit this kind of behavior, but it is the operational practice of major league teams. Sportswriters also apparently believe that major league teams can legitimately sign any player who is sixteen. Rob Neyer, for example said, that "[y]ou're not supposed to sign *anybody* before his 16th birthday."[50] The seventeen-year-old rule is clear, however, that the important date for signing is not the sixteenth birthday but the seventeenth.

In November 1999, the Major League Baseball Commissioner's Office began to investigate whether the Los Angeles Dodgers had illegally signed their Dominican third baseman Adrián Beltré when he was only fifteen years old.[51] The Commissioner's Office concluded that the Dodgers flagrantly violated major league rules in signing Beltré, and it imposed penalties on the Dodgers' organization.[52,*]

The Beltré incident became a window on how major league teams behave in Latin America and on how they violate their own rules on underage signing. The problem of underage signing has been with Major League Baseball for many years. In the mid-1980s, the Commissioner's Office instituted the seventeen-year-old rule to address major league teams' abusive behavior in signing fourteen-, fifteen-, and sixteen-year-old children in Latin America.[53,†]

---

*The penalties imposed on the Dodgers did not, however, have much effect on their Dominican activities. Some of the sanctions, such as closure of the Dodgers' academy, were never put into effect by the Commissioner's Office, and the *Los Angeles Times* noted that, one year after the imposition of penalties in the Beltré case, it was business as usual for the Dodgers. Paul Gutierrez, *Foreign Allegiance: Despite the Beltre Controversy, the Dodger Baseball Camp in the Dominican Republic Remains Open*, L. A. Times, Feb. 27, 2001, at 2001 WESTLAW 2464975.

†Ironically, pressure to adopt the seventeen-year-old rule came from major league teams that had not tapped the Latin American talent pool as early and intensively as franchises such as the Los Angeles Dodgers and the Toronto Blue Jays. Teams getting left behind in the growing hunt for Latin talent criticized the exploitation of children being signed at very young ages. Larry Millson, *Ballpark Figures: The Blue Jays and the Business of Baseball* (Toronto: McClelland and Stewart, 1987), at 226. This dynamic suggests that the seventeen-year-old rule's purpose had less to do with stopping exploitation of Latin children than with helping teams that were losing a competitive advantage to major league rivals.

To the "quality out of quantity as cheaply as possible" tradition, major league teams added the "younger the better" corollary.

The seventeen-year-old rule does not prevent major league teams from inviting children not old enough to sign to play and practice in their Dominican or Venezuelan minor league training facilities—the so-called "baseball academies."[54] The strategy of bringing thirteen-, fourteen-, fifteen-, and sixteen-year-old players into the academies is (1) to build a sense of loyalty in a child that will make it easier for the team to sign him when he is old enough; (2) to prevent other major league teams from approaching promising youngsters; and (3) to begin to develop the child's baseball skills properly to enhance his potential. Major league teams see these young children as commodities to appropriate (bring into academies and keep them away from other teams) and exploit (train them as cheaply as possible for maximum gain).

A classic example of the rapacity of major league teams toward Latin children can be found in the case of Venezuelan Laumin Bessa as reported by Steve Fainaru of the *Washington Post*. The Cleveland Indians signed Bessa in 1998 when he was only fifteen years old in violation of the seventeen-year-old rule, did not use the Minor League Uniform Player Contract in signing Bessa in violation of Major League Rules, hid Bessa in the Indians' Venezuelan baseball academy until he could be legally signed, and misled Bessa about the size of his signing bonus.[55] After the *Washington Post* revealed the facts of Bessa's case, the Commissioner's Office fined the Indians $50,000, forced the Indians to close their Venezuelan baseball academy for July and August of 2002, but allowed the Indians to participate in the Venezuelan Summer League for the 2002 season.[56] Leaving aside the weak sanctions from the Commissioner's Office for such a string of abusive behaviors by a major league team toward a Latin child, more astonishing was the reason the Indians gave for not firing the scout, Luis Aponte, who violated the seventeen-year-old rule, presented Bessa with an invalid contract, hid Bessa in the Indians' academy, and misled the player about his signing bonus. "In a measure of the degree of corruption that exists in Latin American baseball," Fainaru reported, "the Indians opted not to fire Aponte after deciding that *he was following normal business practices at the time*."[57]

Major League Baseball teams' systematic violation of the seventeen-year-old rule equally reveals their rapacity toward Latin children. Though the rule was imposed to stop major league teams' abusive behavior toward young Latin children, major league teams have continued to show contempt for the rule and the policy reasons behind it. As the Beltré incident and others like it demonstrate (see Table 3.1), major league teams routinely violate the seventeen-year-old rule to sign young children. Sandy Alderson of the MLB Commissioner's Office has said that "[t]here continue to be cases where clubs violate the rules."[58] But the problem of underage signing is more prevalent than Alderson's comment and the list of illegal signings in Table 3.1 indicate. The Beltré incident

Table 3.1. Recent MLB Underage Signings That Made the News

Ricardo Aramboles	Illegally signed by the Florida Marlins in 1996
Félix Arellán	Illegally signed by the Los Angeles Dodgers in 1996
Winston Abreu	Illegally signed by the Atlanta Braves in 1993
Adrián Beltré	Illegally signed by the Los Angeles Dodgers in 1995
Jossephang Bernhardt	Illegally signed by the Tampa Bay Devil Rays in 1996
Laumin Bessa	Illegally signed by the Cleveland Indians in 1998
Wilson Betemit	Illegally signed by the Atlanta Braves in 1996

provided the ugly evidence that illegal signings were a major problem for Major League Baseball.

Responding to criticism of the Los Angeles Dodgers' behavior in illegally signing Adrián Beltré, former Dodgers' manager Tommy Lasorda lashed out at critics for attacking the Dodgers for doing what every team does. "I bet you there's 50 Latino ballplayers in the major leagues that have signed illegally," Lasorda told a November 1999 press conference.[59] Lasorda's fifty Latin players represented approximately half the contingent of Dominican and Venezuelan players on Major League Baseball 2000 rosters. Following up on Lasorda's statistic, sportswriter Rob Neyer reported that "I'm told by someone with a background in scouting that the number is actually significantly higher than that."[60]

Lasorda mentioned only major league players, not the numbers of players illegally signed in the minor league system. In connection with the minor leagues, the illegal signings of the Dominican Wilson Betemit, Venezuelan Félix Arellán, and Venezuelan Laumin Bessa are illustrative. The Atlanta Braves signed Betemit when he was fifteen years old.[61] The Los Angeles Dodgers signed Arellán when he was fifteen years old.[62] The Cleveland Indians signed Bessa when he was fifteen years old.[63]

The Associated Press reported that "[t]here are no statistics, but hundreds of underage boys are believed to be signed clandestinely in Latin America every year by [MLB] scouts."[64] Raúl Salmerón, President of the Venezuelan National Sports Institute, says that the Adrián Beltré and Wilson Betemit cases are "just the tip of the iceberg. It's a problem that repeats itself with great frequency in Venezuela and other Latin American countries that are considered authentic sources of raw material for the big leagues."[65] How many Latin players in the minor leagues in the United States, the Dominican Republic, and Venezuela have been illegally signed in the years since the seventeen-year-old rule was instituted? Nobody knows. Nobody ever will know. But nobody should doubt that the number is in the thousands.

Major league teams frequently excuse their underage signings by arguing that determining the ages of prospective ballplayers in the Dominican Republic and Venezuela is difficult. Obtaining authentic birth certificates, the teams claim, is not the quick and easy process that it is in the United States or other developed countries. In addition, the teams accuse Latin players of lying about their ages, suggesting that the teams and not the players are the victims. Post–September 11th events appeared to provide support to the major league teams' claims about bad documentation systems and players misleading teams about their ages when a number of Latin major league players had to admit they were older than previously thought. After September 11th, the U.S. Immigration and Naturalization Service (INS) tightened its requirements for obtaining visas, meaning that major league teams had to deliver authentic documents for their Latin major and minor leaguers playing in the United States for the 2002 season.[66] Quite a few Latin major league players suddenly aged a year or two.[67] As for the Latin minor league players scheduled to arrive in the United States later in the spring, the Commissioner's Office estimated that "as many as 100 of them will show up with different birth dates than they had when they left [the United States after the 2001 season]."[68]

Officials of major league teams did not miss the opportunity to point blame at the players and the Latin American countries for the age discrepancies. Atlanta Braves' general manager John Schuerholz captured these sentiments when he commented that:

> Most of the players who have found themselves in this circumstance are guys in the Dominican, where we all know that, for as long as I can remember, the ability to determine, with finite accuracy, the birth date of a player has been a challenge. And that's whether we're talking one year ago, five years ago, 10 years ago, 20 years ago or 30 years ago. Every organization in baseball has had a situation like this that has scouted in that environment.[69]

Schuerholz added in another interview that "[t]his has been an ongoing problem for as long as we have been signing players from what we'll call Third World countries. We've muddled through as best we can."[70]

Missing from the major leagues teams' spin on the age discrepancies is the nature of the system the major league teams created in Latin America. As demonstrated previously in this chapter, major league teams hunt primarily for Latin players as young as possible. This preference has led teams into massive violations of the seventeen-year-old rule, and it produces a system in which Latin players older than sixteen and seventeen are encouraged to lie about their ages. Andrés Reiner, head of international scouting for the Houston Astros, explains the way the system really works:

> Scouts are looking for 16-, 17-year-old players and a lot of times when they say 18 or 19, most scouts have no interest in them. If you see a player who is 17, the projection is much higher than if he is 19. . . .

Everybody who works in baseball in Latin America, we know what is
going on and what has been going on.[71,*]

At the heart of the recent age discrepancies is the major league teams'
emphasis on signing players as young as possible, the same emphasis that leads
to violations of the seventeen-year-old rule. In addition, the claim by major
league teams that the documentary systems in the Dominican Republic and
Venezuela force teams to "muddle through" rings hollow. When the INS tightened its requirements for documents in connection with obtaining visas, teams
and players apparently had few problems actually producing the proper documents. The media coverage about the age differences does not include reports
about Latin major leaguers being stranded in their home countries because
they could not produce proper documents. This situation suggests that major
league teams have themselves been lax about requiring proper documents
from players. The reason for such laxity with Latin players arises from the major league teams' desire not to check birth certificates and other documents
closely. Authenticating birth certificates, which the INS has shown can be
done even in the Dominican Republic, would eliminate major league teams'
defenses against *underage signings* — the team did not know the player was
underage, and everyone knows how difficult it is to get the proper documents
in Third World countries.

The Commissioner's Office's belated efforts at taking the seventeen-year-
old rule seriously has exposed the nonsense of major league teams' claims that
Latin players and Third World countries are responsible for age discrepancies,
whether they pertain to underage players or to older players claiming to be
younger. Since late 2000, the Commissioner's Office has mandated that major league teams require players to produce authentic birth certificates.[72] Neither this requirement nor the INS's post–September 11th crackdown has
caused the sky to fall on major league teams' efforts in Latin America, demon-
strating that Major League Baseball's attempts to muddle through the effects
of lying children and Third World disorganization have involved more deception than muddle.

The third feature of the "Latin players on the cheap" tradition is the signing of hundreds of Latin children for very little money. Regalado noted that
historically, signing "bonuses were few and far between and moderate, at
best."[73] Kevin Kerrane noted that Joe Cambria, who scouted in Cuba for the
Washington Senators from the early 1930s to the mid-1950s, bragged that he
could sign Cubans for less signing bonus money "than you pay for a hat."[74]
Kerrane went on to argue that Cambria "didn't even bother with the hat" in

---

*Alexi Quiroz faced this age problem during his experience with Major League Baseball. See
chapters 4 and 8.

signing Cuban players.[75] The Detroit Tigers offered Alfonso (Chico) Carrasquel, who would eventually become one of the most famous Latin major
leaguers, a baseball glove and a plane ticket to the United States as a signing
bonus in 1949.[76] Carrasquel was lucky. Regalado states that "[m]ost players
signed contracts that merely paid for their passage to the United States."[77]
Howie Haak, Latin scout for the Pittsburgh Pirates in the 1950s and 1960s,
noted that in his first year of scouting in Latin American he signed "four gems
for about a thousand dollars of bonus money—total. . . . To get four guys that
good in the states might've cost a hundred thousand."[78]

Signing bonuses increased as more and more major league teams began
to scout intensively in Latin America, but the bonuses remained incredibly
cheap for major league teams in comparison to what North American draftees
and major league players commanded. Thomas Fitzgerald noted in 1999 that
the average signing bonus in the Dominican Republic was between $5,000
and $8,000. Dick Balderson, in his 1999 "boatload mentality" statement, used
$5,000 as the signing bonus for his Dominicans. Even with such paltry signing
bonuses as the norm, many Latin players never actually see any money from
the team with which they signed. Sammy Sosa signed with the Philadelphia
Phillies for $2,500 in 1984, but he never received any of this money.[79] Players
and former players in Venezuela report that they saw none or only part of the
signing bonuses major league teams promised them.[80]

The system by which children are brought into contact with major league
teams in Latin American countries often involves more than major league
scouts. In Venezuela and the Dominican Republic, people called *buscones*
and *dirigentes** play a major role in how major league teams get access to
Latin children. Generally speaking, *buscones* have been individuals who hunt
for baseball prospects, attempt to train and develop promising kids, and then
try to direct prospects to specific teams. A *buscón* channels potential prospects
to major league scouts, who make the final decisions about whether to sign a
prospect.

Historically, a *buscón* usually had an exclusive relationship with one
major league team, but the growth in interest in Latin talent has caused the
system to change. In the Dominican Republic, *dirigentes* often serve the same
function as *buscones*, except that *dirigentes* sell players to the highest bidder
and do not have close relationships with any one team. The *buscón* or the *dirigente* is not an employee or agent of the major league team. The *buscón* or
dirigente is self-employed and earns his money from the prospects major
league teams sign. The *buscón* or *dirigente* tells a potential prospect that he

---

Buscón means "one who is searching." *Buscones* is also the term used in the Dominican Republic to describe contractors for sugar plantations who hire Haitians at the Dominican-Haiti bor-
der. The United Nations Commission on Human Rights has likened the conditions under which
the Haitians work to slavery. In baseball, *dirigente* means "manager" or "coach."

can help get the player signed to a contract with a major league team, and, if the player does eventually sign, then the player typically pays the *buscón* or *dirigente* money, usually a percentage of his signing bonus. Players must "give the *buscones* a significant portion of their signing bonuses: at times 50 percent or higher."[81]

Major league teams often also pay *buscones* and *dirigentes* money as "finder's fees" or "'commissions' ranging from $500 to as much as $50,000."[82] Vladimir Guerrero, now a star with the Montreal Expos, signed with the Expos after having been sold to Expo scout Fred Ferraira. Tim Kurkjian of ESPN describes what happened:

> [Guerrero] arrived [at the Expos' Dominican facility] on the back of a motorcycle driven by some guy who delivered prospects to [MLB] camps. He had his workout stuff in his lap, and was wearing two different shoes, one of which had a sock stuffed in the toe to make it fit. He ran a 6.6 60-yard dash (that's moving) and threw the ball exceptionally well from right field. . . . Fred Ferraira, an Expos scout, had seen enough. He signed the kid right there, and paid his biker friend $200 for bringing him around.[83]

Enrique Soto, called the "King of the *Buscones*" in the Dominican Republic, began working for himself after he was fired as a scout for the Oakland Athletics* because Soto realized that "major league teams would pay more for well-trained, well-fed players."[84] Soto's business consists of finding young children with baseball talent and investing in them through training and nutrition until the time comes to sell the kids to the highest major league bidder.[85] Then Soto takes his cut of the signing bonus, which he claims is about 25 percent.[86] Soto is perhaps the most successful of a growing breed of "entrepreneurs." In 1998, Murray Chass reported in the *New York Times* that, in the Dominican Republic:

> Dominican and American baseball officials say local entrepreneurs are hording children as young as 11 into informal training camps and later brokering them to the major league clubs. . . . Often lining up players while they are still playing in one of the 100 Little Leagues around the Dominican Republic, the scouts [i.e., *buscones* or *dirigentes*] frequently house or feed or lend money to the young players to win their loyalty. Then, when the players are old enough, the scouts broker them to major league clubs.[87]

Steve Fainaru of the *Washington Post* noted that "a Dominican congressman, the former director of Dominican operations for the Seattle Mariners and Jose

---

*Enrique Soto appears as a scout for the Oakland A's in Alexi Quiroz's story. See chapter 6.

Rijo, the former major league pitcher," are also in the business of selling children to major league teams.[88]

The *buscón/dirigente* system may seem strange and complicated, but it is actually efficient for major league teams. The teams directly employ scouts, but not enough to scour Latin countries thoroughly for promising baseball players. The *buscón/dirigente* system allows major league teams to have access to more comprehensive scouting for minimal cost because "commissions" for *buscones* or *dirigentes* are less than what it would cost to employ a full- or part-time scout. Players that sign bear the direct cost of the *buscones'* or *dirigentes'* work through a percentage of the players' signing bonuses. From the economic perspective of major league teams, the *buscón/dirigente* system has traditionally been efficient, which is why major league teams have encouraged and supported these practices in the Dominican Republic and Venezuela.

In addition, while scouts are employees of major league teams and are subject to Major League Baseball rules, *buscones* and *dirigentes* are not regulated by Major League Baseball because they are not employees of the teams, but independent contractors. This arrangement works to the benefit of major league teams because the *buscones* and *dirigentes* can begin preparing children for major league teams at an earlier age than major league teams are allowed to sign and train them.

Major League Baseball teams are, thus, at the center of an industry in the Dominican Republic and Venezuela that traffics in children. In analyzing the *buscón/dirigente* system in the Dominican Republic, Steve Fainaru of the *Washington Post* argued that Major League Baseball "decries the abuses but effectively created the system that fosters them."[89]

Buscones and *dirigentes* do not, it should be emphasized, serve the same role as sports agents. *Buscones* and *dirigentes* sometimes negotiate on behalf of their players with major league teams, but their involvement with the players usually ends at signing. Thus, *buscones* and *dirigentes* do not act like agents, whose work for a player continues after the signing of the contract. Because major league teams are prohibited by Major League Baseball rules from making any payment to any person who represents a player in contract negotiations, any "commission" paid by a major league team to a *buscón* or *dirigente* who represented a player in contract negotiations would be illegal under Major League Baseball rules.[90] Further, even if a *buscón* or *dirigente* represents a player in contract negotiations, the sole issue for the *buscón* or *dirigente* is the size of the signing bonus rather than the whole panoply of issues proper representation would address. Sports agent Scott Boras has, for example, lambasted the *buscones* system in the Dominican Republic:

> The *buscones*, Boras said with distaste, often romance underage players, hiding them out while providing the food and lodging they may not have been receiving regularly, and then, when the player is old

enough, delivering them to an [MLB baseball] academy for a $200 to $400 kickback. "The player has no idea of his true value or that he is entitled to representation," Boras said.[91]

The traditional team-scout-*buscón/dirigente* system has in recent years been challenged by increasing participation of sports agents from North America. Seeing the intense efforts of major league teams hunting for Latin talent, agents have sensed a market opportunity. Historically, major league teams have tried very hard to keep agents out of the process of signing talent in Latin American countries because agents usually make their clients more expensive to sign and retain.[92]

Steve Fainaru of the *Washington Post* reported that "[s]ome teams refuse to negotiate with agents at all, effectively denying players representation during contract negotiations."[93] Andrés Reiner, head of international scouting for the Houston Astros, told Fainaru that "he refuses to negotiate with agents because they tend to inflate a player's value."[94] When asked whether it was fair for a major league team to control the market by denying a player an agent's services during contract negotiations, Reiner replied, "I don't want to control the market. I just want to make the decision of how much a player is worth and how much I will pay him."[95] Agents for U.S. players generally try to increase the value of their clients, and major league teams do not refuse to negotiate with U.S. minor league players and draftees who are represented by agents. This double standard reveals the intentional discrimination major league teams use against young Latin players.

Once the prospect is signed, major league teams continue to discourage the Latin players from working with agents by preventing the players from receiving communications from agents and continuing to convince them they do not need agent representation. A frequent persuasive tactic is telling young Latin players that major league teams might treat them less favorably if they sign with an agent because such signing suggests the players are rebels or problematic people. When such "persuasion" is applied to a child from a developing country who speaks no English and desperately wants to escape poverty through baseball, the result is predictable: the player does not sign with an agent.

Today, Latin prospects fortunate enough to retain a competent sports agent can command higher signing bonuses. Sports agent Rob Plummer claims, for example, to have negotiated signing bonuses over $1.4 million for three different Dominican sixteen-year-old players.[96] Plummer's negotiation of such signing bonuses is exactly why major league teams have historically discouraged Latin players from retaining agents.

In addition, agent involvement would threaten to reduce the power major league teams hold over Latin children and their parents, who are often in desperate economic straits and thus vulnerable to the wishes of major league teams. Agents represent a threat to the "boatload mentality" major league teams have historically had in connection with Latin players. Nevertheless, increasing agent involvement in Latin American countries is producing a new system that is less advantageous for major league teams. Because many agents are not angels, the new, emerging system is not necessarily a great improvement for Latin baseball prospects. Some deeply involved in baseball in Latin American countries believe that the increasing involvement of agents, combined with the already fierce competition among major league scouts and *buscones/dirigentes*, has produced an out-of-control, unregulated feeding frenzy over Latin children.

Agents are necessary in the various worlds of professional sports. But in the case of Latin players, the role of agents is even more important than for North American players because of economic, educational, language, and cultural barriers that foreign players face. Many Latin players lack the education or language skills to discuss or even ask for benefits normally given to North American players. Major league teams know that the absence of agents is good for them because the Latin players generally accept whatever is offered to them with no bargaining. Educational and language obstacles put them at a disadvantage when dealing with major league teams. In addition, because many Latin baseball prospects see the major leagues as their escape from poverty, they are less likely to challenge their treatment than North American prospects are. This major league formula is a paradigm of business efficiency: the production of profit-generating talent at low cost. Agent involvement raises the level of signing bonuses and works as a compliance mechanism for Major League Baseball rules—each of which would raise the overall cost of finding Latin baseball talent.

The fourth aspect of the "Latin players on the cheap" tradition involves how major league teams have historically handled the "contracts" signed by Latin prospects. Kevin Kerrane referred to Branch Rickey's use of "desk contracts," or non-binding agreements that allowed the major league team to do whatever it pleased with its Latin prospects.[97] Cy Slapnicka, who scouted for the Cleveland Indians in the late 1930s, followed the same course as Rickey. Sam Regalado argued that "[t]he art of 'cutting corners' and manipulating contracts was the rule of thumb in the Slapnicka era."[98] Regalado's review of the development of major league recruitment practices in Latin America concluded:

> The contract itself was a euphemism. Joe Cambria, for instance, simply held onto contracts until he deemed players ready to move on or move out. And the players, many desperate, had little recourse.[99]

A common theme throughout the history of signing Latin players is the players' ignorance about what they were signing and the intentional efforts of major league teams to exploit this ignorance. Chico Carrasquel, who signed with the Brooklyn Dodgers in 1949, had no idea what he signed, the document was not in Spanish, he was never told what was in his contract, and he never received any copy of any document that he signed.[100]

Two more recent examples help illustrate this Major League Baseball tradition. The first example is Sammy Sosa, who in his autobiography said the following about his signing:

> But to tell the truth, I never knew what was on the paper that I signed with the Phillies [in 1984 when Sosa was fifteen years old]. To this day I don't know. That was the way then. You were totally innocent and unprepared for negotiations—not a good way to be in the harsh business world of baseball, as I would discover over time. It wasn't long before I came to understand that something was wrong.[101]

The second example comes from journalists Marcos Bretón and José Villegas's description of the Oakland A's 1993 signing of Miguel Tejada, who now plays shortstop for the A's:

> The Athletics offered Miguel a contract. At that point, the most they were paying was five thousand dollars and they didn't think Miguel was worth that much. So they offered him two thousand dollars—a low amount even for a Dominican player. At that moment, there was little money to be made off him, so Miguel had no agent. He didn't even know what his contract really said . . . the actual terms of Miguel's deal were out of his hands. Miguel was still alone. Negotiations would be a one way street. His choice: take it or leave it. This was a far cry from the treatment of the bonus babies of America with their parents, their agents, and their lawyers.[102]

When a young American or Latin player signs to play for a major league team today, he signs the Minor League Uniform Player Contract and addenda that specifically relate to him. The Minor League Uniform Player Contract is a lengthy document printed in small type.[103] Under Major League Rules (MLRs), when a drafted player is tendered a contract, he must receive from the major league team specific documents and papers.[104] This MLR ensures that every American, Canadian, or Puerto Rican drafted by a major league team receives copies of the tendered contract and time to read and understand its terms. As seen in the Travis Lee case described above, violation of this rule brings automatic punishment in the form of making the player a free agent.

The MLRs contain *nothing* that affords equivalent protection to Latin players signed as free agents by major league teams. The MLRs contain no rules that require teams to provide Latin players and their parents with a Spanish-language translation of the Minor League Uniform Player Contract and related addenda. Given the decades of major league teams' extensive recruitment of Latin players, the absence of a MLR that requires the simple translation of the player's contract into Spanish cannot be an oversight or an accident. The absence of such a rule is intentional.

Leaving aside that the MLRs protect North Americans but not Domini-cans or Venezuelans in connection with the tendering of minor league con-tracts, contract law argues against the validity of these contracts. Basic contract theory, in both common law and civil law countries, holds invalid contracts that one party cannot read and thus cannot understand.[105] In such a contract, there is no true "meeting of the minds" between the parties about the rights and duties created by the contract.

And yet major league teams routinely present to Latin children and their parents contracts neither the player nor the family can read or understand. In 2000, Angel Vargas argued that no major league teams provided Latin signees with Spanish translations of the Minor League Uniform Player Contract and related addenda.[106] The same problem existed in the Dominican Republic. During an internship with the Caribbean Confederation of Baseball Players Associations, William Gutierrez talked with dozens of Latin players in Major League Baseball academies in the Dominican Republic in May and June of 2000. None of them had any idea what they signed, and none indicated that they had ever been given copies of their contracts.[107]

The failure of the MLB Commissioner's Office to require major league teams to provide Latin players and their parents with Spanish translations of contractual documents did not happen because the Commissioner's Office did not understand the importance of players being able to read their contracts. The Winter League* Agreement negotiated between the Commissioner's Office and professional baseball leagues in Latin America requires that the Winter League Uniform Player Contract "shall be printed in both the English and Spanish lan-guages."[108] This rule exists to allow English-speaking North American players in the major and minor leagues to understand their contracts if they play for a pro-fessional team in Latin America during the off-season.

No similar rule protecting Latin players signing with major league teams exists. In fact, the only MLR on translation is Rule 21—Misconduct (e.g., in-tentionally losing a game or betting on a game), which must be printed in both English and Spanish and posted in each major league team clubhouse.[109] Major league teams and the Commissioner's Office believe that Latin players must be warned about their possible misconduct but do not need to know what their minor league contracts say when they sign with major league teams.

Given the decades of extensive involvement by major league teams in the Dominican Republic and Venezuela, why had these organizations not simply translated the Minor League Uniform Player Contract and related addenda into Spanish for use with Latin players? How hard could this be for any major league team or the Commissioner's Office?

---

*The "Winter League" is the term used to describe the professional baseball season in the Do-minican Republic, Mexico, Puerto Rico, and Venezuela, which occurs during the North Ameri-can winter when major league teams have their off-season.

The absence of a translation requirement for contractual documents signed by Latin minor league players was not an accidental or unfortunate oversight. It was intentional. Major league teams and the Commissioner's Office were simply following the strategy pioneered by Branch Rickey and the early major league scouts, who made extensive use of "contracts" that gave all the power to major league teams and kept the Latin players ignorant about their rights. The teams that signed Chico Carrasquel, Sammy Sosa, Miguel Tejada, and thousands of other Latin players partook of this major league tradition.*

The fifth feature of the "Latin players on the cheap" tradition involves the so-called "baseball academies" that major league teams have operated in Latin American countries since the late 1970s. Major league teams sign far more Latin players than the teams can bring to the United States under U.S. immigration laws. To deal with this situation, major league teams have developed baseball academies and Summer Leagues in the Dominican Republic and Venezuela.[110] These academies and leagues enable major league teams to keep under contract and evaluate the hundreds of Latin prospects the teams sign each year but cannot bring to the United States. Each major league team has approximately 28 visas for foreign players, totaling around 840 visas for all thirty major league teams. Assuming that every foreign-born major league player receives a visa, major league teams have approximately 618 visas to use to bring foreign minor league players to the United States.[†] After awarding 618 visas to foreign-born minor league players, approximately 2,247 foreign-born minor league players are left without visas, or approximately 78 percent of all foreign-born players under minor league contracts. The only locations outside North America where major leagues have minor league operations are in the Dominican Republic and Venezuela. For reasons the reader will soon understand, major league teams do not send U.S., Canadian, or Puerto Rican draft choices to these "baseball academies" and Summer Leagues for training. These academies and leagues are strictly for Latin prospects signed as free agents.

Major league teams are proud of how cheaply they can operate their baseball academies in comparison to the cost of developing North American baseball

---

*Steve Fainaru of the *Washington Post* reported in June 2001 that the MLB Commissioner's Office was "preparing to make contracts *available in Spanish for the first time,* perhaps this summer [2001]" (emphasis added). Steve Fainaru, "The Business of Building Ballplayers," *Washington Post,* June 17, 2001, at <http://www.washingtonpost.com/wp-dyn/articles/A10070–2001Jun16.html> (visited June 18, 2001). Outside pressure and criticism forced the Commissioner's Office to translate the Minor League Uniform Player Contract. Alexi Quiroz made the lack of a Spanish translation an issue in his ordeal with the Chicago Cubs and the Commissioner's Office (see Part II). We repeatedly addressed this problem in correspondence with the Commissioner's Office, and criticism of Major League Baseball on this issue has appeared in published articles by us, Angel Vargas, and Samuel Regalado. We return to this issue in chapter 13.

†We are using 2002 statistics on foreign-born players in the major and minor leagues in these examples (see chapter 1). Some foreign-born major league players do not need visas because they have obtained residency status in the United States.

talent. "Both [the Dominican and Venezuelan] academies?" Omar Minaya of the New York Mets asked when questioned about the cost of running the Mets' Latin academies, "I'll tell you this — it isn't what we pay for the average first-round draft choice."[111] Similarly, Brad Sloan, scouting director for the San Diego Padres, said, "You can sign a whole lot of players down here [in Latin America and the Caribbean] and run your whole academy for a year on what it takes to sign a first-round draft choice now."[112] According to sportswriter Alan Schwarz, "while the typical first-round pick runs about $1.8 million, the Mets spend less than half that — about the cost of a second-rounder — to sign and develop dozens of players in Venezuela and the Dominican."[113] The *Washington Post* reported that in 2000, the Cleveland Indians signed forty players in Latin America for $700,000, more than $1,000,000 less than the team paid its first-round draft pick.[114]

Sports anthropologist Alan Klein sees in the baseball academy system the commercial motives that imperial powers and multinational corporations have long exhibited:

> The academy is the baseball counterpart of the colonial outpost, the physical embodiment overseas of the parent franchise. It operates more or less like the subsidiary of any other foreign company: it finds raw materials (talented athletes), refines them (trains the athletes), and ships abroad finished products (baseball players).[115]

Multinational corporations often locate production facilities in developing countries to access cheaper labor and to operate in a less regulated business environment. Lower wage rates and less costly regulatory regimes mean more profitable production for multinational corporations. Major league teams clearly see their Dominican and Venezuelan baseball academies as cheap ways to produce baseball players for the minor and major leagues in North America. The head of international scouting for the Houston Astros, Andrés Reiner, argued that baseball is "one industry among thousands. There is no difference between General Motors and the Houston Astros. One [product] is to be sold, like GM, and the other one is to be used in the major leagues. It is just like making Cadillacs."[116] This comment again reveals how major league teams look at Latin children as commodities to be consumed in The Show. The equivalent production facilities in North America (largely today universities) and in Asia (Korean and Japanese professional baseball teams) produce much more expensive "commodities" than does the baseball academy system in Latin America.

Behind the major league teams' pride in their efficient Latin American operations lurk, however, disturbing practices. Complaints regularly heard about major league academies in Venezuela include the lack of (1) security against personal and property crimes; (2) consistent and adequate supplies of clean water; (3) consistent and adequate sanitary services (e.g., functioning toilets); (4) well-maintained buildings; (5) sufficient food and nutrition; (6) trained medical staff; (7) serious educational activities; and (8) high-quality playing facilities.[117] Donald Fehr, Executive Director and General Counsel of the Major League Baseball Players Association, noted in February 2000 that "we generally hear horror stories about very young kids who never come into the U.S."[118]

The following tale was related to us by an individual who was involved in a major league team's operations in Venezuela:

> I was in charge of finding somewhere for the Summer League players to live. The budget was very limited, but I knew the area and knew the best places to put the players. I found a clean and decent place.
>
> One day a player from Panama told me, "Thank you for every-thing. I was in the Dominican Republic last year [with the same major league team] and the facilities and the food there were just horrible. What you are doing here [in Venezuela] is better. At least you treat us as human beings."
>
> I informed the organization that I had found a place. The head scout [of the major league team] was in Venezuela at the time, and he wanted to see the place. When he saw the place the next day, he said, "This is a much better place than the one we have in the Dominican Republic and that is going to cause us a lot of problems. You know people are going to compare." The organization moved the players to a different building that was not the best place for the players. The next season the organization fired us all.[119]

Luis Peñalver,* a former pitching coach for the Los Angeles Dodgers, ran the Dodgers' baseball academy in Venezuela from 1997 to 2000. Peñalver de-scribed to us the bad conditions at the Dodgers' Venezuelan facility: horrible living quarters, bad food, no proper medical trainer to deal with injuries, no health insurance to cover injured players' medical expenses, and terrible buses for transportation to and from games.[120] The Dodgers fired Peñalver in 2000 without providing him the benefits he is due from the team under Venezuelan labor law.[121]

The reader may be wondering how major league teams can get away with such treatment of Latin children and young men in baseball academies. Surely Major League Baseball has rules and standards that apply to living and playing conditions in baseball academies and the Summer Leagues in the Dominican Republic and Venezuela. The Major League Rules (MLRs) pro-vide very detailed standards that all minor league playing facilities must meet. Although the Dominican and Venezuelan Summer Leagues are part of Major

---

*Peñalver makes a brief appearance in Alexi Quiroz's story. See chapter 7.

League Baseball's minor league system, the MLR standards for minor league playing facilities are not applied in the Dominican Republic or Venezuela.

One reason we have heard for the lack of MLR application in the Dominican Republic and Venezuela is Major League Baseball's reluctance to regulate activities in foreign countries. This explanation is nonsense. The Commissioner's Office banned Canadian franchises from recruiting Cuban players despite Canada's open commercial policy toward Cuba. More specifically, the failure to apply the MLR has nothing to do with Major League Baseball's reticence to create and demand playing facility standards in foreign countries. Such standards for Latin Winter League teams employing major and minor league players are contained in the Winter League Agreement between Major League Baseball and Latin professional teams.[122] The Winter League Agreement also requires that the Latin Winter League teams "guarantee full medical and hospital expenses" for injured players and provide qualified medical personnel for players during the Winter League season.[123] The Winter League Agreement also incorporates MLRs into its text[124] and allows the MLB Commissioner to issue regulations to effectuate the Winter League Agreement.[125]

All these examples demonstrate that, when it wants to do so, Major League Baseball applies standards and rules in foreign countries to protect players and its other interests. In connection with the academics and Summer Leagues in the Dominican Republic and Venezuela, the case for applying rules and standards on team behavior is more compelling than with the Winter Leagues because major league teams *directly* control the academies and leagues. The Commissioner's Office has no excuse for failing to apply rules and standards for minor league facilities and medical expenses and personnel to the Latin baseball academies and Summer Leagues.

Why does Major League Baseball not enforce MLRs against minor league playing facilities and medical issues in the Dominican Republic and Venezuela? Enforcing these standards would require major league teams to invest money in upgrading their Latin playing facilities and would thus cut against their efforts to find Latin children to exploit as cheaply as possible.

The MLRs do not, however, contain standards on living conditions for minor league players. Nothing in the MLRs requires, for example, that a major league team provide its minor league players with adequate housing, food, and water. In the United States and Canada, such standards are unnecessary given the higher standard of living that prevails in these countries. But why do the MLRs not contain standards on living conditions for minor league players in the Dominican Republic and Venezuela? Is the absence of such rules driven by the Rickey principle of quality out of quantity as cheaply as possible?

Even if the MLRs contain no standards for living conditions, the Dominican Republic passed a law in 1985 that mandates that baseball academies provide players with adequate food, lodging, and medical necessities.[126] This law was passed to deal with abuses perpetrated in the baseball academies by major league teams. When reading the story of Alexi Quiroz in Part II of this book, the reader should evaluate whether the Chicago Cubs showed any respect for this Dominican law.

The reader should remember that the majority of the inhabitants of baseball academies are children. While Major League Baseball prohibits major league teams from signing any Latin prospect in violation of the seventeen-year-old rule, no rule prohibits teams from inviting younger players to the baseball academies to evaluate their skills at more tender ages. This practice is widespread and serves an important purpose: it keeps potential prospects away from the scouts of other major league teams. A former Dominican commissioner of baseball told anthropologist Alan Klein that baseball academies functioned as "hideouts because the scouts didn't want their kids seen by other scouts. It almost seemed like they were concentration camps."[127] From Venezuela, the Associated Press reported in 2000 that "[s]ports officials in Caracas, Venezuela, denounce an increasing tendency to recruit underage players and to crush their baseball dreams through false promises. In the worst cases, the officials say, scouts promise boys lucrative contracts, then take them out of local play to hide them from other scouts."[128] In October 2001, the *Washington Post* reported that major league teams routinely use their academies to "hide prospects from rivals and agents, training 14- and 15-year-olds at remote facilities until they are signed or cut loose."[129]

Embarrassed by bad publicity, the MLB Commissioner's Office circulated in 2001 a memorandum stating that major league teams could not admit anyone under sixteen into their academies.[130] The circulation of this demand in the form of a memorandum and not a formal MLR should provide the reader with a sense of how uninterested the Commissioner's Office is with these abuses of children. And what about the compliance of teams with this memorandum? The Houston Astros' head of international scouting said that his team is reluctantly complying, but he added, "I think we are the only ones."[131]

The vast majority of Latin children who train at academies (whether or not under contract) or play on MLB Summer League teams in the Dominican Republic and Venezuela never make it to minor or major league baseball in North America. The ruthless pursuit of quality out of quantity as cheaply as possible means that major league teams release hundreds of Latin boys and young men every year. Felipe Alou criticized Major League Baseball's signing practices by stating that "[t]hey sign 25 guys and maybe only one is a good player. It's like they throw a net in the ocean, hoping that maybe they'll get a big fish. The problem is, if they don't get a big fish, they'll throw all the smaller ones back."[132]

MLB's frenzied oversigning of Latin children results in a large number of young players being released by teams each year. Released players are in a difficult position because they are unlikely to get another team to sign them to a new contract. Being released gives players a stigma that is hard to shake. In addition, most of the children have left school to pursue baseball, meaning that the release often leaves the players educationally and psychologically unprepared to pursue other professional careers.[133]

This overview of the main features of the "Latin players on the cheap" is not comprehensive, and we return to the problems that this tradition creates for Latin children and for Major League Baseball later in the book (see Part III). But the previous paragraphs are sufficient to communicate the nature of the process through which major league teams bring Latin baseball players into professional baseball. Unlike the way free agency works for major league superstars, it does not produce for most Latin children a pot of gold at the end of the baseball rainbow. For the vast majority of Latin children brought into the system, the opportunity offered proves ephemeral while the exploitation lingers for a lifetime.

The Disbelief Syndrome and the Opportunity Thesis

In our work on Major League Baseball's mistreatment of Latin American baseball talent, the disturbing nature of the way Major League Baseball brings Latin children into professional baseball commonly elicits one of two responses. The first reaction, which we label the "disbelief syndrome," comes mainly from people who have no prior exposure to baseball recruiting in Latin America. They simply do not believe, or have a very hard time believing, that exploitation of children exists in the world of Major League Baseball.

The second reaction, which we call the "opportunity thesis," is more common in people who do know what has happened and continues to happen in Latin America with major league recruitment of baseball talent. These people acknowledge that historically problems have existed but that, overall, Major League Baseball offers children in Latin American countries opportunities they could never otherwise think possible. René Gayo, the Cleveland Indians' director of international scouting, captured the opportunity thesis when he said, "These guys, if they don't play in the big leagues they're going to end up selling mangoes in the street for the equivalent of a quarter."[134] In investigating underage signings and other abuses, Steve Fainaru heard the "opportunity thesis" many times: "Major league officials point out that teams provide opportunities to deeply impoverished athletes who might otherwise have none."[135] Latin superstars such as Sammy Sosa reinforce the opportunity thesis when, with genuine appreciation, they praise Major League Baseball for giving them the chance to escape poverty for baseball fame and glory.[136]

One defense of the mistreatment described above is that it is perhaps better than the daily existence of most of the children who come into contact with major league teams. More flattering descriptions of life in Major League

Baseball for Latin players can be found. Although he retains a critical eye, Alan Klein's description of the Los Angeles Dodgers' baseball academy at *Campus Las Palmas* in the Dominican Republic is, on the whole, fairly positive.[137] A representative of the Chicago Cubs stressed the physical benefits for Latin children of working with major league teams, pointing out that the boys are fed and treated for intestinal parasites, and that they generally grow healthier than they would in their squalor-ridden neighborhoods.[138],* The boys get plenty of physical exercise, learn discipline and teamwork, and become motivated to achieve goals large and small. When contrasted to the grinding poverty in the surrounding society,[139] the atmosphere provided by major league teams can seem positively humanitarian.

The image left by these descriptions is one of opportunity, not exploitation, and it connects with the "rags to riches" mythology of American baseball:

> A kid with nothing to his name except talent and desire works hard, harder even than the other kids working hard toward the same goal. In time, he goes from playing baseball with a cardboard glove and a ball of taped socks on a corner sandlot, through tough times on the road in semi-pro leagues and on to pro ball. One day, and for years after that, he plays in Dodger Stadium. The story is as old as Abner Doubleday and as American as the game itself. . . . This is about Latin baseball players, who they are, how they got to The Show and what it took to get there.[140]

This Horatio Alger mythology also appears in the attitudes of American major league scouts traveling the poverty-drenched areas of Latin America. Deric Ladnier, director of the Atlanta Braves' minor league operations, complained that economic affluence has diluted the passion for baseball in American boys. But, referring to the Dominican Republic, Ladnier gushed: "When you come down here and you're looking for baseball players and you see people playing on street corners and in fields, you think, 'What a great place to come. They play.'"[141] Latin American countries are attractive to Major League Baseball *because* the field of dreams is built upon poverty and near hopelessness.

The assertions by major league teams that they offer an escape from poverty and hopelessness, provide nutrition to malnourished children, and provide medical treatment for diseased players should be challenged because they present a simplistic picture of a more complex reality. In Venezuela, major league scouts and other people connected to professional baseball were offended by René Gayo's claim that but for Major League Baseball many Latin children would be selling mangoes in the street. The attitude behind the rationalization in Gayo's caricature of Dominican and Venezuelan societies

---

*Keep this statement from the Chicago Cubs in mind while reading Alexi Quiroz's story in Part II of this book.

contains the image of Latin children as good for nothing but baseball or hustling mangoes on a street corner.

In addition, major league teams often claim to be providing better nutrition to kids who are vitamin- and protein-deficient. We understand that many people connected with major league teams' practices in the Dominican Republic and Venezuela are concerned about the inappropriate use by major league teams of nutritional supplements, such as the popular supplement creatine (which is widely used to boost athletic performance in many sports in the United States), when training children and adolescents.[142,*] The assertion by the Chicago Cubs and other teams that Latin players are provided medical treatment for diseases is not in accord with the widespread lack of qualified medical and training personnel on the staffs of the Latin baseball academies and Summer League teams.

The projection of the "rags to riches" mythology onto the exploitation of Latin children by Major League Baseball represents profound ethical myopia in the American baseball world. This projection of American baseball mythology essentially holds that it is acceptable to treat poor children worse than affluent children because they are poor.

We learned that in dealing with the disbelief syndrome and the opportunity thesis that more is needed than citations to law review articles, scholarly works, and newspaper reports that presented and discussed both the opportunity and the exploitation in major league recruitment in Latin America. All this was, for many, just "too academic" and not real enough to grasp properly. Where was the "human face" behind these critical academic analyses and investigative reports?

Other books tell the tales of Latin players who made *las Grandes Ligas* and whose baseball dreams came true. And these books, by and large, dwell on the opportunity successfully seized and provide uplifting human stories that reinforce the opportunity thesis. But for every Sammy Sosa there are hundreds of Latin boys and young men who do not make it to the major leagues. For the most part, the stories of these boys and young men are an invisible part of the history of Major League Baseball. The next part of this book is about one Latin player who did not make it to The Show. This is not a story with a happy ending. This is not a story about the opportunity Major League Baseball offers to children in developing countries in Latin America. This is a story about mistreatment, exploitation, and disrespect. The next part of the book tells the true story of how Major League Baseball turned Alexi Quiroz's field of dreams into a tragic, harrowing ordeal.

---

*When we heard these concerns about unregulated, potentially harmful use of nutritional supplements by major league teams, we raised this issue with the Commissioner's Office, which appeared to be aware of the same concerns.

PART II

Exploitation and Mistreatment in the Global Ballpark: The Tragic Story of Alexis Quiroz

CHAPTER FOUR

"PAPÁ, I WANT TO PLAY BASEBALL!"

A FATHER AND SON were spending time together on a lazy, hot afternoon in Aragua, Venezuela, in 1990. The boy was twelve years old, and the father liked to give his son as much attention as his demanding job allowed. All too soon, the boy would be a man, and then the time for father and son to spend time together on lazy, hot afternoons would have disappeared forever.

The father and son left the Universidad Nacional Abierta, located in the Andrés Bello neighborhood in Maracay, where the father was taking some courses in electrical engineering. As the two drove home down Avenida Barrio Independencia, the boy became quiet. He stared out the window, and his gaze locked on something. Because the father had to watch traffic, he could not ascertain what captivated his son. They had driven down this road many times before without the boy fixating on anything in particular.

"Papá, stop the car," the boy suddenly said.

"What?" the father replied, trying to divide his attention between his son and the road.

"There, papá." The boy pointed out the window. "A baseball field. I want to look."

The father glanced in the direction indicated by his son, and he saw some boys playing baseball, perhaps a youth league team. The father parked the car, and he and his son walked over to the baseball field. The boy walked briskly, staring intensely at the field. It was almost as if the boy was a moth drawn to a flame.

When the father and son reached the baseball field, they stood in silence watching a youth league team practice. It was not long before the boy spoke to his father.

"Papá, I want to play baseball!" he said, not taking his eyes off the practicing youngsters. His father smiled, not at all surprised that his boy wanted to play baseball. After all, what Venezuelan boy did not want to play baseball? Smiling, the father told his son that it was good that he wanted to play baseball and that they would work to fulfill this desire soon. The boy looked up at his father with a look of defiance.

"No, papá, I want to play baseball *right now!*" Alexi Quiroz had the baseball bug all right, and he had it bad.[1]

Like virtually all Venezuelans, this father and son—and the rest of the Quiroz family—were baseball fans. The Quirozes lived in Maracay, home town of one of Venezuela's most famous baseball players—David Concepción, who played for Cincinnati's Big Red Machine in the 1970s.[2] At home, the family watched baseball on TV. They followed and, as baseball fans everywhere do, argued about the attributes and failings of teams and players. Antonio Armas, Andrés Galarraga, Ozzie Guillén, Mark McGwire, and Ricky Henderson were household names.[3] Like most Venezuelans, this family divided the year into two seasons determined not by the planet's orbit around the sun, but by baseball: the Venezuelan Winter League season and the Major League Baseball (MLB) season—*las Grandes Ligas*. The Quirozes supported *Los Leones del Caracas* (Caracas Lions) during the Winter League season, and they followed the Oakland Athletics during the major league season. Alexis Sr. liked Oakland because Venezuelan Antonio Armas once played for the A's; and his son, Alexis (or Alexi as he prefers to be called), cheered for Oakland because he liked the big power hitters, Mark McGwire and José Canseco.[4]

Although the desire to play baseball now burned inside him, Alexi Quiroz faced a particularly important hurdle: he knew nothing about playing organized baseball. Up to that point, Alexi had enjoyed baseball with his family but had not demonstrated any desire to play organized ball.[5] Alexi had played catch and *caimaneras* (informal, pick-up games) with his family and friends from age four. He knew how to watch baseball on TV, and he understood how the game was played. He could talk about teams and players because he absorbed so much baseball from his family's habits and the general cultural role baseball played in Venezuela.[6] But he had not yet learned anything about how to play baseball properly.

At twelve, Alexi was getting a late start in organized baseball. Boys in Venezuela begin playing seriously at earlier ages, sometimes as early as six or seven years old, and many of Alexi's friends had been playing the game formally for a few years.[7] Other boys afflicted with the baseball bug had a head start on Alexi.

Alexis Sr. started to help his son make up lost ground. Alexis Sr. began to teach the boy what he knew about playing the game and to practice with him on the weekends, but he also got Alexi involved in *Los Criollitos*, Venezuelan youth league baseball, where Alexi could learn the proper mechanics of the game. As Alexi's participation in youth baseball deepened, his father got more and more excited about his son's potential. Alexis Sr. recalled, "I was impressed with his arm and how hard he hit the ball. When he was twelve, he could hit the ball as far as any adult in *Parque Metropolitano*." Alexis Sr. was also proud of how hard his son worked at learning to play baseball.[8] Alexi's whole family was also supportive. His mother, Belén, always took Alexi to practice, and Alexi's games became events for the whole family.[9] Alexi's plunge into baseball changed the nature of the family's dynamics, but no one complained. After all, this was baseball!

Although Alexi suffered frustrations and failures in *Los Criollitos*, he proved to be a fast learner. When Alexi was fourteen, he made the team as an outfielder representing the state of Aragua in the 1992 national *Criollitos* competition. At the national tournament, Alexi was the best hitter both in batting average and home runs. His performance did not go unnoticed. A scout from a major league team approached Alexi and his father after the tournament and congratulated Alexi on his performance. He encouraged Alexi to keep working hard, and he gave Alexi's father his contact information. He encouraged Alexis Sr. to contact him when Alexi was a little older.[10]

One might think that such interaction with a major league scout caused celebration in the Quiroz household, given Alexi's baseball passion. The reason no such celebration occurred is that this kind of approach from major league scouts for boys Alexi's age was normal. Indeed, Alexi knew that many of his friends had also been approached in the same manner by major league scouts.[11] It is a routine part of youth league baseball in Venezuela that major league scouts approach very young players and their families to plant seeds of loyalty for a potential relationship in the future.[12]

At the time the scout approached Alexi and his father, nobody in the Quiroz family questioned the propriety of such interaction. The systematic evaluation of children by major league teams struck no one in Alexi's family as strange or improper. After all, this was Venezuela, and one of Venezuela's two seasons revolved around *las Grandes Ligas*. Only later would Alexi and his family stop to wonder about the propriety of major league teams' extensive interest in Venezuelan children.

Another reason why the scout's encouragement did not send the Quiroz family into orbit was that the nature of the scout's interaction signaled that Alexi was only a "normal" player. Scouts' interaction with "top" players was, Alexi and his family knew, more intensive. In Venezuela, the top thirteen- to fifteen-year-old players and their families got gifts from major league scouts to fertilize the seeds of loyalty the scouts try to plant with the boy and his family.[13] Major league scouts routinely gave top prospects hats, uniforms, shoes, gloves, bats, and—if the kid is really hot—money.[14] All Alexi and his father got was kind words and a business card. Alexi was not on the fast track to *las Grandes Ligas*.

Alexi's hopes for the future were, however, increasingly focusing on becoming a major league player. Now that he was developing as a player, Alexi began to dream dreams familiar to many generations of boys in the United States. With his family watching from the stands, Alexi would make sparkling defensive plays and hit the game-winning home run in the World Series. Alexi dreamed of playing for the Oakland A's because he wanted to be a big home-run hitter, like Mark McGwire and José Canseco. He had similar dreams of baseball glory in connection with being a star for *Los Leones del Caracas* of the Venezuelan Winter League. Alexi had a dream for all Venezuela's baseball seasons.[15]

Alexi's status as just a "normal" Venezuelan player meant that he had to work very hard if his baseball dreams were to come true. He was not going to hit home runs for the Oakland A's on the basis of unrefined talent. Alexi would have to train hard to have his shot at The Show. Alexis Sr. reinforced this message by telling his son that it would be very difficult to be the best and that only hard work, sacrifice, and discipline would prepare Alexi to fulfill his dreams, whatever they might be.[16]

Alexis Sr. had, however, to restrain his son's desire to be a professional baseball player. Often to Alexi's frustration, his father insisted that baseball take a back seat to school work during the week. On weekends, Alexi could (and did) concentrate on baseball, but during the week, getting an education had to take priority over baseball. Finish high school, Alexis Sr. told his son, and then we will see about your becoming a professional baseball player.[17] Although it frustrated him, Alexi understood the importance of his father's advice. Alexi simply drove himself to finish high school as quickly as he could to free himself to concentrate on becoming a professional baseball player.[18]

Alexi's determination to finish high school early received a boost when he was fifteen. Alexi was again playing well in youth league competition, and he was also playing in a semi-professional adult league. After one game, Ciro Barrios, a *buscón* for the Chicago Cubs, approached Alexi.[19]

Barrios told him that he could help Alexi become a better player and be in a good position to be signed by the Chicago Cubs. Barrios offered to train Alexi to prepare him for a tryout with the Chicago Cubs' scout for Venezuela. Under his father's orders, Alexi could not pursue this offer because he had not yet finished high school.[20] In this respect, Alexi was unusual because many Dominican and Venezuelan children left school at the encouragement of scouts, *buscones*, or *dirigentes* in order to play baseball full-time.[21] While the attention he was getting still was not the kind top players got, Alexi realized that Barrios would not offer to train him unless Barrios believed he had serious potential.[22] The economics of the *buscón* system meant that Barrios had the incentive to expend time and energy only on prospects with a real shot at being signed. Barrios's offer further steeled Alexi's determination to finish high school early and pursue a career in professional baseball.

In June 1994, right before his sixteenth birthday, Alexi graduated from high school. He immediately told his father that now he wanted to train full-time to become a professional ballplayer.[23] Alexis Sr. was proud of his son for finishing high school and not letting his passion for a baseball career undermine the first priority of education. Nor was Alexi's dream of becoming a professional ballplayer ridiculous; Alexi had been given sufficient encouragement, particularly in the offer from Ciro Barrios, to justify the effort. Alexis Sr. gave his blessing to his son's desires, and his pride in his son grew as Alexi continued to apply his father's advice of working hard to be the best.[24] And there was much hard work left to do, more than Alexi anticipated.

Shortly after Alexi's sixteenth birthday, a scout for the Los Angeles Dodgers, Juan Davalillo,* invited Alexi and one of Alexi's teammates from the Aragua state team to a tryout.[25] Major league scouts often traveled to various cities and regions in Venezuela and invited promising players to tryouts. Often the scouts invited players based on recommendations from team *buscones,* but Alexi had never had contact with the Dodgers prior to this invitation. But major league scouts also tapped into youth league coaches for advice on promising youngsters. In Venezuela and the Dominican Republic, some major league teams would "buy" youth league teams to get a head start on the competition. The scheme works like this: In exchange for money, the manager of a youth league team sends reports to the scout to let him know if a good prospect is blooming. The youth league manager then helps facilitate tryouts for those prospects the scout seems interested in.[26] The facilitator of Alexi's tryout with the Dodgers was his youth league coach.[27] Whether Alexi's coach had a financial arrangement with the Dodgers' scout, we do not know.

As the tryout approached, Alexi's excitement grew. He knew that scouts signed players at these tryouts if the players were at least sixteen years old.† If he could impress the Dodgers' scout, he could be signed on the spot and take his first step toward *las Grandes Ligas.* Alexi's big league dreams were starting to feel more and more possible.

Alexi's mother took him to the Dodgers' tryout in Tumeremo. Four or five other players participated, along with Alexi and his teammate. Alexi hit the ball well at the tryout, hitting a towering home run that would have made Andrés Galarraga raise an eyebrow. Hitting was not, however, the problem. Alexi had always hit well, but his speed was a concern. At the tryout, Alexi's lack of speed did not escape the scout's attention. Davalillo told Alexi that he was too slow and that he needed to work on his speed. Nobody was signed after the tryout.[28]

The sting of the failed tryout was harsh, but something happened that rescued the day from being a total disaster. As luck would have it, Ciro Barrios

*Juan Davalillo is not related to the famous Vitico (Vic) Davalillo.

†Alexi believed that major league teams could legally sign players when they were sixteen years old. In fact, major league teams routinely sign players who have just turned sixteen years old. Major League Rules do not, however, authorize this practice. See chapter 3's discussion of the seventeen-year-old rule.

had been sitting in the stands watching the tryout. (With *buscones* and perhaps even scouts from other major league teams watching tryouts, the pressure on scouts to sign hot prospects immediately should be apparent.) Barrios again told Alexi that he could get him into a position to be signed by the Chicago Cubs. This time Barrios was more precise. He invited Alexi to train with him every day, like a professional. Barrios told Alexi that if he trained hard, he could get signed by the Cubs because he was a good player who only needed specific aspects of his game improved. While disappointed that the Dodgers did not sign him at the tryout, Alexi was excited by the prospect of training with someone every day. Alexi began training with Barrios in August 1994.[29]

Although training with Barrios would help, the criticism that he was too slow worried Alexi. He had heard the same criticism when he played baseball in a semi-professional league. He had heard the same criticism from two players, Freddy and Jaime Torres, who played pro ball in the Venezuelan Winter League. This criticism was in both cases followed by the same advice: "go see Emilio Ostos." Because he had to focus on finishing high school, Alexi had not sought Ostos out. But, in the wake of finishing high school and the Dodgers' tryout, Alexi now believed that seeking out Ostos was imperative. Ostos was a high school teacher in the Aragua area who was well known for training young people for track and field competitions at local, regional, and national levels. Ostos trained kids for free because of his devotion to their potential as athletes. The idea was to have Ostos help Alexi improve his running speed.[30]

Alexi's first meeting with Emilio Ostos was ego-deflating. Ostos had Alexi run the 60-yard dash. Alexi ran it in a depressing 7.6 seconds. Ostos told Alexi that he was really slow. He also told Alexi that he looked out of shape and was slightly overweight. (So much for the extra heft Alexi thought a home-run hitter needed.) Not being someone who sugarcoated advice, Ostos told Alexi that improving his speed would require hard training every day. Given what he had just seen, Ostos doubted whether Alexi could do what it would take.[31]

All this was hard for Alexi to swallow. After the Dodgers' tryout, he knew his baseball dreams would never come true unless he ran faster. But he could not tell if Ostos's skepticism was a calculated attempt to motivate him or get rid of him. Ostos had not, however, shut the door. He had simply issued a challenge. If Alexi took the challenge, Ostos would train him. Alexi accepted the challenge. His training with Ostos began almost simultaneously with his training with Barrios.[32]

For the next twelve months, Alexi trained virtually every day with Barrios and Ostos, or on his own. His typical daily schedule had him training with Barrios from approximately 8 A.M. until noon. The afternoons contained approximately three hours of training designed by Ostos. Such a schedule would have been grueling enough, but Barrios and Ostos set out to remake Alexi as a baseball player and an athlete.[33]

Barrios told Alexi that he would have a better chance to sign a contract with a major league team if he played the infield rather than the outfield. Barrios moved him into the infield, and Alexi had to learn positions he had never played. Barrios told Alexi that one of the most important things about being an infielder was to stay on your toes. Barrios put stones in the heels of Alexi's shoes to force him to stay on his toes. Barrios also changed how Alexi held and swung the bat. Alexi had to relearn some of the fundamental mechanics of baseball just when he thought he was close to becoming a professional player. Barrios taught Alexi how far he had to go to be ready to impress the Chicago Cubs when the moment came.[34]

Similarly, Ostos set out to recast Alexi as an athlete. Ostos told Alexi that he would train Alexi to become a sprinter. Alexi thought he needed a little more speed, so being trained as a sprinter was more than he expected.[35] But Ostos was following Barrios and rebuilding Alexi as an athlete to give him the best possible chance to succeed.

The frustrations of rebuilding, along with the day-to-day stress and fatigue of strenuous training, at times got Alexi down. Many times Alexi would become depressed and despair that he would never make it. He sometimes cried when training was not going well. Alexi prayed a great deal to God for strength and perseverance.[36] His family gave him support.[37] No matter how badly training went, however, Alexi never gave up. Gradually, the rebuilding process began to produce the desired results. Barrios and Ostos both thought he was close to being good and fast enough to prompt the Cubs to give him a contract.[38] With the help of Barrios and Ostos, Alexi demonstrated the true depth of his desire to play professional baseball. His single-minded, disciplined pursuit of his dream had placed him seemingly on the brink of securing a contract. It now seemed as if his date with destiny was only a matter of time.

Toward the end of August 1995, Ciro Barrios told Alexi that it was time for the final push. Barrios believed that the Chicago Cubs' head scout in Venezuela, Alberto Rondón, would give Alexi a tryout within the next month. Now was the time to do everything possible to be ready when the invitation from Rondón came. Alexi redoubled his training efforts. This tryout, Alexi encouraged himself, would end with a contract.[39]

In mid-September, the invitation from Rondón came. Rondón would be holding a tryout for prospects in the Maracay area, including Alexi. Rondón was the Cubs' main scout in Venezuela, and Alexi knew he would have the power to sign players on the spot. Although Alexi felt confident, he also knew he might get only one chance to catch Rondón's eye. Even though Barrios was a *buscón* for the Cubs and had invested time in Alexi, Rondón, not Barrios, held the power. If Rondón rejected Alexi, Barrios might cease investing time and energy in Alexi's development. Without the connections of another *buscón*, Alexi might find it impossible to sign with any team. After all, Alexi was now seventeen. Many of his baseball-playing friends had already signed contracts with major league teams. Alexi knew that if he failed at this tryout, he would not be signed in 1995 for the 1996 minor league season. In the fall of 1996, he would be eighteen, and major league teams would think he was too old. Realistically, the tryout with Rondón was his last chance to keep his major league dreams alive.[40]

Alexi and nineteen other players attended the tryout.[41] Such a large number of players would make it harder for any of them to stand out because the size of the group would limit the time each was exposed to Rondón's scrutiny. And each player knew that a pretty good performance in that short amount of time would not produce a contract. Contracts would be offered, if at all, only to the very best of the group.

Alexi performed up to his capabilities at the Cubs' tryout. He fielded grounders smoothly, ran the bases quickly, and hit the ball with power and consistency. After the tryout, both Rondón and Barrios said that Alexi was the best player there. But Rondón did not offer Alexi a contract. Instead, Rondón told Alexi that he would now train with the Cubs' scout rather than with Barrios. Although a contract did not materialize, the tryout and Rondón's positive reaction meant that Alexi had climbed at least one more rung up the baseball ladder. The year of sweat, toil, tears, and sacrifice paid off in a relatively successful tryout. Alexi felt that he now had the complete package: fielding, running, and hitting. He also believed that his year of work with Barrios and Ostos strengthened his work ethic, which would pay dividends as he moved closer to *las Grandes Ligas*.[42]

Alexi worked out with Rondón for approximately two weeks. The workouts were no more strenuous than what he had done with Barrios, but the big difference was that Rondón was in charge.[43] In a sense, these two weeks were an extended tryout as Rondón perhaps wanted to make sure Alexi's performance at the tryout was not a fluke. Alexi maintained the quality of his play throughout his workouts with Rondón. Surely the offer to sign with the Cubs would come soon.[44]

It was a Sunday night, around 10 P.M. The phone at the Quiroz house rang. It was Ciro Barrios. Barrios told Alexi that Rondón wanted to see Alexi and his father the next day. This had to be it! Rondón's request that Alexis Sr. accompany his son must mean that Rondón wanted Alexi to sign a contract with the Cubs.[45] The whole Quiroz family realized that Alexi was on the verge of his first major breakthrough in his ambition to be a professional baseball player.[46] For Alexi, the anticipation of the meeting with Rondón the next day was both unbearable and sublime.[47] He never imagined that what actually transpired the next day would ever happen.

Alexi and his father traveled together to the Cubs' facility the next day. Rondón instructed Alexi to take his position at shortstop. Alexi fielded about ten ground balls, and then Rondón had Alexi take batting practice with a pitcher and catcher.[48] Alexi was not sure why Rondón was making him do these things, but he did not really care what Rondón's reasoning was. He was convinced that Rondón had a contract on hand.[49]

After Rondón asked Alexi to stop taking batting practice, Rondón went over to Alexis Sr., and the two men walked off together in conversation.[50] Alexi was not invited to join them. He could barely stand the suspense. Were they talking about a contract? Of course they were. Why else had Rondón brought them here? Why else was Rondón talking so earnestly with his father? After a few minutes, Alexis Sr. and Rondón broke off their conversation. Alexis Sr. headed toward his son. Rondón walked away in the opposite direction. What was going on? Alexi noticed that his father was not smiling. Alexi began to fret.[51]

What his father told him hit Alexi like a thunderbolt. His father said that Rondón wanted to sign Alexi to a contract for a $4,000 signing bonus.[52] This, of course, is what Alexi had sacrificed so much for and worked so hard to achieve. But then Alexis Sr. told his son that he had rejected Rondón's offer.[53] Alexi could not believe that his father rejected the offer. His first emotion was to choke the living daylights out of his father. "How could he do this to me!" Alexi agonized to himself. Outwardly, all Alexi's anger could produce was a simple, but very terse, question: "Why?"[54]

Alexis Sr. explained his thinking to his son. He knew Alexi was a good ball-player, and he felt that what Rondón offered as a signing bonus was too low. He believed that the Cubs had not made a fair offer. Alexis Sr. told Rondón that $4,000 was too low for him to agree to risk his son's future.[55] Alexis Sr. had no idea what the market for signing bonuses was,[56] so he might well be wrong that the offer was too low. The whole conversation with Rondón did not sit well with his paternal instinct. He wanted to protect Alexi from being taken advantage of by the Cubs.[57]

Although Alexi knew his father was not trying to hurt him, the rejection of Rondón's offer infuriated Alexi. He was not sure his father understood just how difficult it was for him to get to the point where a professional contract from a major league team was within reach. He did not believe his father comprehended that this offer might be his last chance at a contract. Did other fathers stand in their sons' ways when major league teams came calling? Alexi had organized his education and life around having the chance to play professional baseball in the United States. What was his father thinking?[58]

Alexis Sr.'s concern that the $4,000 signing bonus was too low was, of course, precisely on target because Rondón's offer represented the Chicago Cubs' adoption of the "boatload mentality" toward Latin baseball prospects (see chapter 3). Rondón's offer was even below what some consider the average range for signing bonuses for Latin prospects, $5,000 to $8,000. In offering Alexi only $4,000, the Chicago Cubs' scout had initiated Alexi and his father into the Major League Baseball tradition of getting cheap labor from Latin America. Although he was not aware of the intentional strategy of cheapness employed by major league teams for decades in Latin America, Alexis Sr.'s instincts were correct: the Cubs were being cheap in trying to sign Alexi for $4,000.

Alexi realized that he had to persuade his father not to stand in the way of Rondón's offer. He could not sign a professional contract at seventeen without his parents' signatures. After the initial shock and anger subsided, Alexi talked to his father more calmly about Rondón's offer. Alexi told his father that the money was not the most important thing about Rondón's offer. It would be nice if the Cubs offered more money, but he had never been a top prospect at whom major league teams threw lots of money. The most important thing about Rondón's offer was the opportunity to play professional baseball. He needed that opportunity—the chance to show that he was as good as anyone else. Rejecting the offer, Alexi told his father, would destroy the best, and perhaps the only, opportunity he would get to live his dreams. "I want to play baseball," Alexi cajoled his father, "I just want to play baseball. Let me play."[59]

Alexis Sr. knew how much his boy loved the game. Ever since that afternoon five years before when Alexi first expressed a burning desire to play baseball, the boy had been impatient to succeed, to become the best baseball player he could. Alexis Sr. had always been impressed that Alexi channeled his ambition into disciplined strategies, such as finishing high school early and training hard every day for a year, that required strength of character and stubborn faith in his abilities. Alexi's mature pleas to let him play were not the rantings of a spoiled child. Inner forces Alexis Sr. did not understand drove the boy, but he admired his son's perseverance.

After a couple of days, Alexis Sr. relented to his son's desire to play baseball.[60] This decision did not sit well with Alexis Sr. because the offer from the Cubs was about business and not just baseball. He had seen too much of the real world to harbor illusions about the behavior of commercial enterprises. No, the signing bonus was about business, but he no longer felt he knew what was best for Alexi despite lingering doubts.[61] When his father changed his mind, Alexi's spirits soared.[62]

On September 28, 1995, Alexi and his parents met with Rondón to sign the contract with the Chicago Cubs. Rondón was pleased that Alexi would sign. Addressing primarily Alexi's mother and father, Rondón told them that Alexi's contract would be a three-year contract and that the signing bonus would be $4,000. Rondón also said that under the contract, Alexi would play his first season—the 1996 minor league season—in the United States. "Alexi will hit twenty-five home runs a year," Rondón told them, "and he will be a great hitter in the major leagues. Alexi is gonna make millions," Rondón informed Alexi's parents.[63]

Rondón presented Alexi and his parents with the contract and instructed them where to sign. These instructions were necessary because all the papers laid before the Quirozes were in English only.[64] None of the Quirozes spoke or read English, a fact Rondón knew. The Quirozes had no way to confirm for themselves that the three-year term, the $4,000 signing bonus, and Alexi's first season in the United States were in the contract. Rondón also made no effort to explain to the family what the contract contained. The Cubs' scout simply pointed at the places where they should sign. But all this did not bother the Quirozes at that exciting moment. Alexi was going to the United States, and he could become a big star and earn millions. They asked no questions. They trusted Rondón. They signed.[65]

The signing formalities finished, the Quirozes left Rondón and went home happy. Alexi was bursting with excitement,[66] and his parents reveled in their boy's happiness and future prospects.[67] Alexi's sister, Carolina, remembers Alexi being "the happiest person in the world" on the day he signed with the Cubs. "Actually," she said, "that day we were all happy."[68] But Alexi did not lose perspective. He told his parents that the hard work was really only beginning because the next step in making his dreams come true would be enormously challenging with no guarantee of success.[69]

Rondón did not give the Quirozes a copy of Alexi's contract.[70] There was a reason for this, but it had nothing to do with forgetfulness on Rondón's part.

CHAPTER FIVE

GOING TO VIETNAM

JUST BECAUSE ALEXI HAD A CONTRACT with a major league team did not mean that he could relax. He continued to train with Ciro Barrios and Emilio Ostos after he signed with the Cubs. He worked hard to prepare for the Cubs' mini-camp in Puerto Cabello, Venezuela, in February 1996. The minicamp would be the prelude to his trip to the United States a couple of months later. The contract and the opportunity to play his first professional season in the United States gave Alexi more than enough incentive to push himself hard in his training.[1] After all, he was now a professional baseball player, with a contract and a signing bonus.

Alexi was anxious to get the signing bonus, not because he wanted to run around buying expensive things, but because he had to pay Barrios $500 now that he had signed. Barrios had made clear to all the players who trained with him that any player signed by the Cubs had to pay him $500. Barrios helped Alexi get a contract with the Cubs, and Alexi wanted to fulfill his part of the bargain.[2] Alexis Sr. helped Alexi pay Barrios $500,[3] but Alexi needed the signing bonus check to pay back his father.

When the signing bonus check finally arrived in February 1996 via Alberto Rondón, Alexi and his father were confused.[4] The check was for $6,000, not the promised $4,000.[5] Had the Cubs' organization, out of the goodness of its corporate heart, increased Alexi's signing bonus? Or was there some administrative mistake, which would mean Alexi would be unjustly enriched if he cashed the check and kept the entire amount? Alexi and his father turned to Rondón to clarify the situation.[6] Rondón's explanation had never even crossed their minds.

"The extra $2,000 is for me," Rondón told the surprised Quirozes. Now this explanation left a lot to be explained, but Alexi and his father felt awkward pressing Rondón to explain why the Cubs were paying Rondón $2,000 through Alexi's signing bonus check. After all, Alexi did not feel entitled to the $2,000 because his contract, according to Rondón, only provided for a $4,000 signing bonus. But still, Rondón's explanation did not make any sense.[7] Neither did his explanation of his explanation, which he then gave to the increasingly confused Quirozes.

Rondón told Alexi and his father that the $2,000 was to cover Rondón's expenses for Alexi to attend the upcoming Cubs' February 1996 minicamp in Puerto Cabello.[8] Rondón had expenses amounting to $2,000 relating to Alexi's future attendance at a minicamp organized and operated by the Cubs? It was not apparent to Alexi or his father how Rondón had amassed, or would amass, expenses of $2,000 in connection with Alexi going to the minicamp.[9] Did Rondón have to pay the Cubs $2,000 for Alexi to attend? Not likely, given that Rondón worked for the Cubs and that the Cubs operated the minicamp. Further, why would the Cubs reimburse one employee through another employee's check for expenses already borne by the organization?[10]

Alexi paid Rondón the $2,000 even though Rondón's explanation made no sense. Because Alexi had only been promised $4,000, the Quirozes did not feel cheated, but the episode still made them uneasy.[11] When Alexi was at the Cubs minicamp in Puerto Cabello, he asked other players whether they had to pay Rondón for expenses related to the minicamp. They had no idea what Alexi was talking about. Alexi dropped the matter to concentrate on more important things, like playing baseball.[12]

Only much later in the story did Alexi learn what Rondón had done. Alexi's written contract provided for a $6,000 signing bonus, not a $4,000 one.[13] When Alexi learned this after his relationship with the Cubs had deteriorated, the deception became clear. Rondón told the Cubs that he signed Alexi to a $6,000 signing bonus, which amount appeared in the contract. The written contractual provision would have been necessary for paperwork to support the Cubs' writing the $6,000 check at the home office. Rondón set up the Quirozes by offering Alexi only $4,000. The Cubs were not in breach of contract because they issued a $6,000 check in Alexi's name to him. What he did with the bonus was Alexi's concern, not the Cubs'. With the Quirozes only expecting $4,000, and with their level of trust in Rondón, it would be easy for Rondón to make a quick $2,000. No wonder Rondón did not give Alexi a copy of the contract. Disclosure of the $6,000 signing bonus provision that was in the contract would have spoiled the swindle. The plan was clever, but the cleverness did not disguise how Rondón took advantage of Alexi and his parents. Alexis Sr.'s instincts had been correct: the signing bonus seemed too low for a player such as Alexi.

According to Angel Vargas, president of the Venezuelan Baseball Players Association and general secretary of the Confederation of Caribbean Baseball Players Associations, scouts from major league teams often deceive Latin players in order to take a cut of signing bonuses: "We have problems with scouts stealing money from players. The scouts receive the signing bonus check from the team, give it to the player, and then charge the player 'for his services' sometimes as much as 50 percent or 75 percent of the total amount of the check."[14]

Rondón was more modest, taking only 33 percent of Alexi's signing bonus. Such behavior on the part of scouts is apparently widespread despite the existence of a Major League Rule prohibiting this kind of behavior.[15] The prevalence of this practice by scouts suggests that major league teams often turn a blind eye to violations in Latin American countries of an important Major League Rule.

After paying Rondón $2,000 and repaying his father $500, Alexi deposited, with his father's help, the remaining signing bonus in a bank account in the United States in case he needed money while he played there.[16] Alexi attended the Cubs' minicamp in Puerto Cabello in February 1996, where he came into contact with other new signees, as well as players who had already spent time in the Cubs' system either in the United States or the Dominican Republic. Alexi learned that the players who spent the 1995 Dominican Summer League season at the Cubs' baseball academy in the Dominican Republic were very unhappy, but because he was going to the United States and not the Dominican Republic, he did not pay much attention to these rumblings.[17] Soon, his ears were keen to hear what these players had to say.

Not long after Alexi arrived at the minicamp, Rondón told him he needed to talk. Rondón told Alexi that he would not be going to the United States for the 1996 season. Instead, Alexi would be sent to the Cubs' baseball academy in the Dominican Republic to play in the Dominican Summer League, a rookie league organized by major league teams as part of the minor league system. This news shocked Alexi. He did not understand. Rondón had said that his contract provided that he would play in the United States in his first season.

"Why?" Alexi asked, trying not to display the full extent of his concern.

"We don't have enough visas to send you to the U.S. this year," Rondón responded. Alexi knew that Venezuelans needed visas to go the United States, but neither Rondón nor anyone else in the Cubs' organization had conditioned his playing in the United States on the availability of a visa. Alexi did not understand what was happening. Sensing Alexi's confusion and anxiety, Rondón said, "Don't worry, you're going to the Dominican Republic, and you will do well there."[18]

Alexi had just been introduced to another feature of the globalization of baseball. The U.S. government grants major league teams a limited number of visas for foreign players to play in the minor and major leagues in the United States. The "boatload mentality" of major league teams in Latin American countries means that major league teams have more Latin minor league players signed than they have visas for. As discussed in chapter 3, this visa bottleneck is one of the factors that led to the development of the "baseball academies" by major league teams in the Dominican Republic and Venezuela beginning in the mid-1970s and the Summer Leagues in the Dominican Republic in 1985 and Venezuela in 1997. The baseball academies generally operate year-round. The Summer Leagues are part of Major League Baseball's minor league system and operate from May to August using the facilities of the baseball academies.

The decision to send Alexi to the Dominican Republic also unsettled Alexi because he now began to wonder about the nature of his contract with the Cubs. First had come the confusion about the signing bonus and the extra $2,000. Now came the order to go to the Dominican Republic rather than the fulfillment of what Alexi thought was his contractual right to play in the United States. It dawned on Alexi that perhaps his contract did not say that he would play the 1996 season in the United States. He did not know what his contract said about anything. He had not been given a contract in any language. Alexi swallowed hard as worries began to creep into his head. What was his monthly salary? He did not know. Did he have a three-year contract, as Rondón had said? Rondón had also said that Alexi would play the 1996 season in the United States, and now he would not. How credible were Rondón's promises? As troubling as these questions were, they were nothing compared to what Alexi would have to face shortly.[19]

After Rondón told Alexi that he was going to the Cubs' academy in the Dominican Republic for the 1996 Summer League, the rumblings of discontent coming from last year's Summer League players now became more relevant to Alexi. He and other new signees destined for the Dominican Republic listened to what last year's players had to say about playing for the Cubs in that country. The new signees, including Alexi, could hardly believe what they heard. Alexi was not prepared for these stories because they were alien to how he dreamed professional baseball would be.[20]

Horrible. The Summer League veterans of the Cubs' Dominican academy used this word again and again and again. Horrible climate. Horrible living conditions. Horrible food. Horrible manager and coaches. Horrible trainer. These players were thoroughly horrified at how the Cubs had treated them in the Dominican Republic. Most disturbing to them was the almost constant lack of clean water and electricity in the house in which they were forced to live. The inadequate quantities of poor quality food was something else that shocked these players. Rice and plantains, rice and plantains, rice and plantains, over and over and over. Oppressive heat, lack of water, no electricity, bad food. The horror, the daily horror of it. It was as if these players had emerged from some kind of baseball heart of darkness. These players called the academy "Vietnam." It was like being in a war. You just had to try to survive.[21,*]

---

*The Cubs apparently decided to model their Venezuelan baseball academy on the Dominican one. In 1997, one year after Alexi attended the minicamp at Puerto Cabello, fourteen-year-old Laumin Bessa trained at Puerto Cabello at the invitation of the Cubs. As related to the *Washington Post*, Bessa left the Cubs' Venezuelan academy "after the Cubs moved the players into the stadium. 'We were sleeping underneath the stands,' he said. 'The house had been terrible. But it was a little better than the stadium because at least it was a house.'" Oneri Fleita, the Cubs' director of Latin American operations (and someone who becomes a major actor in Alexi's story), told the *Washington Post* that he saw nothing wrong with housing boys underneath a stadium. See Steve Fainaru, "Baseball's Minor Infractions: In Latin America, Young Players Come at a Bargain Price," *Washington Post*, Oct. 26, 2001, at sec. D, p. 1.

The players who had survived "Vietnam" were mad about their mistreatment. They expressed their inability to comprehend how the Cubs could treat them like this. This sound and fury from the Vietnam veterans rattled Alexi because he knew he was going to Vietnam next. Alexi did not know whether the veterans complained to Rondón or other Cubs' representatives about what they had endured. Alexi did not want to think about what he had heard; he wanted to concentrate on baseball. If the Summer League conditions were difficult, then this was simply another challenge he would have to conquer on his way to *las Grandes Ligas*.[22] Visions of home runs and millions still danced in his head.

Alexi was playing well at the minicamp, holding his own with the other boys who also wanted to make the major leagues. He realized at the minicamp that if he got distracted by worrying about the future, then he could lose his mental edge. In reality, all the Cubs' signees were competing for a small number of opportunities in the minor and major leagues in the United States. Alexi was going to have to earn his visa the hard way, by being the best. Of course, these competitive dynamics were not lost on the other players, and the intense individual competition left no room for team spirit and camaraderie. In the minicamp, Alexi got his first taste of baseball not as a game but as a deadly serious business. Only the fittest survive, and even the fittest need a great deal of luck to survive.[23]

The Cubs' minicamp in Puerto Cabello finished at the end of February 1996. Alexi was not scheduled to leave for the Dominican Republic until May, so in the interim, he worked out with Ciro Barrios and Emilio Ostos to retain the competitive form he honed at the minicamp. Alexi knew that the only way he was going to play in the United States was to excel in the Dominican Summer League. The pressure to stay sharp was constant and did not dissipate with the end of the minicamp. In some ways, the pressure was more intense and unsettling because Alexi was, most of the time, working out alone. He did not have the presence of other players to squeeze his competitive juices without mercy. The absence of such immediate competition encourages an athlete to relax, and Alexi fought this tendency hard as he prepared with Barrios and Ostos for the Summer League.[24]

As the date for his departure to the Dominican Republic approached, Alexi became more excited. The horrible tales of what perhaps awaited Alexi in the Dominican Republic were not strongly present in his mind at this point.[25] His family was excited for him as well. Their support meant much to Alexi, and he wanted to perform well in the Dominican Republic to make his family proud of him.[26] As baseball fans, the Quiroz family knew that the Dominican Republic was the breeding ground for amazing baseball talent. Alexi would be competing not only against other talented Venezuelans, but also against Dominicans. The trip to the Cubs' academy in the Dominican Republic would be Alexi's first real test in professional baseball.

The Quiroz family held a big farewell party for Alexi on the night before his departure for the Dominican Republic. Grandparents, aunts, uncles, cousins, and close family friends attended.[27] "It was a very emotional party," Carolina Quiroz recalled, "because we were really proud of Alexi because he was the only one in our family that was reaching his goal in life and living his dream."[28] The excitement Alexi and his family felt about his imminent departure was tinged with some anxiety because this trip would be Alexi's toughest challenge to date in making his major league dreams come true.

On May 19, 1996, Alexis Quiroz left Venezuela bound for Santo Domingo, Dominican Republic. The flight was uneventful, other than Alexi and the other Venezuelans mulling over what awaited them in the Dominican Republic. Alexi and the other Venezuelans were driven from the airport in Santo Domingo to Santana, where the Cubs' academy was located, about one hour's drive. As they drove, the boys from Venezuela looked out the windows at a discomforting level of poverty. Although Venezuela itself was a developing country, Alexi and his teammates, none of whom came from wealthy families, were taken aback by what they saw as they drove to Santana. It was hard not to feel sorry for the people they saw as they drove past on their way to their field of dreams.[29]

The van eventually stopped before a decrepit-looking house. There was no sign or indication that this house was part of the Chicago Cubs' baseball academy. It looked like a derelict building rather than the facility of a Major League Baseball team.[30] Alexi could see no baseball field or any indication that this house was part of a professional baseball facility. But the Venezuelans were told by their driver that this was it. "Oh my God," Alexi thought to himself as he got out of the van with his bags.[31] Reinaldo Padilla, who like Alexi was making his first trip to the Dominican Summer League team, was also shocked by the condition of the house when the Venezuelans arrived.[32] Welcome to Vietnam.*

The exterior of the house was white, but the paint was chipping or entirely gone in many places. Alexi could also see that the walls were stained in many places from water and dirt. He noticed that the windows had no glass but where covered with slats, many of which were missing, exposing the interior to the elements, including insect life. Inside, the house had two rooms for the players, which contained only bunk beds. Alexi saw no other furniture in the house. The interior walls looked just like the exterior walls—faded, chipping paint, and frequent signs of moisture damage. The floors were bare concrete.[33] The house had only one bathroom. "One bathroom for about twenty guys," Alexi thought to himself, "this is going to be disgusting."[34]

---

*Carlos Jaragüi remembered feeling the same way when he first saw the house upon arrival for the 1995 Summer League season. Jaragüi recalled, "When I first saw the house, I felt really bad. My dad had always taken care of my family. It was a shocking experience to leave my family to live like this. It didn't make any sense." Carlos Jaragüi, interview.

The stories from the Vietnam veterans that he heard during the mini-camp came pouring back into Alexi's memory.[35] All the excitement and anxiety he had felt during his trip to the Dominican Republic now congealed into a terrible, sinking feeling. Horrible, they had said. What had remained abstract to Alexi, what he had allowed himself in his competitive zeal to subordinate mentally at Puerto Cabello, was now staring him in the face. "How could they treat us like that?" the Vietnam veterans complained in their anger and frustration. Alexi was getting his first glimpse of the living conditions that were the source of this incredulity. And this was just the first glimpse.

Alexi was assigned to one of the rooms in the house with nine other players. Alexi's room had bunk beds, so each player got his own bunk. But there was no closet space. The boys looked around in vain for somewhere to put all their gear. The only place was on the floor next to the bunk beds. Luggage from nine baseball players quickly covered the floor, making walking in and out of the room difficult.[36]

Alexi also began to notice the Dominican climate for the first time. The airplane and the van had sheltered him from the heat and humidity, but now, in the house, Alexi felt the oppressive heat. Sweat was forming fast on his body and starting to roll down his face and neck. Alexi noticed that this house had no fans. Nine teenage boys in a room tripping and falling over their luggage in attempts to make themselves comfortable added a few degrees of heat and discomfort to the room.[37]

When Alexi arrived at the Cubs' facility in Santana, the house had no running water.[38] It would continue to have no running water for most of the time Alexi was in the Dominican Republic.[39] No running water, of course, makes it difficult to have water to drink, to bathe in, and to use for flushing toilets. The problem of drinking water is handled below, but the reader has probably already conjured up disturbing images of nineteen teenage boys sharing one bathroom that has no running water. Alexi's word to describe the condition of the bathroom was, not surprisingly, "horrible."[40]

The bathroom was so dirty and disgusting that all but one of the players refused to use it. And even the lone holdout eventually abandoned its use. During his entire stay at the Cubs' academy, Alexi did not see the bathroom cleaned. The woman who did the cooking was responsible for cleaning the house as well, but she did not do it.[41] The reader is also invited to engage his or her other senses to appreciate what Alexi and the others lived on a day-to-day basis. A stinking, fetid bathroom with no running water stewing in the tropical heat of the Dominican Republic in a house with poor ventilation. Without proper sanitation facilities in the house, the players urinated and defecated outside the house.[42] The area surrounding the house became a giant toilet for nineteen teenage baseball players for the Chicago Cubs.

The lack of running water made it impossible to shower and bathe at the house. Alexi and his teammates were playing baseball almost eight hours a day. Teenagers who play baseball for eight hours a day need showers. Alexi and the other players decided to do what the locals in and around Santana did for clothes washing and personal bathing. They walked to the River Nizao, approximately 1.5 kilometers (a twenty- to thirty-minute walk) from the house.[43] Alexi and the other players used the River Nizao as their source of water for personal hygiene for their time in the Summer League.[44] Toward the end of the Summer League, running water was restored to the house.[45] But, given that there was only one bathroom that had not been properly cleaned, Alexi and others continued to bathe in the River Nizao rather than use the bathroom in the house.[46] The choice to continue to bathe in the river rather than the bathroom reinforces how disgusting the bathroom was. Alexi had heard the stories from the Vietnam veterans about the poor quality and quantities of food that the Cubs offered in the Dominican academy during the Summer League. Carlos Jaragüi, who attended the Cubs' academy during the 1995 Summer League season, reported that "the whole food thing—this was a disaster."[47] The reports proved to be no exaggeration. The lack of running water in the house made it impossible to get potable water from the house for most of the Summer League season. The River Nizao offered a possible source of drinking water, but Alexi did not drink from the river. Those who did often got stomach cramps and diarrhea.

Alexi normally drank water in the morning at breakfast from a barrel that sat in the yard of the woman who cooked the boys' meals. Alexi had no idea from where the water in the barrel came, but he was not in a position to refuse to drink any water.[48] After all, Alexi and his teammates were playing baseball around eight hours a day in the Dominican heat and humidity. Their bodies needed water, lots of water. But the Cubs provided no running water in the house itself, forcing Alexi to choose between slurping from the River Nizao or drinking from a barrel that sat in some woman's yard.

When Alexi and his teammates had a chance (which was not often given their rigorous baseball schedule), they bought bottled water from a *colmado*, a local grocery store (if it had any bottled water at the time) about one kilometer from the house.[49] Alexi and the other Venezuelans who followed his drinking habits often suffered severe stomach pains that they attributed to the barrel water. But what other options did they have? To add insult to injury, Julio Valdez, manager of the Cubs' Summer League team and the one responsible for running the academy, would say that the players who got sick were simply weak.[50]

As for food, the Vietnam veterans' dreary complaint of rice and plantains *ad nauseam* accurately described the menu presented to Alexi and his teammates. The woman hired to cook for the boys lived two houses down the street.[51] According to Alexi, the woman seemed to get a salary and money to buy food to cook for the players. But often the woman told the players she had no money to buy food, and that they would have to lend her money so she could purchase food for their meals. Needing food to eat, the players lent her money. She never paid them back. In fact, Alexi and the others later learned that this woman was something of a loan shark. She would lend money to people in the area in order to make money on the interest payments.[52] Food money from the Cubs and the players' pockets was going not to feeding the players but to providing the local economy with credit liquidity and the woman with profit.

The menu from which the players had to choose each day at the academy was almost always the same. For breakfast, the players were served a green plantain with a fried egg on top (one serving only).[53] For dinner, rice and beans, with a sprinkling of meat (one serving only).[54] The players had to bring their own drinks or take water from the barrel in back of the woman's house.[55]

The players ate lunch at the baseball field. The lunch menu, provided by the manager of the Cubs' academy and his assistants, consisted every day of either a banana or an orange. No water or other drinks were provided. Except for one unusual day (see below), Alexi and his teammates were never served cheese, milk, or vegetables.[56]

Under this dietary regimen, Alexi and his teammates were perpetually hungry and thirsty. There was no way to get more food from the Cubs' academy, so the players had to spend their own money to get more food. Another player we interviewed who attended a different team's academy in the Dominican Republic told us that, in order to get more food, players would grab fruit from trees growing outside the ballpark when they were retrieving balls hit over the fence. Home-run hitters were player favorites because their long balls provided the opportunity to snatch some fruit.[57] Alexi and his teammates did not have the option of stealing fruit from nearby trees. If the players wanted extra food, they had to buy it with their own money. The boys sometimes bought food at the local *colmado,* and often in the evenings they frequented *Pico Pollo,* a Dominican fried-chicken shop located ten to fifteen minutes by foot from the house. Alexi and his teammates also would spend serious money on food when they would go to Santo Domingo, the capital of the Dominican Republic, on Sundays, their day off.[58] The only time the dreary food routine changed was when Scott Nelson of the Cubs' head office in Chicago came to Santana to watch the Summer League team. The players knew something was afoot when Julio Valdez began running around trying to make the house look better. The day Nelson came to town, the players were served vegetables in the form of salad and were able to eat as much as they liked. Nelson came and watched the Summer League team play, but he did not talk to the players. Nor did Nelson ever set foot inside the house where the players lived. Unfortunately for the dietary needs of Alexi and his teammates, neither Scott Nelson nor anyone else from the Cubs' front office visited the Summer League team again that season. The normal menu and living conditions resumed.[59]

The deplorable living conditions and the inadequate provision of food and water did not pass without discussion among the Venezuelan and Dominican players on the Cubs' Summer League team. Alexi and his fellow Venezuelans talked among themselves and with the Dominican players about the atrocious treatment they were receiving from the Cubs.[60] The Venezuelans, according to Alexi, were more upset than the Dominican players about the conditions. Alexi attributed this to an unwillingness on the part of the Dominicans to criticize living conditions in their own country.[61] But the Dominicans were probably less vocal about their feelings for a different reason, as the Venezuelan players shortly discovered.

The Venezuelan players, upset about the conditions at the academy, agreed that they should call Alberto Rondón and complain about their treatment. Three Venezuelan players, including Reinaldo Padilla, called Rondón on behalf of the Venezuelan contingent and told him everything. The players left no doubt in Rondón's mind about the anger the Venezuelans felt about how they were being treated. The players ended their conversation with Rondón with the impression that he was going to do something about the situation, although Rondón did not promise anything specific.[62] What happened next was a disturbing turning point for Alexi and his Venezuelan teammates.

The day after Padilla and two other Venezuelans called Rondón, Julio Valdez came to see the Venezuelan players.[63] Valdez had played shortstop in the major leagues for four years with the Boston Red Sox.[64] His nickname was *El Diablo*, or the Devil, apparently because he was devilishly good at stealing base hits from batters.[65] Now Valdez was forty years old, and he was in charge of the Cubs' Summer League team and academy in the Dominican Republic. This position made Valdez an important person in the Cubs' organization because of the significance of the Dominican Republic as a source of baseball talent. Valdez's place in the Cubs' organization also meant that *El Diablo* had significant power over the prospects of the Cubs' signees at the academy. The road to *las Grandes Ligas* ran through Valdez's hands. It would be best to stay on his good side. The Dominican players seemed to understand this intuitively. The Venezuelans were about to learn this lesson the hard way.

When he came to see the Venezuelan players, Valdez was angry. He separated the Venezuelan players from the Dominican players. In a menacing tone, Valdez verbally attacked the Venezuelan players for complaining about the living conditions in the academy. Apparently Rondón had either called Valdez or the Cubs' head office in Chicago, which then contacted Valdez to inquire about the players' complaints. Valdez made no effort to explain the living conditions or to apologize for them. He focused on one thing: keeping his job. "I am not going to lose my job because of you," he shouted at the Venezuelan players. "If I lose my job because of you," he spat at them, "I will find you and break your knees with a baseball bat." The Venezuelans were now scared. Nobody said anything in reply to Valdez's threats.[66]

Alexi recalled this confrontation with Valdez as a particularly difficult moment for him during his stay in the Dominican Republic. Not only were the players subject to deplorable living conditions and inadequate food and water, but they were also now being threatened with physical violence by the manager of the Cubs' Summer League team for complaining about their mistreatment. Professional baseball was turning out to be different than he had imagined it would be. Alexi did not tell his family about this confrontation with Valdez because he was afraid they would worry about his health and safety. Alexi and the other Venezuelan players realized after their chat with Valdez that they had only one option: shut up and survive.[67]

For the rest of their stay in the Dominican Republic, relations between the Venezuelan players and Valdez were bad. Reinaldo Padilla told us that after the phone call to Rondón, Valdez was hostile toward the Venezuelan players.[68] Alexi and his fellow Venezuelans could not escape Valdez because he was the manager of the Summer League team, so they had to see and work with him every day. The Venezuelans avoided talking to Valdez unless they had no choice.[69] But Alexi recalled that after the confrontation with the Venezuelans, Valdez began to pick on them by playing mental games.[70] Valdez would pit Venezuelan players against each other by spreading rumors designed to sour their relations and solidarity. Sometimes Valdez would come to where the players were eating with a huge plate of rice and demand that a player eat it all because they had complained about the food.[71] Once Valdez told Alexi that one of the other Venezuelans was a drunkard and a lousy baseball player.[72]

Reinaldo Padilla believed that Valdez thought Alexi had been the one that called Rondón, making Valdez's anger at Alexi more visible. Padilla remembered Valdez often making derogatory remarks about Alexi, such as "he's never going to make it."[73] This bothered the other Venezuelan players. Other players told Alexi that Valdez told them that Alexi practiced witchcraft against them to ruin their chances to play major league ball.[74] While some of Valdez's attempts to foment trouble were eccentric (witchcraft?), they indicated how bad relations between the Venezuelans and Valdez, and between Valdez and Alexi, had become. And the Venezuelans knew their futures as baseball players rested with Valdez because he reported to the Cubs.

Valdez gave the players other reasons to fear for their immediate and long-term baseball futures. The Venezuelan players often saw Valdez drinking. While they never saw him drinking during games, they often saw him drinking after games.[75] One evening the boys were walking into the town of Nizao to get some food, and they passed Valdez's house. He was drinking in his yard, and he called to the players that he was getting ready to write reports to the Cubs about their performances.[76] This did not fill the players with confidence about how Valdez might write the reports. But the boys experienced something much worse in connection with Valdez's drinking. One night the play-

ers witnessed behavior from Valdez that shook them to the core. Alexi's teammates related to him the following event, which he missed because he was
getting food at *Pico Pollo.*

Valdez arrived at the house about 9 P.M. one evening, and the players
noticed and smelled immediately that Valdez was drunk. Valdez also had a
gun in his hand, and he was mad. He started yelling, "Who is the macho guy
who wants to fight? Who is the macho guy with the big knife who wants to
fight?" Earlier that evening, one of the players, Jesús Sánchez, had showed his
teammates a large knife he kept in his bags. One of the men who looked after
the academy's equipment at the house, whom the players called *Rollo Loco*,
must have told Valdez about the kid with the big knife. "Who wants to fight
with me?" Valdez kept yelling, glowering at the boys with the gun in his hand.
Valdez walked up to Reinaldo Padilla and asked him who had the knife.
Frightened, Padilla did not respond. Valdez showed Padilla the gun and pointed it at his face. "You're playing with a weapon," Valdez said to Padilla, "but
this is a weapon too."[77]

Padilla and the rest of the boys were scared because they did not know
how to react to an angry, drunk man wielding a gun, trying to pick a fight.
Eventually Valdez went outside the house and fired two shots into the air.

When Alexi returned to the house after Valdez had left, he found his
teammates in a frightened condition. When they told him everything, Alexi
became frightened as well. To the threat of having their knees broken, the boys
now had to fear getting shot by Valdez during a drunken tirade.[78]

Alexi and his teammates faced other disconcerting problems less life-
threatening than a drunken Valdez with a gun. One was their monthly salaries.
Alexi's monthly salary, and that of a number of other players at the academy,
was $850 under their contracts.[79] The players were told that they would be paid
every two weeks by the Cubs while they were on the Summer League team.[80]
This meant the players should have received a check for $425 every two weeks.

Alexi and the other players often did not receive their checks every two
weeks. Often the date the checks were delivered was long after the date on
which they were issued. More worrying than these delays was the discrepancy
between what the players thought they should be receiving and what actually
appeared in their paychecks.[81] Alexi and his Venezuelan teammates received
checks for $237.50 "biweekly."[82] Their monthly pay was, thus, only $475 not
$850. Alexi and his teammates had no idea where the other $375 per month
went.[83] The check stubs contained no information about why so much money
was missing. Nor did any Cubs' employee or official explain why the money
was missing.*

---

*Later in his ordeal, Alexi learned why the Cubs deducted so much money from his paychecks.
See chapter 12.

The missing salary was not the only financial concern the players faced. Alexi and his teammates had to incur expenses that ate up the money they did receive. The cost of extra food and water came straight out of the boys' pockets. Telephone calls to Venezuela from the Dominican Republic were expensive, on the order of $30 a call.[84] To stay in touch with family back home was an expensive proposition. Alexi's girlfriend, Elisa Pino, recalled that Alexi phoned her often in the early days after he arrived in the Dominican Republic.[85] The frequency of calls from Alexi tapered off as the expense took a toll on Alexi's finances. The resulting lack of communication with Alexi was difficult for Elisa.[86]

In addition, the players had to pay to have their regular clothes washed. (Players did not have to pay to have team uniforms washed.) The players also had to pay something they called a "clubhouse fee." Two men seemed to have the responsibility of taking care of the house. (Of course, taking care of the house did not include cleaning the bathroom or fixing the water problem.) These two men organized the team's baseball equipment, made sure the boys went to sleep at night at the appointed time, and hung around looking important. Every two weeks (or whenever the boys actually got their biweekly salary checks), they had to pay each of these men 100 Dominican pesos, which is roughly seven dollars.[87] Each of these men received approximately $133 every two weeks from the nineteen players on the Summer League team.

Valdez also "fined" the players for mistakes they made during games. The money collected through the fines, Valdez told the boys, was to be spent at the end of the Summer League season for a big party. Reinaldo Padilla remembered being fined $35 for an error in a game.[88] There was, however, no party at the end of the season.[89] The boys had no idea where all the money they had paid in fines went.

The boys also had expenses related to their Sunday trips to Santo Domingo. Sunday was their day off, and no food was available on Sundays at the academy. Because there was no baseball and nothing else to do in the neighborhood except hang around a house with a stinking bathroom and no food or water, the boys headed every Sunday they could for the big city. The boys had a familiar routine in Santo Domingo. They would EAT. They walked around in the Plaza Mayor, a shopping mall. And they went to the movies, not to watch movies but to sit in air conditioning for a few hours and sleep.[90] The boys left much of their salaries in Santo Domingo. With money missing from their paychecks and the expenses they were incurring, professional baseball was not proving lucrative for Alexi and his teammates.

And then there was the daily baseball routine. The players woke around 6:00 A.M. Every morning Alexi's bunk was soaked in sweat because of the heat and humidity and the lack of fans or ventilation in the house. He and the others walked down to the cooking woman's house for their green plantain and

Table 5.1. Alexi Quiroz's 1996 Dominican Summer League Statistics

AVG	G	AB	R	H	2B	3B	HR	RBI	BB	SO	SB	E
.223	52	148	20	33	5	1	4	15	15	25	4	15

fried egg breakfast. Alexi usually arrived at the baseball field at 7:30 A.M., a little before the other players so he could practice hitting with the baseball tee. Stretching began at 8:00 A.M., followed by running. After these preliminaries, the players practiced until approximately 10:30 A.M. Games against other teams in the Dominican Summer League usually began at 11:00 A.M. The game would last roughly until 2:00 P.M., at which point Alexi and his team-mates enjoyed their banana or orange.[91] After the game, practice resumed until around 4:00 P.M. The players then returned to the house for their dinner of rice and beans sprinkled with meat, followed by a stroll to, and a bath in, the River Nizao. In the evenings, the players often went in search of more food, with *Pico Pollo* being a convenient and popular destination. Back to the house, and shortly thereafter it was time to go to bed.[92]

In purely baseball terms, Alexi and many of the other players were not performing well.[93] They were all worried about how this would affect their prospects. Was Valdez filling his reports to the Cubs with all their failings? During the first weeks of the Summer League, Alexi could not even touch the ball at the plate, let alone get a hit. Alexi recalled that, until the last few weeks of the Summer League season, he batted poorly. In the last few weeks, Alexi's hitting exploded, as he batted over .400 and hit four home runs. Tables 5.1 and 5.2 provide Alexi's and Reinaldo Padilla's 1996 Summer League final statistics from the Chicago Cubs' *1998 Information Guide*.[94]

Alexi attributed his problems at the plate partly to his efforts to accommo-date changes in his swing that Julio Valdez required. Ciro Barrios changed how Alexi held and swung the bat, which caused Alexi much frustration. Valdez changed his swing again, and Alexi's efforts to adjust his swing to Valdez's speci-fications caused his batting numbers and confidence to plummet and his anxiety to skyrocket. The improvement in his batting statistics toward the end of the Summer League season resulted from his shift back to his old batting style.[95]

Table 5.2. Reinaldo Padilla's 1996 Summer League Statistics

AVG	G	AB	R	H	2B	3B	HR	RBI	BB	SO	SB	E
.133	39	90	7	12	0	0	0	3	21	35	0	14

Alexi was deeply frustrated because his efforts to follow Valdez's advice produced poor results at the plate. How would Valdez report this back to the Cubs? In addition, all the players attributed their poor showings to the conditions in which they lived,[96] but this legitimate excuse gave them no comfort in terms of how their performances would be reported to the Cubs. The team as a whole did not do well that season, winning fifteen but losing fifty-seven against Summer League opponents.[97] Alexi did not think Valdez was a good manager and coach.[98] Alexi and the other players watched in astonishment as Valdez's twelve-year-old son often made the lineups for games.[99] This was professional baseball?

Vietnam proved to be all Alexi had been told it would be. The warnings from the previous year's Venezuelan contingent proved accurate in every respect. Now it was Alexi and his fellow Venezuelans who were disgusted and disillusioned about how the Cubs had treated them. It was all so wrong. It was dehumanizing. It was horrible. The players felt helpless. Rondón knew about the conditions. Nothing changed. Perhaps even the head office in Chicago knew after the Venezuelans complained. Nothing changed. Worse, the Venezuelan boys were threatened with physical violence by the manager of the team if their complaints persisted. Alexi's youthful dreams of playing in *las Grandes Ligas* received a terrible shock at the Cubs' Dominican academy.

Alexi's memories from his first trip to the Cubs' academy in the Dominican Republic haunt him to this day. During our interviews with Alexi, his descriptions about the conditions in which he and the other players were forced to live—the lack of sanitation, running water, and adequate food and water—brought him to tears. We had to stop the interview to allow him time to collect himself. The precise moment the memories overwhelmed him came as he described how he had to walk to the River Nizao to bathe. His pain and humiliation were palpable. After Alexi excused himself from the room to fight back his emotions, we sat stunned, trying to fathom how degraded Alexi felt by the whole experience at the Cubs' facility. Even Alexi doubted our ability to understand the full horror of it. "You really had to be there," he said, looking into the distance as if still struggling to make sense of the ordeal himself. Alexi visited the baseball heart of darkness that he had been warned awaited him and his fellow Venezuelans. But, for Alexi, the nightmare had only just begun.

On August 26, 1996, Alexi's plane landed in Caracas, Venezuela. His family met him at the airport,[100] and they hardly recognized him. Alexi had lost fifteen pounds in the Dominican Republic.[101] Carlos Jaragüi had lost thirty-one pounds.[102] Another of his teammates had lost twenty-five pounds.[103] In addition to the emaciation, his family sensed immediately that Alexi was a changed person. "What happened to you?" his family members asked.[104]

During his time in the Dominican Republic, Alexi told his family little about what he was going through. He had not wanted to worry them.[105] He revealed some of the awful things to his father, who advised him not to mess with Valdez and to be patient.[106] "Things will be all right in the end," his father reassured him.[107] His family's worried questions prompted him to tell them a little of what happened, but he refused to expose them, particularly his mother, to the truth.[108] There are some things that a mother should not know. Alexi survived Vietnam, but he came back a different person. Some of the excitement and hope Alexi packed with his gear four months earlier had been severely bruised. Further, Alexi had no idea whether surviving Vietnam was good enough to allow him to continue a career in professional baseball. "Things will be all right in the end." As he came home from Vietnam, for the first time in the pursuit of his baseball dreams, Alexi was not so sure.[109]

CHAPTER SIX

IN BASEBALL PURGATORY

"So, how was the Dominican?" Alberto Rondón asked the Venezuelan players upon their return from the Cubs' Summer League team.[1] Rondón knew what their stay was like in the Dominican Republic because the Venezuelan players had called him to complain about it. But because Rondón asked, the players told him the whole story about their experiences at the Dominican academy.[2] For the second time, the Cubs' chief scout in Venezuela got an earful from his Venezuelan signees about the horrible conditions and treatment the Cubs made them endure. Rondón could not, of course, deny what the players told him. In fact, he seemed to know the story only too well. He told the players that what happened to them was a "big problem" with the Cubs. Rondón acted like he was upset; he called Valdez a "piece of shit."[3]

Rondón told the players there was really nothing he could do about the situation. Valdez was an important person in the Cubs' organization. Rondón said the Cubs had a high opinion of Valdez, which meant Rondón had no power to do anything about what he knew was wrong with the Cubs' academy in the Dominican Republic.[4]

The Venezuelan players at this little get-together had the same question for Rondón: "Why didn't you tell us about this before we went?" But no one asked.[5] There seemed no point. It was clear to the boys after Vietnam just how much they meant to the Chicago Cubs. Besides, the Venezuelans had already angered Valdez. The last thing their major league dreams needed was Rondón's revenge directed either at Valdez or them. Shut up and survive.

Neither Rondón nor anyone from the Cubs' organization told Alexi or the others what the future held. The Venezuelan Winter League season was to begin in October, and Alexi wanted to play for one of the Venezuelan teams. Rondón told him and the other Cubs' players not to play pro ball in the Winter League. Only Mariano Medina played for a Venezuelan team during the

1996–1997 Winter League season. Alexi and the rest of the players practiced with Ciro Barrios and Rondón from their return from the Dominican Republic until the Cubs' February 1997 minicamp in Puerto Cabello. During this time, Rondón told Alexi and the rest of the players that visa availability would determine whether they played in the United States or the Dominican Republic during the 1997 minor league season.[6] At least Alexi had not been released; this was some comfort given how badly everything had gone in the Dominican Republic. Alexi's sister, Carolina, recalled being with Alexi one day when he learned that one of his friends had been released by a major league team. Alexi said to Carolina, "I hope I never have to live through that experience."[7] But the thought of returning to the Cubs' academy in the Dominican Republic brought bad memories back, disturbing Alexi's concentration and his hopes for a professional baseball career.[8]

Alexi attended the Cubs' minicamp at Puerto Cabello in February 1997. Alexi's game had bounced back to its normal sharpness after his return to Venezuela. Oneri Fleita, the Cubs' coordinator of Latin American scouting, praised him during the minicamp. "You have a lot of talent, and you seem smarter than the others," Fleita told him. "If you ever have a problem, give me a call." Such praise and the offer of help boosted Alexi's confidence a little.[9] Fleita was more important than either Rondón or Valdez.

Shortly after the minicamp ended, Alexi and the other players received new contracts directly from the Cubs. When the new contract arrived, Alexi and his parents were perplexed.[10] Rondón had told them they had signed a three-year contract. What was this new contract for? Should they sign it? More importantly, what exactly did it say? They could not read it because the papers were in English. No explanation of the contract accompanied the documents. All this was bizarre. What should they do?

After the minicamp, Alexi felt a little better about his prospects with the Cubs. He and the other Cubs' players in Venezuela returned to practicing with Ciro Barrios and Rondón. Alexi continued to play well in practice. He was running fast, fielding sharply, and hitting with power and consistency. One day in early April 1997, Alexi felt sick, and he stayed home. In the evening, while Alexi was resting at home, the telephone rang. On the other end was David Osorio, a friend of Alexi's who was practicing with the Cubs. Osorio told Alexi that at practice Rondón announced that Carlos Jaragüi, Jairo Rebollaro, and Alexi had been released by the Cubs.[11]

Alexi was immediately in a state of shock. His thoughts and feelings ran wild. How could this happen? Didn't he play well at the minicamp? Hadn't Oneri Fleita praised his abilities? What was going on? For a boy who had dreamed of playing in *las Grandes Ligas* and who had worked so hard to be a professional baseball player, the news of his release was devastating. Alexi was suddenly filled with fear about his future. He had never wanted to be anything but a baseball player. What was he going to do now? Panic gripped Alexi.[12]

His first action was to call Rondón. It was about 10:00 P.M. "Why was I released?" Alexi asked Rondón. Trying to sound sympathetic, Rondón said he fought hard for Alexi but there was nothing he could do. "Why didn't you tell me in person? Why did I hear about this from someone else?" Alexi angrily inquired. Rondón replied that he had planned to call Alexi. How could Rondón be so insensitive? He was planning to call? Rather than follow his urge to berate Rondón, Alexi returned to the central mystery: "Why was I released?"[13]

Rondón told Alexi that Julio Valdez was responsible for Alexi's release. Oneri Fleita called Valdez to get a report on the players who played on the 1996 Dominican Summer League team. Rondón told Alexi that he was with Fleita when Fleita spoke with Valdez by telephone. Valdez told Fleita to fire Quiroz. Rondón said that he fought for Alexi, but he was powerless against Valdez's recommendation and Fleita's decision. Alexi asked how he could be released when he was under a three-year contract. Rondón knew that Alexi was not under a three-year contract, but he simply said again, "I'm sorry, there's nothing I can do."[14]

The conversation with Rondón unhinged Alexi. Neither of his parents was home. He desperately wanted to talk with his father, who had been such a pillar of support. But his father was working at a dam construction site about three hours away. Alexi called one of his cousins to ask him to drive Alexi to the construction site. It was very late at night. Alexi's cousin, appreciating the gravity of what had happened to Alexi, agreed to drive him.[15]

They drove for seven hours trying to find the construction site. They never found the right road. As they drove around in an increasingly futile effort, Alexi stared out the car window in shock. He was very afraid for his future. He was in emotional free fall. His father was not there to stop the pain. Alexi and his cousin had no choice but to return to Maracay.[16]

When Alexi returned home, he told his mother what had happened. She was as surprised as Alexi because there had been no indication that his relationship with the Cubs would be abruptly terminated.[17] During the morning, Alexi's father called to check in, and Alexi told him that the Cubs had released him.[18] Alexis Sr. was shocked. He promised to come home to help Alexi. Alexi's father could not believe that the Cubs had released his son. "Try not to worry too much," Alexis Sr. told his son. But he knew this advice would not do much good in the circumstances.[19]

Upon his return from the construction site, Alexis Sr. called Alberto Rondón to get an explanation for Alexi's release. Rondón asked Alexis Sr. to give him some time to do something for Alexi. This was a different response than Rondón had given Alexi. But Rondón did not call back. Alexis Sr. had to call Rondón again. This time Rondón repeated what he had told Alexi, "I'm sorry, but there is nothing I can do."[20]

The whole episode disheartened the Quirozes. If Julio Valdez told Oneri Fleita to release Alexi, then that recommendation should have come immediately or shortly after the end of the Dominican Summer League season in August 1996. How could seven months elapse between the end of the Dominican Summer League season and when Alexi learned of his release? Was there a dispute in the Cubs' organization about Alexi between Fleita, Rondón, and Valdez? That possibility did not seem credible. Why had they let him attend the minicamp in February 1997? Did Oneri Fleita not praise Alexi at the minicamp? Did this suggest that Valdez told Fleita to release Alexi after the minicamp? If so, why did Valdez wait so long to recommend firing Alexi? If Valdez recommended releasing Alexi before the minicamp, why had Fleita praised Alexi and told him to call if there was ever a problem?

Further, the timing of the release was terrible because it came so late that it would be next to impossible for Alexi to find another team willing to take him on board with only a month before the 1997 minor league season started. Alexi faced the immediate prospect of losing an entire season of baseball because the Cubs had released him late in the baseball cycle. Alexi knew that not playing competitive baseball for an entire season would severely affect his ability to impress scouts from other teams next year. With whom would he practice? He could not practice with Barrios and Rondón because the Cubs had released him. Did he have to find another *buscón* to promote him to a new team? What was he going to do? His dreams of playing in the United States now started to seem like hopeless fantasies. Was it time to give up?[21]

Following Alexis Sr.'s fruitless attempts to get an explanation from Alberto Rondón, Alexi stumbled across another possibility. One day Alexi told the father of José Luis Mora, one of Alexi's friends, about his predicament. Mora's father advised Alexi to contact Marcelino Alcalá, a Puerto Rican lawyer who was in Caracas on business. Alexi had the new contract the Cubs sent prior to his release. Perhaps Alcalá could advise them if the contract provided any possible strategy. While they did not have a copy of Alexi's original contract, perhaps this new contract was the same type of contract Alexi signed in 1995. They needed a lawyer's help. First, they could not read the English language contract; and even if they could, the contract might be difficult to understand without a lawyer's assistance.[22]

Alexi and his father met with Alcalá toward the middle of April 1997. Alcalá's first response was that the contract was unfair because most of the provisions favored the Cubs. Alcalá read the Minor League Uniform Player Contract as well as the addenda that related to Alexi. Alcalá asked the Quirozes whether they read or spoke English and whether the Cubs explained the contract to them. When they answered no to both questions, Alcalá expressed his astonishment. Alcalá said that even people living in the United States who speak English need lawyers to explain such complex contracts to them.[23]

A provision in the Minor League Uniform Player Contract caught Alcalá's eye and provided the basis for the strategy he suggested: Paragraph XIX on Termination, which provided that the "Club may terminate this Minor League

Uniform Player Contract upon the delivery of written or telegraphic notice to Player."[24] The Cubs had not provided Alexi with any written or telegraphic notice of his release. Under the terms of the Minor League Uniform Player Contract, Alexi had not been properly released from his earlier contract. He was still a Chicago Cub.

Or was he? Alexi recalled Rondón's statement that Alexi originally signed a three-year contract. Because they did not have a copy of the original contract, Alcalá could not analyze it. But the cover memorandum from David Wilder, Director of Minor Leagues for the Chicago Cubs, sent with the new contract said "RE: 1997 Contract" and "[e]nclosed please find your 1997 addendum C for the Dominican Summer League club."[25] These items suggested that the Cubs signed minor league players to contracts on a year-by-year basis. Perhaps Alexi's original contract had not been a three-year deal. This reasoning opened up the possibility that Alberto Rondón had lied to the Quirozes about the length of Alexi's original contract. No wonder Rondón did not give the Quirozes a copy of that contract.

For whatever reason, Alcalá did not draw the Quirozes' attention to Paragraph VI on "Duration and Conditions of Employment" in the Minor League Uniform Player Contract, which provides:

> Unless a different term of this Minor League Uniform Player Contract is set forth in Addendum A, Club hereby employs Player to render, and Player agrees to render, skilled services as a Minor League Player in seven (7) separate championship playing seasons, commencing with the beginning of the championship playing season identified in paragraph 3 of Addendum A, or that portion of that regular championship playing season remaining after the execution date of this Minor League Uniform Player Contract, as specified in paragraph 4 of Addendum A, whichever is later.[26]

Addendum A of Alexi's original contract contained a section called "Contract Term (For Previously-Signed Players Only)."[27] Because Alexi had never previously signed with a major league club before, this section did not apply to him. This meant that Addendum A did not modify the seven-year term contained in the Minor League Uniform Players Contract that Alexi had originally signed.[28] The contract term had not expired.

Even though Alcalá did not point out this provision and its consequences to the Quirozes, he reached the same answer that that analysis of Paragraph VI produces: Alexi was still under contract because the Cubs had not properly terminated the contract under Clause XIX and the term of the original contract (seven years) had not expired. Alcalá advised the Quirozes to sign the new Addendum C* that the Chicago Cubs sent in March 1997 and send it to the

---

*Addendum C to the Minor League Uniform Player Contract sets the player's salary for the upcoming season and has to be signed with a new salary amount with each successive season.

Cubs with a request for information about when Alexi should report to play. Alcalá helped the Quirozes draft the cover letter to the Cubs forwarding the signed Addendum C and asking when Alexi should report.[29]

The thought of returning to Vietnam horrified Alexi, but what Alcalá offered was a way to keep Alexi's dreams of a major league career alive. They signed Addendum C, dated their signature April 1, 1997 (before Alexi had been told of his release), and sent it in with the letter recommended by Alcalá.[30] Now they had to wait for the Cubs to respond. Alexi found himself in baseball purgatory, stuck between the heaven of still having a chance to make the major leagues and the hell of being rejected and seeing all his dreams destroyed.

Although the Quirozes did not dig further into the contract issues at this point, further analysis of Addendum C for the 1997 season deepens the mystery of why the Cubs released Alexi when they did. David Wilder, then director of minor leagues for the Chicago Cubs, signed Alexi's Addendum C for the 1997 season on January 10, 1997.[31] Alexi's time on the Cubs' Dominican Summer League team ended in August 1996. Wilder's January 10th signature suggests that Valdez's recommendation to Fleita to release Alexi had either not been made between the end of August 1996 and January 10, 1997, or Fleita had not passed along the release decision to Wilder by January 10, 1997. This raises the following questions: Why had Valdez not passed along his release recommendation to the Cubs before January 10, 1997; and why had Fleita not passed Valdez's release recommendation to Wilder by January 10, 1997?

What subsequently happened to Alexi's Addendum C for the 1997 season does not resolve the mystery. Wilder's cover memo to Alexi enclosing the contract and the 1997 Addendum C is dated February 28, 1997,[32] a month and a half after Wilder signed the Addendum. Apparently the decision to release Alexi did not reach Wilder between January 10th and February 28th. Alexi received Wilder's cover memo, Addendum C, and the Minor League Uniform Player Contract in mid-March 1997.[33] Only at the beginning of April 1997 did Alexi receive word he had been released.[34] But Alexi's signed Addendum C for the 1997 season was received by the Cubs and sent to the MLB Commissioner's Office for approval. It was signed by Roy Krasik of the Commissioner's Office on April 28, 1997—almost a month after the Cubs released Alexi.[35] Had Valdez, Fleita, and Rondón all acted on Alexi's release without notifying Wilder, even after Alexi had been let go?

As a matter of contract law, when Krasik approved the Addendum C for the 1997 season on April 28, 1997, Alexi was under contract to play for the Cubs at the Dominican academy for the monthly salary of $950. The Cubs had not provided Alexi any written notice of his termination as required by the Minor League Uniform Player Contract, so his contract was not technically terminated. What this conclusion means is that the Chicago Cubs were in breach of contract because they refused to let him play in 1997 and thus owed

Alexi $950 per month for the 1997 season, plus accrued interest from the first day of the 1997 season.

The Quirozes received no response from the Cubs to their letter and the signed Addendum C for the 1997 season.[36] As the days and then weeks passed in May 1997, Alexi grew more alarmed and frustrated. He had too much time on his hands to reflect on what had happened to him in his relationship with the Cubs, particularly the degrading experience in the Dominican Republic.[37] Alexi talked a great deal with his father during the weeks after they sent in Addendum C, and they decided toward the end of May 1997 to send the Chicago Cubs a letter outlining the problems that Alexi had experienced.[38]

In a letter dated May 26, 1997, Alexis Sr. wrote in Spanish to the Cubs detailing the nature of Alexi's treatment by the Cubs, especially the mistreatment Alexi endured during the 1996 Summer League season.[39] This letter told David Wilder about, among other things, the lack of water in the house, the cramped living conditions, the inadequate food, Valdez's threats to break the Venezuelan players' knees with a baseball bat if he lost his job over their complaints to Rondón, Valdez's twelve-year-old son making up game lineups, Valdez's frequent drinking, and the episode where a drunk Valdez threatened the players with a gun.[40] Alexis Sr. wrote that he felt obligated to denounce his son's treatment in order that the problems might be fixed. Alexis Sr. told Wilder, "I have seen my son cry at nights because of this. . . . We think you have caused moral and psychological damage to a kid whose only sin was to trust people that offered him help."[41]

The Quirozes sent the letter to David Wilder by certified mail to the Chicago Cubs' head office in Chicago so they would know that the letter had been received.[42] Neither Wilder nor any one else at the Chicago Cubs ever responded to this letter.[43] At the very least, the May 26th letter is evidence that, for the second time, the head office of the Chicago Cubs had been told in detail about the problems that Alexi and the other Venezuelan players experienced during the 1996 Summer League season. It would not be plausible for the Cubs to claim they did not know what was going on in the Dominican Republic at their academy.

After the letter to Wilder had been sent, Alexi decided to call Oneri Fleita. "Call me if you ever have a problem," Fleita encouraged Alexi at the February 1997 minicamp. Alexi had a problem, so he called Fleita. Fleita did not remember him. Alexi reminded Fleita of their conversation at the minicamp, particularly what Fleita had said about how promising Alexi's baseball skills were. Alexi told Fleita that the Cubs had released him. Fleita responded that players get released all the time, and that he did not remember Alexi. Alexi hung up the phone with Fleita's "I don't remember you" still ringing in his ears.[44]

Alexi decided that one option was to go to the United States and take the issue up with David Wilder at the Cubs' minor league facility in Mesa, Arizona. This option seemed kind of far-fetched, but perhaps it was a way to resolve the problem Alexi confronted. Alexi applied for a tourist visa to visit the United States in case he wanted to pursue this strategy.[45]

Apart from trying to get some response from the Cubs, Alexi's only other strategy to keep his professional baseball dreams alive was to find another major league team to take him on board. During May 1997, Alexi tried to convince teams with operations in Venezuela to take a look at him. To his delight, the Tampa Bay Devil Rays invited Alexi to practice with their Venezuelan prospects at the beginning of June 1997. The Devil Rays' scout in Venezuela, Freddy Torres, watched Alexi at some of the practices and told him he was a good player with plenty of potential. This boosted Alexi's hopes, but then came the cruel reality. Before Tampa Bay could think of signing Alexi, he had to produce the written release letter from the Cubs. It became apparent to Alexi that the Cubs' failure to provide a written release letter had consequences more dramatic than the contract issues raised by Marcelino Alcalá, the Puerto Rican lawyer, in April. Here was another major league team that was at least open to the possibility of signing him, but it could not act without written evidence that the Cubs had released Alexi.[46] Tampa Bay was following the rules: teams had to provide written notice of contract termination. The release letter made the player a free agent. Without the letter, Tampa Bay did not want to risk getting embroiled in a "player poaching" controversy with the Cubs and the MLB Commissioner's Office.

Alexi confronted the same problem with the St. Louis Cardinals. Alexi managed to get invited to a tryout with Miguel Navas, who worked as a scout for the Cardinals in Venezuela. Navas liked what he saw and told Alexi that he had promise. But Navas, like Freddy Torres of the Devil Rays, wanted to see Alexi's release letter from the Cubs. All Alexi could do was tell Navas that the Cubs had not given him a letter. The Cardinals, like the Devil Rays, needed a release letter before they could proceed with Alexi.[47] Ironically, for Alexi the release letter was simultaneously a source of anguish because it concerned the Cubs' rejection of him and a source of hope because he was perhaps catching the eye of some other major league teams. If he could just get the release letter . . .

At the same time Alexi was trying to land a spot with the Devil Rays and Cardinals, he called Enrique Soto, a scout for the Oakland Athletics. Soto saw Alexi play for the Cubs in a game against the A's late in the 1996 Dominican summer season, a game in which Alexi had hit two home runs. Soto approached Alexi after the game and told Alexi he had a sweet swing and an overall great game. He gave Alexi his card and encouraged Alexi to contact him, which Alexi now did. After hearing Alexi's situation, Soto told Alexi to call Miguel Machado, who was Soto's boss. Alexi called Machado, who told Alexi to find Julio Franco,* a *buscón* for the A's in Venezuela. Machado said

---

*This is not the famous Dominican player Julio Franco.

that Franco had to check Alexi out before things proceeded. Soto had also apparently called Machado because Machado told Alexi that Soto said Alexi was a good player. If Franco agreed, then maybe Alexi and the A's could work something out. The A's had always been Alexi's favorite major league team.[48] Maybe everything would be all right in the end.

Alexi arranged a tryout with Julio Franco at the A's facility in Puerto La Cruz. Franco picked Alexi up at the hotel early in the morning and drove him to the baseball field. The field was muddy because of overnight rains. Alexi could immediately see that it would be difficult to run fast. Other players were at the field, and others arrived just after Alexi. The tryout began well for Alexi as he beat all the other players in the sixty-yard dash. But Alexi's lack of competitive playing time and practicing caught up with him quickly. He was not in top playing condition, and the tryout revealed that to Franco, and Franco told Alexi that he was out of playing shape. Alexi explained to Franco that he had not played competitively since the Cubs' minicamp in February 1997, nearly four months before. Franco made it clear, however, that he could not submit a favorable report to Machado and Soto based on the tryout.[49]

Alexi called Soto and Machado after he returned home from the tryout. Alexi begged them for a chance to have another tryout with the A's. He explained why he was out of shape, and in desperation, he said that if the A's gave him a chance to train in the Dominican Republic, he would show them just how great a baseball player he was. Machado and Soto were apparently impressed with Alexi's determination because they invited him to train at the A's facility in the Dominican Republic in July 1997. After Alexi worked himself back into playing shape, Machado and Soto would make a decision on him. Neither Machado nor Soto asked to see a release letter from the Cubs. Maybe this was Alexi's big break. Although Alexi's application for a tourist visa for the United States had been granted by this point, he did not believe he would have to use it now that the A's were giving him a chance.[50]

When Alexi arrived at the A's facility in La Victoria, Dominican Republic, on July 10, 1997, he could not believe his eyes. After his hellish experience at the Cubs' academy in Santana, what he saw before him was nothing short of heavenly. The living quarters were clean, had running water, and were well cared for by the A's. There was good food and lots of it. The playing fields were also superior to the run-down facility at which the Cubs' Summer League team practiced and played in Santana. Alexi also experienced a much better level of coaching and training than what Valdez and his assistants (including his twelve-year-old son who made up game lineups) provided. The A's clearly invested in their academy, and the resulting better treatment of the players flowed from such financial and human resource investments. Much to Alexi's surprise, the A's academy even had English lessons for the players, taught by an American from Iowa. One hour every day, the Iowan taught boys aged thirteen to nineteen rudimentary English skills.[51]

In the midst of all this, Alexi wondered why the A's had little boys aged thirteen and fourteen at the academy. These boys were not signed by the A's, and they did not play in official games, but they participated in the academy's regimen. Alexi noticed that often the regimen was hard for the thirteen- and fourteen-year-olds. "What are these little guys doing here?" Alexi asked himself.[52] Major League Baseball knows that "these little guys" attend baseball academies. In fact, Major League Baseball does not seem to think that having such young boys in baseball academies is questionable. Posted on MLB's official Web site in connection with the 1999 All-Star Game was a story from *Baseball America* that included the following: "The two Latin summer leagues have led to an academy-based scouting system in Latin America, where players as young as 14 are brought into baseball academies, trained and taught until they are eligible to sign. Virtually every Major League club now has at least one academy in Latin America."[53]

Seeing the young boys trying to keep up with the big kids brought a bad memory back from Alexi's time with the Chicago Cubs' Dominican Summer League team. After the Cubs had lost a game to the St. Louis team, Julio Valdez had lost his temper. Valdez ordered his players to run until he told them to stop. The players ran and ran and ran. An hour passed. Players started falling down exhausted, but Valdez yelled at them to get up and keep moving. Alexi fell down but had to get up. A fifteen-year-old Dominican on the team, nicknamed *Monguito*, was having a hard time staying on his feet. *Monguito* did not play during the games because he was too young to be signed, but he had to endure the punishment like the older boys. This struck Alexi as both unfair and unwise given that *Monguito* was younger than the other players. Alexi remembered *Monguito* as he watched the little boys in the A's academy train with the older players.[54]

Alexi spent most of July 1997 at the A's academy in La Victoria. Enrique Soto was there during most of this period, but Alexi's best test would come when Miguel Machado came to the academy to watch him and the other players. Machado, not Soto, would be the one to decide whether Alexi should be given a chance. Near the end of July 1997, however, Machado told Alexi via Soto that he was not coming. Machado advised Alexi to go home. This development hit Alexi hard. His big break turned out to be a big bust.[55]

Soto sympathized with Alexi's disappointment, but he told Alexi that he had no authority to sign players released by other major league teams without Machado's approval. There was nothing Soto could do. Despite Soto's sympathy, Alexi was angry. The A's had dangled an opportunity in front of him, only to pull it away just as he reached to grasp it. He received no good explanation for why Machado would not see him play. He felt as if he had been led down the base path and then abandoned before he could score.[56]

The trip to the A's facility was also painful for Alexi because it highlighted just how badly the Cubs had mistreated him and his teammates during the

1996 Dominican Summer League season. The A's invested in their academy in La Victoria, and they treated their players like human beings. The contrast between the A's academy and the Cubs' academy drove home the extent of the degradation meted out by the Cubs to their Dominican and Venezuelan prospects. How could two major league teams run such radically different baseball operations in the Dominican Republic? Why had the Cubs for years been allowed by the major leagues to mistreat their Latin players in the Dominican academy? The contrast between the A's investment and the Cubs' exploitation also allowed Alexi to sense that the fictitious three-year contract and the failure to provide a release letter were part of a general attitude the Cubs had toward Latin baseball players.[57] There was a different way to behave toward Latin children and young men with promising baseball skills, as illustrated by the A's operation. Even though Alexi wondered about whether it was wise or even necessary to have thirteen- and fourteen-year-olds in the A's academy, that concern seemed minor compared to what Alexi suffered in Vietnam.

Upon his return to Venezuela on August 2nd, Alexi's options were few. He called Edgar Tovar, a Venezuelan player Alexi had met sometime earlier. Tovar played for an independent baseball league in South Dakota, and Alexi wanted to know if there were any opportunities for him in the independent league. Tovar told Alexi it was too late in the year to land a spot in that league.[58]

It seemed like Alexi's last hope for rescuing his baseball career was to go to Arizona and get a release letter from the Cubs so he could pursue possibilities with other teams. After all, if he had had the release letter, he might have been signed by now by Tampa Bay or St. Louis. Without that release letter, there was simply no hope. He had to go to Mesa, find David Wilder, and get the release letter. Alexi had his visa for the United States, so now all he needed to do was get on the plane and go.[59]

As Alexi finalized his plans for a trip to Arizona, Alexis Sr. called Alberto Rondón for advice about how to deal with the Cubs in Mesa. Rondón said that if Alexi "had the guts," he should walk into the Cubs' facility in Mesa and tell them he was the best player in Arizona. Rondón, perhaps sensing that this strategy might not work, gave Alexis Sr. some names and numbers of people at other major league teams with facilities in Arizona.[60] This information gave the trip to Arizona a different trajectory. Perhaps Alexi could interest some other major league teams and get the release letter all in one trip. To help Alexi pull off this double play, his uncle, Juan José Quiroz, who spoke English and had lived for a short time in Arizona,[61] agreed to accompany Alexi on his Arizona adventure.[62] Alexi and Uncle Juan left Venezuela for Mesa on September 25, 1997.[63] Neither Quiroz anticipated what would happen next. It would be nothing short of a miracle.

CHAPTER SEVEN

THE MESA MIRACLE

ALEXI DID NOT CALL THE CHICAGO CUBS IN MESA in advance of his visit. His plan was to show up unannounced and ask for the release letter. It would be hard to ignore him if he was standing in front of David Wilder, director of minor leagues, as the Cubs had ignored him and his father from afar. He was not going to follow Rondón's advice and try to convince the Cubs that he was the best player in Arizona. All he wanted from the Cubs was the release letter, and then their relationship would be at an end. The future lay with some other team.[1]

Upon their arrival in Mesa, Alexi and Uncle Juan did not visit the Cubs right away. They went hunting for a new team. Alexi had to persuade some other team that he was the best player in Arizona, not the team that had released him. Alexi and his uncle first called at the facility of the Los Angeles Dodgers, where Alexi spoke first with Luis Peñalver, a pitching coach from Venezuela. Peñalver told Alexi and Juan to talk with Glenn Hoffman, who was "the boss." Through Uncle Juan's translation, Alexi explained to Hoffman that the Cubs had released him, and he was in Arizona seeking another opportunity to play baseball. "Let me show you how good I am," Alexi told Hoffman. Hoffman expressed surprise that Alexi, a Venezuelan teenager, was in Arizona. But Hoffman quickly got to the central issue: He needed a release letter from the Cubs before he could do anything. No problem, thought Alexi, because they were going to get the release letter in person.[2]

The next stop was the Anaheim Angels. Alexi and his uncle spoke to Eddie Rodríquez, who once managed *Los Tigres de Aragua* in the Venezuelan Winter League, so Alexi and Juan thought he might help. Like the others before him, Rodríquez told Alexi he needed to see the release letter before the Angels could talk to him.[3] After cold-calling two teams, Alexi had not been sent away without any chance to come back and talk. Alexi and his uncle knew that their preliminary conversations with the Dodgers and the Angels did not mean Alexi was close to getting offered another contract. All Alexi wanted at this stage was not to have doors slammed in his face. Doors were not slamming in his face. It was time to get the release letter from the Cubs.

Alexi and his uncle went to the Cubs' facility and found the place nearly deserted. Someone told them that the Cubs' Mesa team was playing a game at the A's facility, so Alexi and his uncle drove to the A's complex. As Alexi approached the field, he saw some of his former Cubs' teammates from Venezuela: Elvis Polanco, Dennis Abreu, Franklin Font, and Ricardo Palma. Alexi started chatting with his old friends, and they were curious to know why Alexi Quiroz had suddenly appeared in Arizona. Someone else took an interest in Alexi's appearance as well. A man in a Cubs uniform approached Alexi and asked, "Who are you?"[4]

The man was Sandy Alomar Sr. Born in Puerto Rico, Alomar entered the major leagues in 1964 and played fifteen years for the Milwaukee Braves, Atlanta Braves, New York Mets, Chicago White Sox, California Angels, New York Yankees, and Texas Rangers.[5] He is the father of the current major league stars Roberto Alomar and Sandy Alomar Jr. Suddenly, Alexi found himself under interrogation by one of the most well-known and well-respected former Latin baseball players.

Alexi told Alomar that he played shortstop for the Cubs in the Dominican Summer League, was released, and was in Arizona to get his release letter, which the Cubs never provided. Alomar seemed perplexed. "Why did they release you? We need good shortstops," Alomar said to Alexi and his uncle. Alomar had to break up the conversation because the game between the Cubs and A's was to begin shortly, but he wanted to talk to Alexi after the game.[6]

Alomar, Alexi, and Uncle Juan hooked up after the game to continue their conversation. Alomar brought along Jesús Marcano "Manny" Trillo, a former Venezuelan major leaguer who also worked for the Cubs. Trillo started in the majors in 1973 with the Oakland A's and played seventeen seasons, finishing in 1989 with the Cincinnati Reds.[7] Alomar and Trillo listened to Alexi tell a longer version of his story and why he was in Arizona. When Alexi finished, Alomar said that he had a vague recollection that Alexi's name had appeared on a player's list in Mesa earlier in the season but that it had been removed, perhaps because Alexi had never showed up.[8] Confusion hovered around the conversation. Something did not seem right. Alomar said that Alexi needed to speak to David Wilder.[9]

Alexi and Uncle Juan again appeared unannounced at the Cubs' facility in Mesa. They walked into Wilder's office and talked with Patti Kargakis, Wilder's assistant. They were ushered into Wilder's office. Through Uncle Juan, Alexi told Wilder that he had been released by the Cubs but had never received a written release letter. He needed the written release letter in order to talk to other major league teams.

"That's impossible," Wilder responded. "I haven't fired anyone." Wilder then told Alexi to go to the clubhouse, put on a uniform, and start practicing with the Mesa Cubs.

In a flash, the nightmare of living in baseball purgatory vanished, and Alexi got very, very excited. Wilder called ahead to let the clubhouse know that Alexi was coming down to get a uniform. Alexi left Wilder's office and went to the clubhouse, where he was measured for a uniform. Uncle Juan stayed behind with Wilder, who invited Juan to lunch and apologized to Juan. He realized there must have been a terrible misunderstanding somewhere, and that the Cubs had made a mistake of some sort. Juan's sense of relief was nearly as great as Alexi's excitement about getting to play baseball again.[10]

After Alexi put on his Cubs uniform, he went out onto one of the practice fields, where he found Sandy Alomar, Manny Trillo, and John Pierson (another Cubs' coach) waiting for him. Alexi was the only player on the field. Alexi warmed up, ran some sprints, and fielded ground balls. As the workout concluded, Alomar told Alexi that he liked what he saw. For Alexi, this was almost too good to be true. After the workout, Wilder told Juan that Alexi would stay and play in Arizona. Wilder apologized for the season that Alexi lost because of the Cubs' mistake, and said that he would try to straighten things out.

Alexi and Juan could not believe what had happened. They had come to the Cubs' facility to get a release letter, a piece of paper that would terminate Alexi's connection with this team. Instead, Alexi was wearing a Cubs uniform, working out for Alomar and Trillo, and getting the chance to play for the Cubs in Mesa. The last-ditch strategy of coming to Arizona had produced an unbelievable result. Alexi was going to play minor league ball in the United States for the rest of the season.[11] Even though only about three weeks were left in the season, the breakthrough for Alexi was more than he or Juan could ever have expected.[12]

Alexi began practicing with the Mesa Cubs. After a couple of days, Wilder told Alexi and Juan that, well, the Cubs had released Alexi, but that they wanted to sign Alexi again. It had all been a big mistake. Wilder apologized again. Juan thanked Wilder for giving Alexi another opportunity, and Wilder returned the thanks, praising Juan for bringing Alexi back to the Cubs. With Alexi now practicing with the Cubs, and the Cubs seemingly enthusiastic about Alexi's prospects with the team, Juan returned to Venezuela happy in the knowledge that his nephew's baseball dreams were back on track. Before he left, Wilder assured Juan that there would be no more problems concerning Alexi.[13, 14]

In the midst of his euphoria about being a professional baseball player again, Alexi had some serious concerns. Foremost was that he had not played competitive baseball since July at the A's academy in the Dominican Republic. It was now October, and Alexi was not in playing condition. He had no rhythm at the plate. In the three weeks of the season that Alexi played with the Mesa Cubs, he batted between twenty-five and thirty times in games without getting a hit. Alexi realized that the pitching in the instructional league was better and the competition in Arizona was a notch or two above anything he had faced in the Dominican Republic. Alexi performed better in the field than at the plate, fielding the ball well at shortstop and ending his time in Mesa with no errors. Alexi even remembered Coach Pierson comparing him to Vinny Castilla, the famous major league third baseman. When Castilla first came up to the major leagues with the Atlanta Braves, he was a poor hitter. As his game progressed, Castilla developed into a power hitter.[15]

Alexi was one of six Venezuelans playing for the Mesa Cubs. He remembers two players were from the Dominican Republic. The rest, about thirty players in all, were American. Alexi's time in Mesa was his first experience with Americans generally and with American baseball players specifically. For the most part, the Americans on the Mesa Cubs ignored the Latin players, and the Latin players ignored the American players.[16,*]

A small number of the American players tried to be friendly with the Latins. Alexi remembered Todd Noel, Diego Rico, and Matt Mauck as making an effort to reach out to the Latins.[17] But these guys were the exceptions and not the rule as far as the American players went. Alexi sensed resentment from most of the American players toward the Latins. In fact, one of the American players, whom Alexi only knew as Jerry, said to Alexi, Franklin Font, and Ricardo Palma, "Why are there so many Latinos on this team? Why are you even here?"[18] Alexi had the opportunity to contrast how he and the other Latin players were treated by the Cubs during the Dominican Summer League to how the predominantly American Mesa team was treated. The playing facilities were far superior to the run-down field and dugouts at which Alexi had played in the Dominican Summer League. Alexi and his Mesa teammates stayed in a hotel, so the living conditions were light-years better than the squalid house in Santana. The players often ate at the Mesa clubhouse, and the food was diverse and plentiful. The players also got "meal money." Every Monday, each player was given $160 for meals not provided by the Cubs. Nobody got meal money in the Dominican Republic. Even though Alexi was not paid a salary

*Compare Alexi's experience in Mesa with the following observation about racial relations in the major leagues: ". . . [John Rocker will walk back] into a major league clubhouse that is arranged like nearly all major league clubhouses. White guys dress in one corner. Black guys dress in another corner. Latin guys in a third corner. . . . On many teams, the blacks keep mostly to themselves. . . . Then there are the Latinos, a group often unnamed and ignored. . . . It starts in the minor leagues where . . . [r]acial attitudes are not broken down, they are reinforced." Bill Plaschke, *Game Is Really Off Its Rocker*, LATimes.com, Jan. 7, 2000 (visited Jan. 7, 2000).

during his stay in Mesa, he actually made some money by saving his meal money. Alexi experienced how the Cubs treated American players, and he was able to compare this luxurious treatment with the degradation he and the other Latins endured during the Summer League season.[19]

One of the most powerful contrasts for Alexi came when he was hit on the knee by a ground ball during practice. As soon as Alexi fell to the ground after being hit by the ball, two trainers rushed to his assistance. They told Alexi to stay still, and they thoroughly checked out his knee. Alexi lay on the ground wondering what the big deal was about. The trainers eventually escorted him to the medical station in the dugout where they checked the knee again. Alexi had the feeling these guys really knew what they were doing, even though Alexi was not really hurt. The trainers decided that an X-ray was not needed, but they put ice on the knee and told Alexi not to play the rest of the day. Alexi's Venezuelan teammate, Franklin Font, also experienced the high-quality medical attention provided by the Cubs at the Mesa facility. Font was spiked in the arm during practice, and the trainers immediately got him to a nearby hospital for stitches. Font never paid a penny for this medical treatment because the Cubs took care of everything. And Alexi was also told that in addition to the highly skilled trainers, the Cubs also had a medical doctor on staff.[20]

Alexi never saw anything like that as a member of the Cubs' Dominican Summer League team. Nor had he seen many Summer League teams with any kind of properly trained medical staff, even though Major League Rules require that major league teams provide minor league teams with qualified trainers.[21] The Dominican Cubs' "trainer," whom Alexi had only known by his nickname Chuchúa, appeared to have no training at all in dealing with sports-related injuries and medical problems. For example, Chuchúa had refused to ice down pitchers after games. He dismissively told them to do it themselves. Anyone seriously injured playing for the Dominican Cubs would have been in serious trouble.[22] Again, there was a startling contrast between what was available for the predominantly American Mesa team and what was available for Latins in the Summer League or the Dominican academy.

Alexi had further conversations with Sandy Alomar Sr. and with Rubén Amaro about what had happened to him. Amaro, who was born in Mexico, played for eleven seasons in the major leagues from 1958 until 1969.[23] Both Amaro and Alomar said the whole situation was weird and that Alexi ought to be compensated for the season he lost. Alomar even advised Alexi to stay away from Rondón in the future because Rondón was primarily responsible for what had happened. One night while Alexi was in Mesa, Rondón called Alexi's hotel room. Alexi was not there, but Dennis Abreu answered the phone. The next day, Abreu told Alexi that Rondón had called. Alomar overheard the conversation and told Alexi not to talk to that "son of a bitch" anymore. Alexi sensed there was some history between Alomar and Rondón that was not pretty. Alomar gave

Alexi his home telephone number and told him to call if the Cubs gave him any more problems.[24]

Toward the end of Alexi's time in Mesa, Wilder summoned him to his office. Rubén Amaro was also there. Wilder wanted Alexi to sign a contract for the upcoming 1998 season. A new contract! Alexi's concerns about his performance during his time in Mesa had not apparently been shared by the Cubs because they wanted him to sign a new contract. The ugly episode of the release was now becoming ancient history. As Wilder's assistant laid out all the paperwork, Alexi talked with Amaro and told him that the Cubs had promised him a three-year contract when he had signed in 1995, but he was not sure that the original contract had in fact been a three-year deal. Alexi wanted this contract to be a three-year contract. Amaro went to talk to Wilder.[25]

Wilder came back out of his office with Amaro and told Alexi that the new contract Alexi would be signing would not be a three-year contract, but the Cubs would give Alexi three years anyway. Alexi had no idea what that meant. Juan Quiroz had already gone back to Venezuela, so Alexi had no one to talk with about Wilder's promising a three-year contract without the three years being in the contract. Wilder then told Alexi that he would play the 1998 season in the United States.[26] The contract did in fact state that the "Club initially directs Player to perform for the Mesa Cubs Baseball Club of the Arizona League" and Addendum C, which set Alexi's monthly salary at $1,050 per month, listed "Mesa/Williamsport" and "Rockford" as examples of clubs for which Alexi would play.[27] The Dominican Summer League was not mentioned, as it had been in the contract Alexi signed in April 1997.[28]

On October 22, 1997, Alexi signed the contract and other documents. No one from the Cubs explained anything to him. All the documents were in English, and no Spanish translations were provided. He had no idea what he was signing or why he was signing the documents. Fingers just pointed to where he should sign. So he signed. In addition, the Cubs never gave Alexi a copy of anything he signed that day. (It was only later in the story that Alexi obtained a copy of the contract he signed in October 1997.)

But Alexi's excitement over signing a new contract overcame any concerns he had during that signing session.[29] His worries about his baseball career were transformed into a renewed determination to make it to *las Grandes Ligas*. The trip to Mesa had begun as a last-ditch effort to salvage his baseball career. The most he had hoped for was to return to Venezuela with the release letter. If he was lucky, he had thought, he might also come home with some names of Venezuelan scouts for other major league teams. Instead, he returned to Venezuela as a newly signed professional baseball player, who would play in the United States in the 1998 season.[30] Everything seemed almost too good to be true.

Reinaldo Padilla poses in batting stance at the front of the house in Santana that served as the living quarters for the Cubs' 1996 Summer League team. The run-down nature of the building is evident in the water damage and the peeling paint on the façade. Near Padilla is a primitive piece of weight-training equipment.

A room inside the house in Santana. The metal bunk beds, bare cement floors, and windows covered only by slats are evident in this picture, providing a sense of the environment in which the Cubs' players lived.

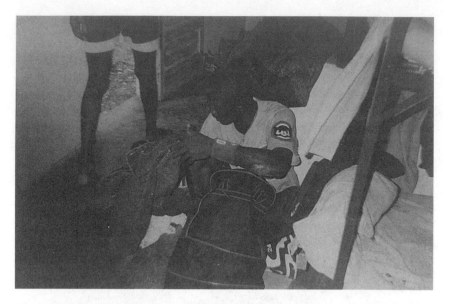

Another room inside the house in Santana. The players had no closets and piled all their clothes and gear on the cement floor, as shown here. The room is also very exposed to the outside elements because of the flimsy doors (left side of picture). Note also the large, open, and untreated injury on the player's forearm, an indication of the lack of proper medical attention for Cubs' players.

Alexi (in the batting helmet) poses with his roommates for a picture in the house in Santana. The picture provides a sense of how the players were crowded together in their accommodations in Santana.

Alexi practices batting at the Cubs' playing facility in the Dominican Republic. Alexi noted that this primitive practice device was dangerous if you hit a ball against the cinder blocks because the ball would ricochet back at the batter.

Alexi bats in a 1996 Summer League game. Alexi noted that the open dugouts (right of picture) were dangerous because players had no protection from foul balls coming from home plate.

Entrance to the Cubs' minor league facility in Mesa, Arizona, which made a very different first impression on Alexi than the Cubs' decrepit house and playing facilities in the Dominican Republic.

Alexi sitting in front of his locker in the Cubs' minor league clubhouse in Mesa during his brief time with the Mesa Cubs in the fall of 1997. Compared to what the Cubs' provided Latin players in the Dominican Republic, the clubhouse and other facilities in Mesa were beyond luxurious for Alexi.

Batting cage at the Cubs' minor league facility in Mesa, a far cry from the primitive cinder block and net provided at the Cubs' facility in the Dominican Republic (see p. 101).

Alexi relaxes in his room at the hotel in Mesa where he and his Cubs' teammates lived during his time with the Mesa Cubs in the fall of 1997. Alexi took note of how different the living arrangements were in Mesa from what he and his Latin teammates experienced in the Dominican Republic.

The Quiroz Family, 2002. From left to right: Elisa (Alexi's wife), Alexis Sr. (father), Alexi, Daniel (brother), Carolina (sister), and Belén (mother).

CHAPTER EIGHT

THE DOMINICAN DISASTER

ALEXI ARRIVED BACK IN VENEZUELA on November 2, 1997. With a new contract, Alexi was able to interest a Venezuelan professional team, *Los Cardenales de Lara*, in retaining his services during the Venezuelan Winter League season. This opportunity would allow Alexi to keep his baseball skills sharp in advance of the Cubs' February 1998 minicamp in Puerto Cabello and his trip later in 1998 to play minor league ball in the United States. Alexi did not just waltz into *Los Cardenales'* camp and join the first-string team. Professional baseball in the Venezuelan Winter League is very competitive. From November 1997 to February 1998, Alexi played most of his games with *Los Cardenales'* second team in the "parallel league,"* and he hit well, around .340. He played three games for *Los Cardenales'* first team, but he did not get any hits. *Los Cardenales* won the Venezuelan Winter League championship for the 1997–1998 season.[1]

Alexi's return from Arizona caught the attention of more than *Los Cardenales*. Alberto Rondón called Alexi almost as soon as he returned from Arizona, and Alexi was not sure what to do when Rondón called. Still fresh in Alexi's memory was Sandy Alomar Sr. telling Alexi to stay away from Rondón. Rondón invited Alexi to practice with him after the Venezuelan Winter League season was over, and Alexi decided not to beat around the bush with Rondón. He told Rondón what Alomar had said.[2]

Rondón then went on the offensive, emphasizing everything he had done for Alexi and telling Alexi a new story. According to Rondón's new story, Wilder and Alomar had called Rondón from Mesa to ask who had fired Alexi Quiroz.

---

*The "parallel league" is the Venezuelan minor league in which younger, less-experienced players play in the hopes of being called up to the main Winter League team.

In April 1997, Rondón had told Alexi that Valdez had been responsible for releasing Alexi, but Rondón now said he played dumb with Wilder and Alomar and said he did not know who was responsible. After finishing with Wilder and Alomar, Rondón called Oneri Fleita to ask who fired Quiroz. Fleita told Rondón that Valdez had recommended that the Cubs release Alexi. Then, later, Rondón, Fleita, and Valdez were all present at a meeting at the Cubs' facility in Mesa. At this meeting, Valdez denied that he had said Alexi should be released. Rondón told Alexi that both he and Fleita got angry with Valdez because they knew Valdez had been responsible. At this meeting, Fleita accused Valdez of being two-faced. Rondón finished this story by saying that the reports on Alexi from Arizona were good and that Alexi should be feeling great about his future with the Cubs.[3]

After the Venezuelan Winter League season, Alexi returned to practicing with Rondón, not because Rondón was back in his good graces but because Alexi did not have much choice. All the other Cubs' minor league players in Venezuela were practicing with Rondón, so Alexi decided it was best not to aggravate him given how important Rondón was in the Cubs' organization in Venezuela. Because Alexi would play in the United States during the 1998 season, he wanted to minimize problems that might stand in his way. Alexi already had experienced the impact of one man's opinion (Valdez), and he wanted to stay on the good side of Alberto Rondón.[4]

The Cubs held their Venezuelan minicamp in February 1998 at Puerto Cabello. At the minicamp, Alexi performed well. He felt strong, ran fast, played the infield well, and hit consistently with power. Playing during the Venezuelan Winter League season helped him maintain the competitiveness he had achieved in Mesa. He would be ready for the level of competition he would face in Arizona when he returned there in a few months. Now all he needed was his visa from the Cubs.[5]

At the end of the February 1998 minicamp, the visa information arrived from the United States. Alexi went to see Rondón to collect his visa paperwork. Rondón looked through all the papers. As he looked through them again, Alexi sensed something was wrong. The Cubs sent no visa information for Alexi, and all Rondón could say was, "I don't know what happened." There was no use yelling at Rondón. Alexi felt as if he had been run over by a truck. As soon as the minicamp broke up, Alexi went home depressed.[6]

Alexi called his uncle Juan Quiroz, who had accompanied him to Mesa, to tell him that the Cubs had not given him a visa. This news shocked Juan after all the apologies and nice things Wilder and the other Cubs' officials had said in Mesa. "There'll be no more problems with Alexi," Wilder had told Juan in Mesa. Well, here was a big problem. Juan called Wilder, who told Juan that the Cubs changed their minds and that Alexi would play in the Dominican Republic during the 1998 minor league season, not in the United States. Juan could not believe what he heard. Alexi could not believe it either.[7] What happened to the three-year contract under which he was going to play in the United States? Why had the Cubs for the second time reneged on their promises? Back to Vietnam? Alexi felt the progress he made in Arizona dissipating. This could not be happening to him. Not again.[8]

Alexi decided to go back to Mesa and talk with Wilder to sort out this mess. He did not want to go back to the Cubs' Summer League team in the Dominican Republic. If Wilder would not change his mind, Alexi would ask for a release letter. Alexi realized that getting a release letter rather than going back to Vietnam was dangerous because it was already late in the cycle of the new baseball season and he might not be able to sign with any other team for the 1998 season. Alexi was staring at the prospect of sitting on the sidelines two years in a row while his chances of playing in *las Grandes Ligas* continued to evaporate. Not only would two idle years hurt his baseball skills but they would also make him less attractive to major league teams because he would be older. Major league teams dislike signing Latin baseball players over seventeen years old. They like to get them as young as possible. Alexi was now nineteen. It would not help that the same team had released Alexi twice. Alexi faced a crisis.[9]

On March 8, 1998, Alexi traveled to Mesa. He stayed with a friend of Uncle Juan's, Cheryl Huskey, who spoke Spanish and agreed to translate for Alexi in his dealings with the Cubs.[10] Huskey repeatedly called Patti Kargakis at the Cubs' Mesa facility to get copies of Alexi's contracts. Kargakis said the contracts were in Chicago, but she promised to contact the Chicago office to get copies sent to Alexi. Alexi did not get copies of his contracts after these phone calls.[11]

Before Alexi went to the Cubs' facility, he called both Sandy Alomar Sr. and Rubén Amaro. Alomar asked why Alexi was not in Mesa. When Alexi told Alomar that the Cubs had ordered him to the Dominican Republic, Alomar advised Alexi to find a lawyer and clarify matters. Alomar again thought the whole situation was strange. Amaro had the same reaction when Alexi called him. Alexi asked Amaro about Wilder's promises of a three-year contract and playing in the United States, and Amaro agreed that Wilder had promised these things. But Amaro said he could do nothing. That was the system. Alexi had to talk to Wilder.[12]

Before Alexi went to see Wilder, he called Rondón to tell him what Alomar and Amaro had said. Rondón told Alexi that he had talked to Wilder, who confirmed that Alexi had a three-year contract, but that he had to go to the Dominican Republic for the 1998 Summer League season. Rondón advised Alexi not to worry and to go to the Dominican Republic and prove how good a player he was. "Kill the Dominican league and all will be well," Rondón encouraged Alexi.[13]

Was Rondón serious? The Venezuelan players twice complained to Rondón about the degrading treatment they had received during the Cubs' Summer League season. Rondón admitted that what they told him was a "big problem" with the Cubs. Now Rondón was advising him to go back? Alexi knew better than to believe that the situation would be improved from his experience in 1996. After all, he had first heard about Vietnam from the Venezuelan players who had been there in 1995. Why would the Cubs improve things for the 1998 season when the mistreatment of players had been going on for years?[14]

With Cheryl Huskey, Alexi went to David Wilder's office at the Cubs' facility in Mesa. "Why are you sending me to the Dominican Republic?" Alexi asked.

The apologetic Wilder of October 1997 had vanished: "I'm the boss, and I can do whatever I want with you." Alexi told Wilder that he did not want to go back to the Dominican Republic and that he would rather have a release letter. Wilder said that Alexi could have a release letter but that he would suspend Alexi for six years, meaning that he could not sign with any other team during that period. Alexi had not expected this kind of threat. He thought Wilder would just give him a release letter and be done with him.[15]

A suspension? Alexi had no idea what Wilder was talking about. All Alexi could say was "why?" Wilder responded that six years might be too harsh, but he would suspend Alexi for two years if Alexi wanted a release letter. Two years, six years, it did not make any difference. Either would end any chance Alexi, at age nineteen, would have of signing with a major league team. The meeting with Wilder clarified Alexi's choice: either go to the Dominican Republic with the Cubs or never play professional baseball with a major league team. Take it or leave it was Wilder's posture at the end of the meeting. Alexi wanted to talk it over with his family. He and Cheryl Huskey left Wilder's office.[16]

Alexi was depressed. He left Cheryl's house two days before he was to fly back to Venezuela, and he wandered around Mesa. As he moped around Mesa, he remembered that in October 1997 he and Juan had met a woman, Magdelena Schwartz, who ran a Latin community center. He found her number and made an appointment to see her. He checked into the Super 8 Motel[17] and then went to see Schwartz. At her house, Alexi also met a lawyer, Gelly Valero. Alexi told them what had happened to him, and they talked about his situation for an hour or so. Valero and Schwartz both said that if Alexi wanted to pursue his baseball dreams, the only option was to go back to the Dominican Republic. Even though that was not what Alexi wanted to hear, he also knew that their analysis of the situation was correct.[18]

On April 3rd, Alexi returned to Venezuela, depressed as he had never been before. Not even the dark days of self-doubt he had while training with Ciro Barrios and Emilio Ostos could match the emotional funk in which he now found himself. Apart from confirming that he would go to the Dominican Republic, Alexi did not have contact with Alberto Rondón. Alexi did not practice much during April 1998. He did not want to practice. Practicing reminded him of what he was going to experience again in the Dominican Republic. Baseball was no longer fun. Baseball now simply brought to Alexi memories of his mistreatment that made him shudder. Many times during the weeks before he left for the Dominican Republic Alexi felt like quitting. Why should he subject himself to degradation again?[19]

But Alexi did not throw in the towel. Deep inside he still wanted to play baseball. He still wanted his dream of a major league career to come true. It was his dream, and he was not going to let the Cubs take that from him, no matter how many lies they told, how much disrespect they showed, and how badly they mistreated him.[20] Although his family members supported his decision, he felt alone. Alexis Sr. knew that his son was depressed, but he also knew that Alexi had to make his own decisions.[21] The Quiroz household was somber on the eve of Alexi's departure for his second tour of duty in the Dominican Republic. The familial excitement over Alexi's career had disappeared. There was no family party this time to celebrate Alexi's departure.[22]

When Alexi arrived in the Dominican Republic, he discovered that the living quarters for the Cubs' Summer League team were no longer located at the squalid house in Santana. The living quarters were now in the larger town of Nizao, near Santana. Most of the Venezuelan players, including Alexi, were assigned to a house located in one of the ghettos of Nizao. People in the neighborhood told the players that the house had formerly been a brothel. Under its previous owner, the first floor of the house served as a bar; prostitutes turned their tricks on the second floor. When Alexi and his Venezuelan teammates arrived, the first floor was abandoned, wrecked, and filthy. Alexi and his teammates got to live and sleep where prostitutes once earned their living.[23]

This former use of the property suggests it was in a tough part of town. Alexi and his teammates realized they were not living in a safe area. Despite their precautions, many of Alexi's teammates were robbed in the neighborhood during the Summer League season. Thieves also broke into the house and stole money, clothes, and valuables.[24] How the Chicago Cubs could do this to their players was again a source of anger and frustration for the Venezuelan players, but Alexi and other Vietnam veterans knew it was hopeless to complain.[25] For starters, Julio Valdez was still in charge.

Worse for Alexi was the history between him and Valdez. Valdez was responsible for the Cubs' release of Alexi in April 1997, and he probably did not take kindly to being confronted by Rondón, Fleita, Wilder, and Alomar about Alexi's release. Fleita had even called Valdez a liar in connection with the Quiroz case. But perhaps worst of all for Valdez, Quiroz was back, which meant Valdez's authority had been challenged and overruled. Alexi had not been in the Dominican Republic long before he found himself living in a crime-ridden neighborhood, sleeping in a room formerly used for prostitution, and coached by a man who possibly detested him. Welcome back, Alexi.

The house in which Alexi stayed had running water for most of the time he remained in the Dominican Republic, so Alexi and his Venezuelan teammates could use the one bathroom in the house. They cleaned it themselves because no one else was responsible for keeping the bathroom clean. Instead of walking to a river to bathe when the house did not have running water, the players went to a shower at a club in Nizao. The players did not drink water from the house's pipes but instead bought bottled water from stores in Nizao.[26]

The Cubs had not changed their approach to food. The daily menu was the same as it had been in Santana. Alexi and some of the other players did not bother with the food the Cubs provided. Alexi, like many of the players, paid a local woman to cook for him,[27] and he ate his dinner at her house.[28] In addition, being in a city made it easier for the players to get food from other sources. Alexi was glad not to have to frequent *Pico Pollo* again and again and again and again.[29]

The rooms on the second floor of the former brothel were slightly bigger than the rooms in the house in Santana, but the players still had no closets. All their gear went on the floor, which made walking around an adventure. As at Santana, the Nizao brothel house had no fans or proper ventilation, but Alexi bought a fan in Nizao and used it to circulate some air for himself and his roommates. The players soon learned why clients of the prostitutes probably cursed their luck when it rained. The house had a flimsy, leaky metal roof that was full of holes and leaked profusely during the rain. When it rained, everything got wet.[30]

The routine with salary payments was the same as it had been at Santana. Roughly every two weeks Alexi and his teammates would receive paychecks. Alexi received a check for $330 for each two week period, or $660 a month.[31] At the time, Alexi was not sure why he received more money than some of the other players, even players who were also second- or even third-timers in the Summer League.

When Alexi was in the Dominican Republic, he did not know what his contract said about his salary, so he had no idea how much money he should receive.[32] The contract Alexi signed in Mesa said that his monthly salary was $1,050.[33] Under his contract, Alexi should have received $525 every two weeks, not $330. At the time, Alexi did not know this because he had not been given a copy of the contract he signed in Mesa. As during his first stay in the Dominican Republic, the Cubs provided no information about why $390 per month was not paid to Alexi.

On the baseball field, the tension between Alexi and Julio Valdez became immediately apparent.[34] Valdez began to play mental games with Alexi as soon as the Dominican Summer League season started. Valdez played mind games with other players too, but Alexi sensed that with him things were personal. "Quiroz, you have no future here," Valdez told him one day.[35] Reinaldo Padilla remembered Valdez saying in front of the team, "Quiroz, you're a mommy's boy, a sissy."[36] Valdez also repeatedly told players that Alexi was too small to play baseball and that he was not going to make it.[37]

In the first five games of the Summer League season, Alexi hit three home runs (which surprised Alexi given how little he had practiced during April). Valdez then benched Alexi.[38] People in the stands who had watched Alexi belt those early home runs called for Valdez to "put in number 20" (Alexi), but instead Valdez let Alexi warm the bench.[39] Other players on the team could not understand why Valdez would not play Alexi.[40] Alexi realized he was not going to get many opportunities to prove himself with Valdez in charge.[41]

Valdez also had not given up his drinking since Alexi was last in the Dominican Republic. The players often saw him drinking after games,[42] and one night there was a disturbing incident that brought to mind Valdez's 1996 pistol-toting tirade. One evening when Alexi was eating at the house of the woman who cooked for him, two of the Cubs' players got into a fight. After tempers had cooled, Valdez appeared at the brothel house drunk. He went berserk and began yelling, "Who wants to fight me? Who wants to fight THE MAN? I'm the man." Frustrated at the players' reluctance to fight, Valdez threw and kicked their clothes and gear around, then began to throw the players' stuff into the street. Alexi returned to the brothel house after Valdez left, and he found his teammates scared about what happened.[43]

As if things were not bad enough, Alexi got sick in the third week of June 1998. He was coughing painful and unproductive coughs that were keeping him from running efficiently. The Cubs' academy had no one who could provide Alexi with medical advice, and he had been advised not to go to the Nizao community medical center,[44] so he had to take himself to a hospital in Bani, not far from Nizao.

On June 20, 1998, Dr. William Mejía diagnosed Alexi with bronchial pneumonia, and he prescribed some drugs and Tylenol.[45] Alexi paid for the medicines with his own money.[46] Dr. Mejía said Alexi was crazy to be playing baseball and that he needed at least two weeks of rest without baseball.

When Alexi got back to Nizao, he told Valdez what the doctor had advised. Valdez allowed Alexi one week off, offered no assistance to Alexi, and never showed any interest in whether he recovered from the infection. Alexi wondered how the Cubs would have handled his pneumonia in Mesa.[47] But bronchial pneumonia was nothing compared to what Alexi soon would endure.

Alexi took his medicine and slowly began to feel better. He took only one week away from the team, and when he returned, he felt better but not completely well. He still had trouble breathing and would cough now and again. The twelve hours per day of practices and games were physically grueling, even for players who were not fighting bronchial pneumonia, and all the nourishment they got during the day was an orange in the afternoon.[48] No water.

No juice. Just an orange in the mid-afternoon. Players frequently passed out from the combination of the tropical heat and the lack of water, and Chuchúa, the Cubs' "trainer," would respond by splashing a little water on their faces. No other medical or other attention was given to players lying prostrate on the turf, and Valdez seemed unconcerned. Alexi knew this would never happen in Mesa.[49]

On July 25, 1998, Valdez included Alexi in the lineup at third base for a game against the New York Mets. Since Valdez had been benching him, Alexi was going to try to make the best of every opportunity Valdez grudgingly gave him. Alexi tried to put out of his mind all the anger and aggravation the Cubs' mistreatment of him and his teammates caused. Alexi knew that he played his best when baseball was a joy, and he wanted to separate the game between the lines from what happened to him outside the baseball diamond. When it came time to take the field, Alexi sprinted to third base with extra vigor. As he fielded warmup grounders, he recalled the stones that Ciro Barrios used to put in the heels of his shoes. "Stay on your toes, stay on your toes." Alexi would stay on his toes, ready for anything that came his way.[50]

In the third inning, a Mets' batter hit a low line drive to Alexi's left, between shortstop and third base. Alexi dove for the ball and almost caught it, but it continued into left field. Alexi hit the ground hard, left shoulder first. When he hit the ground, Alexi heard a terrible pop in his shoulder. Prostrate on the ground, he looked at his left shoulder and was horrified to see it sticking awkwardly up near his neck. Alexi's teammates came running when they heard Alexi scream for help. They knew something very bad had happened to Alexi's shoulder by the way he hit the ground and from the way he screamed. It was a terrible moment.[51]

Chuchúa and the Mets' trainer stood over Alexi, without any idea what they should do as Alexi writhed in pain on the infield. Eleazar Medina recalled that the trainers tried to pick Alexi up by grabbing his jersey, which caused Alexi to scream even louder, horrifying and scaring the other Cubs' players. Next the trainers slipped their hands underneath Alexi's legs and back and carried him to the Cubs' dugout, where they again started to take off Alexi's uniform shirt. Again, Alexi howled in pain, but the trainers persisted with removing Alexi's shirt.[52]

Once the shirt was removed, Alexi and everybody else in the dugout saw that the shoulder was either badly dislocated, broken, or something equally horrible. Alexi was nearing panic, but the trainers for the Cubs and Mets decided that they should rotate Alexi's left arm to see whether it would move. They grabbed his left arm and tried to move it back and forth and up over his head. Alexi screamed at them to stop because of the pain, and he begged them to get a doctor. "We know what we are doing," the trainers reassured Alexi, but neither Alexi nor his teammates were reassured. Oblivious to his pleas, the two trainers yanked, twisted, and pulled at his left arm from several different angles, but they could not get it to move much. Perplexed, the trainers then said, "We should take you to a hospital."[53]

Valdez's assistant and Chuchúa then bundled Alexi into Valdez's car, and off they sped toward the hospital in San Cristóbal, about thirty minutes away from Nizao. Why they did not go to the hospital in Baní, which was closer than San Cristóbal, Alexi did not know.[54] Perhaps the San Cristóbal hospital was better for Alexi's kind of injury. This would have made sense if Alexi had actually been treated in the hospital at San Cristóbal by a doctor.

Alexi cried and moaned grotesquely during the excruciatingly painful drive to San Cristóbal. After the half-hour drive, they reached the public hospital in San Cristóbal—the Hospital y Centro Sanitario Juan Pablo Piña—but they did not go inside. Instead, Chuchúa asked some hospital staff members who were outside the building where García was. They replied that García was at home. Chuchúa then sent someone to fetch García. Alexi, trying to deal with the pain, did not understand what was happening,[55] but he thought García must be a doctor, maybe a sports doctor since García had been recalled from home. But when García arrived, he was dressed in a T-shirt, shorts, and sandals and was covered with splotches of paint. Maybe García was painting his house and had been brought back to the hospital to care for Alexi. García took Alexi into the hospital to have X-rays taken as the pain continued to eat away at Alexi. At this point, Alexi believed that García was a doctor because how else could someone walk into a hospital and take X-rays. But instead of going to another room in the hospital after the X-rays, García and Chuchúa took Alexi outside to the parking lot.[56]

García and Chuchúa led Alexi to a "storage room" located near the hospital but still in the parking lot, as best as Alexi remembers. Whatever it was, the room was not a hospital room or a doctor's office. Neither García nor Chuchúa explained anything to Alexi, who started to worry about what was happening. García and Chuchúa seemed to Alexi to be on familiar terms, but in the circumstances, Alexi was in no condition to evaluate whether García and Chuchúa were friends or colleagues.[57]

Inside the storage room, García and Chuchúa tried to move Alexi's left arm, just as the two trainers had attempted at the baseball field. These efforts caused Alexi more pain. García and Chuchúa next laid Alexi down on the ground and tried to move his arm. Still the arm would not move much. García then decided that a more aggressive strategy was required.[58]

García pressed down on Alexi's shoulder with his foot. Then García stomped on Alexi's shoulder. The stomping was followed by García's kicking his shoulder, trying apparently to get the shoulder to pop back into place. Despite Alexi's protests, García continued kicking, with Chuchúa holding Alexi down to prevent him from moving out of the way. Then García suddenly stopped. The arm and shoulder had not moved at all. García then said something to Chuchúa that Alexi did not hear because of the pain in his shoulder and the shock of what was happening. Alexi felt helpless and weak as the pain drained away his strength. García then left the storage room, and Alexi was alone with Chuchúa. Alexi managed to ask Chuchúa who García was, but Alexi does not remember what Chuchúa said in response.[59]

In a few minutes, García returned with a nurse, who gave Alexi a shot of something, perhaps a painkiller. After a few moments, García resumed stomping on Alexi's shoulder, but this time with more force. Then Alexi heard his shoulder crack and pop very loudly, and the shoulder seemed to snap back into place. Almost immediately the pain went away, and Alexi almost believed that García's primitive treatment method had worked. But before this belief could take root, the pain returned. When Alexi told García that the pain was back, García told Alexi such pain was normal with these kinds of injuries. García immobilized Alexi's arm in a plastic sling, told Alexi to buy 500 milligrams of something he did not understand, and handed him a note referring him to an orthopedic doctor.[60] Then García walked out the door of the storage room with the nurse, and Alexi never saw him again.[61]

Valdez's assistant and Chuchúa then drove Alexi back to the Cubs' baseball facility in Nizao. As they drove back, Alexi was in pain and was also worried that the injury might threaten his baseball career. When they arrived back at the baseball field, the game between the Cubs and Mets was just about finished.[62] Alexi came over to the Cubs' dugout, and Julio Valdez glanced at Alexi and simply said, "Your season is over." Valdez said nothing more to Alexi about the injury.[63] Strangely, such coldness from Valdez shocked Alexi.[64] His teammates showed compassion and concern for Alexi and took care of him for the rest of the day, and the support from his fellow players made Alexi feel a bit better emotionally. But even though his teammates were compassionate, they were not doctors. They did not know how to help the pain go away.[65]

Alexis Sr. was stunned by what his son told him about how he had been treated in San Cristóbal. He knew his son was in serious trouble because, when Alexi called his father that evening and told him what had happened, Alexi cried during the entire conversation. Alexis Sr. felt as helpless as Alexi.

At first, Alexis Sr. wanted his son to get on the first plane back to Venezuela. He was concerned that Alexi would not be given proper medical treatment by the Cubs in the Dominican Republic. But he also worried that if Alexi left and came home to Venezuela, the Cubs would not help Alexi in any way, especially in paying for the medical expenses that Alexi was sure to have. Alexis Sr.'s experiences working for big companies had taught him that procedures must be followed before such companies will live up to their responsibilities to employees. He advised his son to talk to Valdez the next day and ask the Cubs for help because the Quirozes did not want the Cubs telling them later that they did not follow the correct procedure. It was a gut-wrenching thing to tell his injured and frightened son.[66]

That night Alexi did not sleep. Fear, anger, and wild thoughts raced through Alexi's mind. Why was this happening to him? What had he done wrong? What had he done to deserve this treatment? Would he ever be able to play baseball again? He spent all night crying because of the pain, trying desperately to cry quietly so as not to disturb his teammates.[67] Eleazar Medina slept in a bunk close to Alexi, and he heard Alexi's efforts to deal with his pain during the night. Medina said it was a "tragic night."[68]

The next morning, July 26th, Alexi saw Valdez at the Cubs' baseball facility and asked him for help, just as his father had recommended. Valdez responded to Alexi's pleas for help by saying, "I can't do anything for you. I'm not a doctor." Alexi begged Valdez to arrange for Alexi to go to a hospital and have his shoulder examined and treated properly. All Alexi got in return was, "I can't do anything for you. I'm not a doctor." In Alexi's eyes, Valdez just wanted him to go away.[69]

After his conversation with Valdez, Alexi returned to the brothel house by *moto-concho*, a kind of moped used in the Dominican Republic. It became clear to Alexi that the jarring and bumping of the *moto-concho* was bad for his shoulder, and the trip back made him feel worse. The first thing Alexi did upon his return from the baseball field was call his parents.[70] Alexis Sr. told his son he should now try to get to a hospital himself. It sounded to Alexi's parents that the injury needed immediate attention and that Alexi could not wait until he was back in Venezuela to get proper treatment. Alexi's entire baseball career, and perhaps his future ability to use his left arm and shoulder, now seemed to be at stake. Valdez's attitude about the injury disgusted Alexi's parents.[71]

Alexi hung up the telephone thinking he would try that day to go to the hospital in Baní, but the pain in his shoulder so debilitated him that all he could manage to do was walk back to the brothel house and collapse on his bunk. Because it was a Sunday, Alexi's teammates were not at the baseball field, and they spent the day caring for Alexi.[72] Medina remembered that the second night after the injury was just as bad for Alexi as the first.[73]

The next morning, July 27th, Alexi went to see Valdez again. He told Valdez about the pain and how it would not go away, and again begged Valdez to help him get to a hospital for treatment. Valdez responded again, "There's nothing I can do." Then Valdez offered a new bit of advice: "Go back to Venezuela if you want treatment." Alexi left Valdez and went back to the brothel house. There he met Valdez's assistant, who told Alexi that he was taking Valdez's wife, who had recently given birth, to the hospital in Baní for a postpartum examination. Alexi asked if he could ride with them to the hospital, and the assistant said yes.[74]

At the Hospital Nuestra Señora de Regla in Baní, a Dr. Márquez examined Alexi. Alexi told Dr. Márquez the whole story of the injury at the game and the "treatment" he received from García in San Cristóbal. Dr. Márquez was incredulous. "How is it possible that a major league team didn't send you to a proper doctor for this injury?" Dr. Márquez asked.

"You mean García is not a proper doctor?" Alexi replied. Dr. Márquez said he had heard of this García and that he was not a doctor. Somehow García had convinced people in San Cristóbal that he knew something about medicine, so García got involved in medical situations. Dr. Márquez told Alexi that García was not the proper person to treat this kind of injury and that García had probably done more harm than good in how he had "treated" the injury. Dr. Márquez said the pain should have subsided by then if the injury had been properly handled,[75] but he could not diagnose Alexi's injury without another X-ray being taken.[76] Dr. Márquez told Alexi where to go to get X-rays of his shoulder, and then advised him to take the X-rays to one of two orthopedic clinics in Baní to have his shoulder examined by a specialist. Alexi paid Dr. Márquez from his own pocket.[77]

At the Baní hospital, many people were waiting to get X-rays. The hospital staff told Alexi that he could have his X-rays taken at a nearby private clinic and avoid waiting. Alexi walked to the private clinic, Grupo Médico Baní, and had X-rays taken of his shoulder.[78] Alexi paid for the X-rays himself.[79]

He took the X-rays to the Centro Médico Regional, where a Dr. Miranda looked at the X-rays and told Alexi that the reason he was in pain was because his shoulder was still out of place. Alexi had a luxation, or dislocation, of the shoulder. Dr. Miranda could not believe that Alexi had been without proper medical attention since the injury occurred on July 25th. He told Alexi that dislocated shoulders need immediate medical attention, that he feared Alexi might have permanent damage in his shoulder, and that Alexi needed surgery to repair the damage already done. Alexi began to cry at this devastating news. As Alexi fought back the tears, Dr. Miranda told him he would put the shoulder back in place but that Alexi needed to have surgery soon to prevent further damage to the shoulder. Alexi was distraught. He had to talk to his father.[80]

Alexis Sr. tried to calm his son down as Alexi cried during the whole telephone conversation. The only reasonable thing to do, Alexis Sr. advised his son, was to have Dr. Miranda put the shoulder back in place and then get back to Venezuela as soon as possible for whatever surgery was needed.[81] Alexi went back to Dr. Miranda, and the doctor gave Alexi anesthesia so he would not be awake for the reduction of the dislocated shoulder. When Alexi awoke, his left shoulder and arm were heavily bandaged, and he could not move his left arm at all.[82] Alexi paid for the reduction procedure with his own money.[83]

It was early in the evening when Alexi returned to the brothel house in Nizao. Much to Alexi's surprise, Julio Valdez was waiting at the house for Alexi to return. He had a salary check to give to Alexi.

"How are you?" Valdez asked.

"How do you think I am?" Alexi angrily responded. Alexi told Valdez that his shoulder might be permanently damaged and that he could lose his baseball career. "This is your fault," Alexi vented at Valdez. "How would you like this to happen to one of your sons?"

That hit a nerve with Valdez, who yelled at Alexi not to talk about his sons. "I don't care about your future," Valdez retorted. "I am not going to lose my job over you. I will hunt you down if I lose my job over you." Valdez then left. Alexi's teammates, who witnessed this encounter, came up to Alexi and congratulated him. Someone had finally stood up to Valdez, they said to Alexi.[84]

But Alexi did not feel as if he had won any moral victory over Valdez. His baseball career may have been destroyed by the failure of the Chicago Cubs to provide him with proper and timely treatment for a badly dislocated shoulder. His relationship with the Cubs had proved personally and professionally devastating. Here he was, living in a former house of prostitution in a crime-ridden neighborhood with his arm and shoulder damaged by the "treatment" made available by the Cubs and with threats of physical violence from Valdez ringing in his ears. All he had wanted to do was play professional baseball. What he experienced was degradation, exploitation, and physical abuse.

Alexi called his parents. Alexis Sr. was beside himself with fury about the confrontation with Valdez. Even after everything Alexi had experienced at the hands of the Cubs before the injury, Alexis Sr. could still not comprehend how the Cubs could treat his son this way. Alexi remembered his father wanting to come to the Dominican Republic and bring Alexi home, but his mother thought that that was not a good idea. Alexis Sr. would want to confront Valdez if he came to Nizao, which would be a recipe for trouble and perhaps violence. Alexi and his parents agreed that Alexi should catch the first flight home to Venezuela the next day. They would pick him up at the airport.[85]

That evening, Alexi's teammates helped him pack. It was a sad occasion. The other players understood the severity of Alexi's injury and the unlikely prospect that he would ever play professional baseball after that. Perhaps adding to the somber mood was the realization that what had happened to Alexi could have happened to any one of them, maybe tomorrow.[86] For whatever reason, fate frowned on Alexi on July 25, 1998, but every player knew that injuries could happen at any moment. Each player also knew that the Chicago Cubs had nothing in place for its Summer League team to take care of sports injuries properly.

Alexi had suffered a minor bump on the knee in Mesa, Arizona, and was smothered with treatment and care from highly skilled sports trainers. When he was seriously injured in the Dominican Republic, all the Cubs made available to Alexi was brutal "treatment" reminiscent of the dark ages of medicine. Alexi felt depressed, angry, and helpless. More had been taken from him than his baseball dream. Why was he, a Venezuelan, a Latin, forced to endure squalid living conditions, inadequate food and water, disrespect, threats of violence, and now physical abuse and permanent damage in pursuit of a baseball dream? It was time to go home.[87]

On the morning of July 28th, Alexi's teammates bundled his luggage into a taxi. After they said their good-byes, Alexi went to the Cubs' facility to pick up his plane ticket from Julio Valdez. (Valdez kept the return portion of the players' tickets to the Dominican Republic on file.) In a tense meeting, Valdez gave Alexi his return ticket. Alexi asked Valdez if he had the X-ray taken in San Cristóbal that Chuchúa brought back from the García incident. Valdez told Alexi that he had sent it to Arizona already, and Valdez gave Alexi the FedEx receipt for the package. Alexi then left.[88]

The taxi took Alexi to Santo Domingo,[89] where he first went to a travel agent to exchange his return ticket for the first flight back to Caracas. The travel agent was able to get Alexi on a 5:00 P.M. flight from Santo Domingo to Panama City on Copa Airlines. Alexi would have to change planes in Panama City and catch an Antillean Airlines flight to Caracas.[90] This would mean he would have to carry his bags at the airport in Panama City, which was not a good idea given his condition. He would also have to pay $169 on top of the value of his existing ticket. But Alexi wanted to get home as fast as possible. This way he would arrive in Caracas about 11:30 P.M. Alexi booked the tickets and got on the plane.

Alexi's mother, sister, brother, and girlfriend met him at the airport in Caracas. Alexis Sr. could not get permission to leave his work site to come to the airport.[91] While they were happy that Alexi was finally out of the Dominican Republic, they were also very worried about him. Alexi's sister, Carolina, described Alexi's return: "We went to the airport, all our family and his girlfriend, to pick him up. When I saw him I almost cried, he was thin and in pain. The trip back to our house was a hard one for everybody, Alexis was crying and in pain. My hero."[92]

As every lover of fairy tales knows, heroes pursue justice and right against seemingly insurmountable odds. But Alexi was not living a fairy tale.

CHAPTER NINE

"THAT'S JUST YOUR STORY"

ON JULY 29, 1998, the day after Alexi arrived home in Caracas from his ordeal in the Dominican Republic, Alexi saw Dr. José Luis Caicedo Yrumba, a specialist in sports injuries.[1] Dr. Caicedo listened to Alexi's story of his injury and "treatment" in the Dominican Republic by the Chicago Cubs, and he was horrified.[2] He later wrote in a medical report on Alexi that the attention Alexi received in San Cristóbal from García caused more damage to Alexi's shoulder.[3] Dr. Caicedo's medical report also included the following observations about how Alexi had been handled in the Dominican Republic:

> [I]n my opinion, for an injury so severe as that of Mr. Quiroz, he
> should have had an immediate evaluation and treatment from a spe-
> cialist in this area. His return to Venezuela under these conditions
> caused much pain and discomfort, due to the difficulty of carrying his
> luggage and his posture or the way in which he was seated on the
> airplane and on other motor vehicles, which influenced negatively . . .
> the tissue already wounded. . . . Without a doubt, I consider that what
> I have written and seen on the medical reports shown by Mr. Quiroz,
> that the way that the traction and reduction operations were per-
> formed and the time lapsed without the appropriate medical attention,
> were not the most appropriate, causing greater damage than that
> which was incurred by the initial injury.[4]

Dr. Caicedo took off the bandages and sling placed on the arm and shoulder by Dr. Miranda in the Dominican Republic and proceeded to examine Alexi's injury. Alexi's skin was cleaned, and Dr. Caicedo performed an examination that included cryotherapy and electroanalgesic procedures.* According

---

*Cryotherapy is medical therapy that involves the use of cold treatments, such as ice packs. Electro-
analgesic therapy involves the use of electrical impulses to treat damaged tissue and muscle.

to Dr. Caicedo, this examination revealed injury to the long portion (tendon) of the biceps, injuries to the labrum and glenoid, and a torn articular capsule.[5] In layman's terms, Alexi's left arm and shoulder were seriously damaged.

Dr. Caicedo prescribed some anti-inflammatory medication for Alexi to reduce swelling and pain in the shoulder.[6] He also believed that Alexi should undergo an MRI (magnetic resonance imaging) scan of his shoulder to reveal the extent of the damage. Dr. Caicedo recommended a specialist in Valencia, Dr. Gilberto Ojeda Mirón, who could provide a more thorough diagnosis of Alexi's injury.[7]

The next day, July 30th, Alexi visited Dr. Ojeda's office in Valencia. Once again Alexi told his tale, and Dr. Ojeda, like Drs. Márquez, Miranda, and Caicedo before him, could not believe what he heard.[8] He examined Alexi and diagnosed that Alexi had anterior instability of the shoulder with a lesion of the labrum and pain if rotational motion was attempted.[9] He told Alexi that the best way to find out how much damage the shoulder and arm had sustained was to conduct an MRI,[10] and he scheduled one for the next day.

On July 31st, Alexi underwent an MRI in Valencia.[11] On August 3rd, Dr. Ojeda delivered very bad news to Alexi. The MRI revealed a lesion of the gleno humeral labrum and gleno humeral ligament.[12] Alexi needed surgery on the shoulder to repair the damage, specifically arthroscopic surgery and a procedure known as Bristow surgery, which involves surgically implanting screws and other hardware to repair the shoulder.[13]

Even though this news did not surprise the Quirozes, it was still hard to take. Surgery and the subsequent rehabilitation period would mean that Alexi, in all likelihood, would miss the 1999 baseball season. The chances that any major league team would sign for the 2000 season a twenty-one-year-old Venezuelan who had not played in the 1997 and 1999 seasons, and who had suffered a serious shoulder injury in the 1998 season were less than nothing.[14]

But a more immediate problem confronted the Quiroz family. Dr. Ojeda estimated that the cost of the surgical procedures would be approximately 3.2 million bolivars (about $6,000 on August 3, 1998).[15] Alexi's parents did not have this kind of money. Alexis Sr. would have to find the money either by borrowing from other family members or by getting the Chicago Cubs to pay for the surgery.[16] Alexi had a health insurance card that the Cubs had issued him,[17] but in Venezuela the card was not worth the plastic on which it was printed. Venezuelan health care providers generally do not have arrangements with U.S. insurance companies.[18] Dr. Ojeda's clinic needed to be paid for the surgery before it took place, which meant Alexis Sr. had to come up with the required money fast. Each day that passed represented more pain for Alexi and more potential damage and deterioration to Alexi's shoulder and arm.

Alexis Sr. called Alberto Rondón, who told him he knew about the whole episode. Who called Rondón about the injury is not clear. Rondón said he would try to find some money, but he recommended that Alexis Sr. "pay for the surgery and then try to get reimbursed" from the Cubs, a response that shocked Alexis Sr. He did not have the kind of money needed to pay for major surgery. The Quirozes did not live in poverty, but they were not a wealthy family. How could Rondón suggest that they pay for this surgery? The Chicago Cubs were responsible, and that organization could afford to pay for the surgery. Alexis Sr. was also taken aback by Rondón's tone: just pay for it and then try to get reimbursed. *Try* to get reimbursed? Where was a commitment that Alexis Sr. could trust? The whole conversation was unbelievable, and Alexis Sr.'s anger and fear grew.[19]

"Don't worry," Rondón told Alexis Sr., trying to calm him down. Despite sounding supportive and promising to call back, Rondón did not call back. Alexis Sr. called Rondón for seven consecutive days, but Rondón never called back. Alexis Sr. was beside himself with anger and anguish. His son was badly injured, in a great deal of pain, and in immediate need of major surgery he did not have the money to pay for. The Cubs were not only not providing assistance for Alexi's urgent medical situation, they were not even calling him back. As a father, Alexis Sr. was hurting—his son was in intense pain because of mistreatment. His fury against the Cubs mounted.[20]

Alexis Sr. asked his company for an advance on his salary, and he began to borrow money from family members and close friends, slowly scraping together money to pay for Alexi's surgery. Even though his family was supportive, the process of having to borrow money from his employer, relatives, and friends was painful and humiliating. But however deeply this process wounded Alexis Sr.'s pride and bank account, he was determined to help his son.[21]

Alexis Sr. called Rondón again, and his wife said that he was in Maracaibo with someone from the Cubs' organization. She gave Alexis Sr. the phone number of a hotel. Rondón answered the phone, but he put Oneri Fleita, the Cubs' coordinator of Latin American scouting, on the line. Barely able to control his anger, Alexis Sr. told Fleita that he was collecting money to pay for surgery that was the responsibility of the Chicago Cubs. He asked Fleita for help. When Fleita promised Alexis Sr. that he would call the head office in Chicago and see what he could do, Alexis Sr. made it clear that he needed a response quickly.[22]

When Fleita did not call back, Alexis Sr. decided he was not about to be ignored again by Cubs' officials. He again telephoned Fleita, who said he would call the head office in Chicago. Alexis Sr. told Fleita that the Cubs had to come forward with some financial assistance quickly because, according to the doctors, Alexi should not wait any longer for surgery. Fleita told Alexis Sr. to go ahead with the surgery and the details could be worked out later.[23]

Fleita's response was not acceptable. If Alexis Sr. was going to spend money he did not have, he needed a letter from the Cubs, by fax, stating that the organization was responsible for the financial expenses of Alexi's surgery and subsequent medical expenses. Although Fleita promised to see what he could do, Alexis Sr. did not hold out much hope after all Alexi had been through with the Cubs. After many days and much pain and anguish, he cobbled together enough money so that the surgery could be scheduled for August 12th.[24]

On August 12th, a letter dated August 11th from the Chicago Cubs arrived by fax for Alexis Sr. It stated: "This letter will verify that Alexis Quiroz was injured while playing for the Chicago Cubs in the Dominican Republic. This is a worker's comp injury and all bills will be handled by the Chicago Cubs worker's comp carrier listed below: Kemper Insurance Company."[25]

Alexis Sr. breathed a sigh of relief because he now had a letter from the Cubs in which they took responsibility for Alexi's medical expenses incurred and yet to be incurred because of the injury. While it was a relief to have this letter, Alexis Sr. was still furious that Rondón and Fleita had not acted more quickly when Alexi needed a swift response.[26] Nine days had come and gone since Alexi was told he needed surgery as quickly as possible, nine days for Alexi to suffer more pain and during which the damage to his body may have been getting worse. Was there no end to the insensitivity of the Chicago Cubs? The Quirozes would shortly learn the answer to this question.

Fortunately, the surgery went well. On August 18th, Dr. Ojeda examined Alexi and found that he was recovering excellently from the surgery.[27] On that day, Dr. Ojeda instructed Alexi to begin physical therapy to rehabilitate his left arm and shoulder.[28] Dr. Ojeda sent Alexi to Mario Ricardo Páez Plazola, a physiotherapist in Valencia.[29] Páez discussed with Alexi the various steps through which his rehabilitation would have to progress,[30] and indicated that each session would cost 6,000 bolivars (about $10 on August 24, 1998) and that the rehabilitation would probably last for seven to nine months.[31] If Alexi ever played baseball again, it would not be during the 1999 season.

The seven to nine months of rehabilitation expenses now facing the Quiroz family brought the question of the Cubs' financial responsibility back to the forefront of the family's concerns. After the initial visit with Páez, Alexi, his sister Carolina, and his aunt Alcira Castellanos went to Alberto Rondón's apartment to discuss their financial worries.[32] Rondón told Alexi to go ahead with the rehabilitation. "Here we go again," Alexi thought to himself. "We have to pay the money out of our pockets and hope the Cubs reimburse us?"[33] Alexi told Rondón that he would give all medical receipts from the Dominican Republic, the surgery, and the rehabilitation to Rondón. Rondón assured Alexi that he would forward them to the Chicago Cubs' head office for reimbursement.[34] Alexi brought for Rondón's review detailed schedules, dated August 24, 1998, of the medical and other expenses that Alexi had already incurred because of the injury.[35] Alexi had Rondón sign these schedules.[36] Alexi left with Rondón copies of the receipts for expenses already incurred.[37]

Alexi also presented Rondón with copies of three letters, two dated August 3, 1998, and the third dated August 24, 1998. The first letter, written by Alexi and addressed to the Chicago Cubs with a duplicate to Rondón, described what happened to him after he was injured on July 25th until his flight home to Venezuela on July 28th.[38] The second letter, written by Alexis Sr. and addressed to the Chicago Cubs with a duplicate to Rondón, denounced the behavior of Julio Valdez in connection with Alexi's injury.[39] The anger of Alexis Sr. was apparent in this letter. He called Valdez's conduct in this affair "unacceptable and inhuman" and argued that "people like this cannot be in charge of . . . the development and care of young people that begin in this difficult career."[40] Alexis Sr. called for the Cubs to investigate Valdez's behavior and told the Cubs that he was also sending a copy of the letter to officials in the Dominican Republic and Venezuela.[41] He also threatened to take Alexi's case public "if it is necessary."[42]

The third letter, written by Alexis Sr. on August 24th and addressed to the Chicago Cubs with a duplicate to Rondón, accused the Chicago Cubs of failing to live up to their promises of financial support.[43] Alexis Sr. said that after Alexi returned home after his "totally inhuman and even cruel" mistreatment in the Dominican Republic, all that the family had received from the Cubs was the letter of August 11th.[44] Alexis Sr. mentioned the phone calls with Rondón and Oneri Fleita in this letter. The August 24th letter also contained Alexis Sr.'s complaints about how the Cubs had mistreated Alexi from the very beginning of their relationship, including the "incomplete promises" of Alberto Rondón, the dramatic reversal of David Wilder's attitude toward Alexi, and Julio Valdez's hostility toward Alexi during his 1998 time with the Cubs' Summer League team.[45] Alexis Sr. observed, "All these events let me see that Alexis's career in the organization has been managed in an irresponsible way."[46] Alexis Sr. also told the Cubs that "I would like to get . . . answers to these letters."[47]

Neither Alexi nor Alexis Sr. ever received a response from any person at the Chicago Cubs to any of these letters.[48] The next piece of correspondence the Quirozes received from the Chicago Cubs further demonstrated how uninterested they were in how they had mistreated Alexi.

Alexi began his rehabilitation in late August. He had shown his discipline and determination to overcome physical and mental challenges during his earlier training with Ciro Barrios and Emilio Ostos, but these tests of endurance were nothing compared to what he confronted in rehabilitation. When he first began rehabilitation, Alexi could not move his left arm at all, and he could not even close his left hand. No movement and no strength. In the first rehab sessions, Alexi could not complete the most basic exercises.[49] He was faced with literally rebuilding his arm and shoulder.

Even though the surgery went well, no one knew how far Alexi could bring back his arm and shoulder. In Alexis Sr.'s August 24th letter to the Chicago Cubs, he asked, "I would like to know what your position is for Alexis' future and the chances he is going to get . . . to . . . recover."[50] This question suggests that Alexi and his father held out hope that Alexi would play baseball again. Alexi recalled that even in the dark, early days of his rehabilitation, he believed that he might play baseball again.[51]

Dr. Ojeda had already told Alexi that his arm and shoulder would never be the same again because there was permanent damage from the injury and how it had been mishandled in the Dominican Republic.[52] Alexis Sr. told us he knew Alexi would never again play baseball, but he said nothing to his son about this.[53] It was just something that Alexi would have to accept in his own time and in his own way.

Slowly, painfully, Alexi made progress in his rehabilitation. The steely determination and grit he showed in his training with Barrios and Ostos reappeared as Alexi tackled the challenge of bringing his left arm and shoulder back to life. After two months, Alexi was able to lift his arm a little bit. On Mario Páez's instructions, Alexi went to a toy store and bought clay to squeeze in his left hand to build up its strength. Alexi worked at his rehabilitation very hard, even though it was generally a painful, frustrating process. He would work at Páez's clinic every morning from Monday to Friday for three hours. After he returned home, Alexi continued to work out on his own for another two to three hours per day. Sometimes he would go to the stadium where he had trained with Ostos and jog around the track. When the arm and shoulder began to recover some semblance of motion, he went to a nearby pool in the evenings to swim laps in an effort to push the rehabilitation faster.[54]

Just as when Alexi trained to be a professional baseball player, in his rehabilitation he showed a fierce determination to overcome the challenges before him. At one point, Páez even got angry at Alexi for pushing the rehabilitation too hard. Alexi could not rush the rehab process because the arm and shoulder had been badly damaged, and the shoulder needed time to regain strength and movement. "Have patience," Páez advised. Páez eventually told Alexi to exercise at home only every other day in order to give the arm and shoulder some rest, which was important for the rehabilitation process. Páez's guidance and support became an enormous source of strength for Alexi, both physically and mentally, throughout the hard road of rehabilitation. Páez also saw in this young man an example of how he would like all his patients to respond to rehabilitation. Páez held Alexi up to his other clients as a model rehab patient.[55]

But rehab was at times difficult. One of the early rehab exercises required Alexi to grab a pencil with his left hand. He could not do it. As strength and movement started to return, there would be relapses where neither Alexi nor Páez could get the arm and shoulder to work properly. Sometimes weeks passed without Alexi making any improvement, which frustrated Alexi enormously. "Have patience, Alexi," Páez would say. Alexi still had great difficulty sleeping, even when taking medication to reduce the pain and discomfort in his arm and shoulder. He often would fitfully sleep and then wake up suddenly in a cold sweat with his heart racing in his chest. Sometimes the pain and frustration would cause Alexi to cry at night.[56] His mother, sister, and aunt often took turns caring for him at night as he tried to get some sleep to be able to tackle rehabilitation with vigor.[57]

As the rehabilitation process progressed, Alexi realized that he would not play baseball again. Páez tried one rehab exercise with Alexi that brought this point painfully home. After Alexi had recovered some strength and movement in the left arm and shoulder, Páez told Alexi to bring his baseball glove to the clinic. Páez had Alexi put on the baseball glove. "Now, catch the ball," Páez said as he tossed a baseball to Alexi. Alexi tried in vain to maneuver the glove toward the ball, but instead the ball grazed his head. No, Alexi would not play baseball again. In fact, Alexi began to worry less about baseball than about being able to have a normal life. Would he ever be able to recover normal use of his left arm and shoulder? Would he ever be able to sleep at night without pain? Was the damage to the arm and shoulder so bad that he would have chronic problems, such as arthritis, for the rest of his life? Suddenly baseball did not seem all that important.[58]

But baseball matters were never far away. On October 8, 1998, less than two months after Alexi's surgery, the Chicago Cubs sent Alexi a letter,* signed by David Wilder, that contained the following statement:

> Under terms of your Minor League Uniform Player Contract, you have exhausted the term described in paragraph 6A of your contract. You will, therefore, become a Free Agent on October 15, unless, prior to 5:00 P.M. (EDT) on October 15, you are re-signed by this organization or are assigned to a Major League roster. This is your official notification.[59]

The Chicago Cubs had released Alexi Quiroz again. For the Quirozes, the Cubs were rubbing salt into Alexi's considerable wounds by releasing him in this way and at this difficult time. Because the Cubs had never given Alexi a copy of his 1997 contract, he had no idea what paragraph 6A of the contract said about the term of his employment with the Cubs. Alexi believed he was being released because he had been badly injured and had become expendable. Neither he nor his father were going to take this slap in the face from the Cubs lightly.[60]

Although Alexi believed he had been released because he had been injured, the language of the release letter is curious. The letter says that the term of Alexi's contract with the Cubs had been exhausted, not that Alexi was being

---

*In keeping with the Cubs' traditional practices, this letter was sent in English with no Spanish translation attached. The Quirozes had to get the letter translated so they could read it.

released because he had become disabled.[61] Under the Minor League Uniform Player Contract, the club may terminate the contract if the player becomes disabled in accordance with Paragraph VIII of the Uniform Contract.[62] Paragraph VIII deals with the obligations of the club to the player if he is disabled during employment under the contract, but it does not prevent the club from terminating the contract with the disabled player.[63]

But the Cubs did not rely on these provisions of the Minor League Uniform Player Contract in releasing Alexi. They said instead that the term of Alexi's contract with the Cubs had been exhausted,[64] even though David Wilder had promised Alexi a three-year deal in 1997. Rubén Amaro confirmed this during Alexi's second trip to Mesa.[65]

The Minor League Uniform Player Contract provides in Paragraph VI.A (this is the same provision referred to in Wilder's termination letter to Alexi) as follows:

> Unless a different term of this Minor League Uniform Player Contract
> is set forth in Addendum A, Club hereby employs Player to render,
> and Player agrees to render, skilled services as a Minor League Player
> in seven (7) separate championship playing seasons . . ."[66]

In Addendum A to the contract Alexi signed in Mesa in October 1997, the contract term was expressly set at one year.[67] The contract was signed by the Cubs on October 14, 1997,[68] and the termination letter stated that Alexi was a free agent as of October 15, 1998.[69] The Cubs were simply applying the term of the contract.

This brings to mind the trouble Alexi had had with the Cubs ever since 1995, when they offered him a three-year contract. As mentioned in earlier chapters, Rondón originally promised Alexi a three-year deal, which proved to be a false promise. In Mesa, Wilder confused Alexi by telling him the contract would not expressly be for three years but that the Cubs would give Alexi three years anyway. They expressly gave him only one year. Alexi never knew at the time what the contracts said because they were in English only, the Cubs never explained them to him, and the Cubs never gave him copies at the time he signed.

The termination letter from the Cubs also contained something that further bothered the Quirozes. The letter told Alexi that as of October 15, 1998, "your personal insurance coverage with our club will terminate."[70] While the insurance coverage provided by the Cubs was useless in Venezuela, this part of the letter raised the fear among the Quirozes that the Cubs would not pay for Alexi's medical and other expenses related to the injury.[71] Alexi had given Alberto Rondón all the receipts he had in late August. Now it was October, and the Cubs had not reimbursed the Quirozes for any expenses. Were the Cubs going to renege on this promise and responsibility as well?[72]

Alexi and his father contacted both Rondón and Fleita about the termination letter.[73] Rondón told Alexi that the release letter was nothing to worry about and that Alexi was still a Chicago Cub. Alexi and his father did not understand how Alexi could simultaneously be a free agent and a member of the Chicago Cubs. Not wishing to take Rondón at his word, Alexi and his father met with Oneri Fleita and Rondón at the Cubs' facility in Puerto Cabello in November 1998. Fleita gave the Quirozes the impression that he did not want to talk with them. Alexis Sr. told Fleita it was irresponsible for the Cubs to release Alexi when he was still in rehabilitation, and he reminded Fleita and Rondón that he still had not received any money from the Cubs for the surgery although nearly three months had passed since the operation.[74]

Fleita told the Quirozes that the normal procedure was for the Cubs to send that letter to all the players and then re-sign them, and that Alexi would still have a chance to play with the Cubs. Fleita would be ready to watch Alexi practice and play in January 1999 and make a decision then. January 1999? Alexi told Fleita that a January 1999 date was ridiculous because his rehabilitation would not be completed by January 1999 and that only his doctors could determine when he would be ready to play baseball.[75]

Fleita responded that the Cubs were not going to give Alexi anything for free. Fleita told the Quirozes of other injured players who did not work hard on their rehabilitation yet expected to play again. Fleita said he would be ready to see Alexi play in January, that Alexi must work hard to obtain a visa, and that if he did work hard, he would play A ball in Lansing, Michigan. Alexi Quiroz would play A ball in the United States in 1999? Alexis Sr. asked Fleita how he thought Alexi would be ready to play baseball in January. Fleita did not respond.[76]

Alexi told Fleita and Rondón that it was impossible for him to be ready to play in January because of the damage that his arm and shoulder had sustained in the Dominican Republic from the Cubs' failure to provide the medical attention he needed. Fleita was unmoved. He told Alexi that the tryout in January was his "last offer." Fleita wanted to make sure he gave Alexi one last chance so that Alexi could not accuse the Cubs of walking away from him. When Alexi again protested that he could not be ready by January, Fleita replied, "Quiroz, that is my last offer."[77]

The dam holding back Alexi's emotions burst, and he angrily reminded Fleita that it was his family, not the Cubs, who had helped him with this injury. All Alexi and his family had received from the Cubs were broken promises, disrepect, and now this debilitating injury. "You have never helped me," Alexi said, "and now you have fired me." Alexis Sr. jumped in, accusing the Cubs of breaking their promises, and now their representatives in Venezuela would not even listen to Alexi.

Fleita became angry, saying that "Oneri Fleita always fulfills his promises." Furious, Alexi peeled back his shirt and showed Fleita and Rondón the scar on his shoulder from the surgery.

"This is the Cubs' fault," Alexi said, "because there was no medical attention for me at the academy." What Fleita said next took the Quirozes by surprise and was chilling to hear.[78]

"That's just your story," Fleita coldly responded.

The possibility that Fleita or anyone else in the Cubs' organization would
not believe Alexi's account of what happened to him in the Dominican Republic had never occurred to the Quirozes. But now Fleita had accused Alexi
and his father of lying about what had happened in the Dominican Republic.
It was just Alexi's story; it was not what really happened. Fleita's accusatory remark brought a new ugliness to the problems the Quirozes had with the Cubs.
What larger implications did this remark have for the Quirozes? Did this mean
the Cubs would refuse to pay for Alexi's considerable medical expenses? In this
awful moment, Alexi challenged Fleita to investigate his story and check all
the documents Alexi had collected. Fleita did not take up the challenge. The
tense meeting ended with the Quirozes asking about the medical expenses.
Fleita said that they would get the money in a few days. The Quirozes did not
believe it.[79]

The Quirozes' disturbing meeting with Fleita and Rondón was in stark
contrast with the attitude taken by *Los Cardenales de Lara*, the Venezuelan
team Alexi played for during the Venezuelan 1997–1998 Winter League season. *Los Cardenales* did not release or fire Alexi. In fact, they offered their
training facility to Alexi for his rehabilitation, and even offered to find a major
league trainer to help Alexi. On advice from Dr. Ojeda, Alexi stayed with Mario
Páez rather than do his rehab at *Los Cardenales*' facility, but Alexi appreciated
the sensitive way *Los Cardenales* dealt with him.[80] It was a moment of respect
before the next stormy confrontation with the Cubs.

On February 1, 1999, Alexi received a phone call from John Acosta, a former
Cubs' teammate, who told Alexi that Rondón had a check from the Cubs for
Alexi. Was this the long-awaited, desperately needed reimbursement check from
the Cubs? Relief washed over Alexi, as perhaps now his father could pay back
those who had kindly lent money for the surgery. The Quirozes met Rondón the
next day outside a car wash in Valencia near Rondón's apartment,[81] and Rondón
handed them a check for $6,043.75 from the Chicago Cubs.[82]

The Quirozes immediately told Rondón that the check did not cover all
their medical expenses.[83] The Quiroz family had paid almost $9,000 out of
their own pockets for expenses related to Alexi's injury.*

For the Quirozes, this was unacceptable. How could the Cubs, eight
months after the surgery, produce a check that was insufficient to reimburse

---

*Alexi's claims for reimbursement totaled $8,934.06. In the end, as future chapters describe, the
Cubs ended up reimbursing Alexi for $8,913.81, demonstrating that Alexi and his father had been
justified in their protests about the Cubs' failure to reimburse medical expenses.[84]

the family? Alexis Sr. warned Rondón that someday the Cubs were going to pay for the irresponsible way that the Cubs had treated Alexi.

When told the check was insufficient, Rondón at first said he needed more receipts. Alexi reminded Rondón that he had already provided Rondón with all the receipts. Incredibly, Rondón said that he had lost some of the receipts, and could he have them all again? There, in front of the car wash, Alexi handed Rondón another set of receipts. Rondón promised to take care of it and that the Quirozes would receive the rest of the money shortly. This would turn out to be another empty promise.[85]

Alexi and his father considered not cashing the check. If they accepted the check, then they worried that the Cubs would interpret this as the end of the matter, and it would then be hard to get the Cubs to pay for the remaining amount they owed the Quirozes. Against these considerations was the Quirozes' need to pay back family members and friends who had lent money for the surgery. In the end, the need for the money trumped the Quirozes' concerns about how the Cubs would interpret acceptance of the check,[86] and they cashed the check. But events proved the Quirozes right in their worries about the Cubs.

Frustrated and fed up with the Cubs, Alexi went on the offensive. He called Rondón and said he was ready to practice. Alexi still had another two months of rehabilitation to go, and he was nowhere near ready to play baseball; but Fleita had opened this door, and now Alexi was going to walk through it, whatever the consequences. He was calling Fleita's bluff. He wanted to show them just how badly injured he had been and how the Cubs had destroyed his baseball career.[87]

Alexi traveled to Puerto Cabello to practice on February 8, 1999. Alexi had walked out onto the baseball field and was trying to field some ground balls when Rondón and Fleita arrived. Fleita took Alexi aside and chastised him, asking Alexi where he had been in January. "I waited for you and looked for you, but you did not show up," Fleita said. Alexi responded by saying that if Fleita had wanted to contact him, Fleita could have easily done so. Fleita then reminded Alexi of who was in charge: "*You* should call *me*."[88]

Abruptly, Fleita told Alexi that he could not play at the Puerto Cabello facility because the Cubs would not be responsible if he got injured. "You are not a Cub," Fleita said.

The same reasoning, of course, would have applied to Alexi's practicing in Puerto Cabello in January 1999, as Fleita had previously requested, but Alexi had called Fleita's bluff, and Fleita looked silly. Alexi then asked Fleita and Rondón if tomorrow he and his father could meet with them at Puerto Cabello. Fleita, perhaps sensing that this meeting would be a showdown between the Quirozes and the Cubs, reluctantly agreed.[89] A showdown was exactly what Alexi and his father wanted.[90]

The next day, Alexi and his father had a tense meeting with Fleita and Rondón in Puerto Cabello. Fleita started by saying, again, that he had expected

Alexi to practice in January, and that Alexi had not contacted Fleita to inform him that he would not be coming. Now Alexi could not practice with the Cubs because the Cubs were not going to be responsible if something happened to him on the practice field. Fleita then told the Quirozes that, in January, he had everything ready for Alexi to play in the United States—Fleita even had a visa for him. But now, because Alexi had not contacted him in January as he should have, Alexi was not on the team and the Cubs had no more obligations to him.[91]

Alexi told Fleita that the claims about Fleita's expecting Alexi to practice in January were ridiculous because Alexi had repeatedly said at their November meeting that there was no way he would be ready to play in January. Just as ridiculous was Fleita's claim that he had a visa for Alexi to play in the United States. When he had been healthy, the Cubs had promised but had never delivered a visa. Now that Alexi could not play baseball, the Cubs were going to award him a visa to play baseball in the United States? The moment was comical.[92]

Then Alexi raised the problem of the insufficient reimbursement check from the Cubs. Alexi told Fleita that the Quirozes had received an insufficient check for Alexi's medical expenses at the beginning of February 1999, a long time after the injury was sustained. Fleita retorted that the Quirozes had received the check in January, not February, and that they were lying about when they received it. Alexi told Fleita that, no, they had only received the check from Rondón in February not January.

"Do you think I'm a liar?," snapped Fleita. Then Fleita looked at Rondón. He asked Rondón when he had received the check from Chicago and when he had delivered it to the Quirozes. Rondón did not answer.[93]

Although the Quirozes, Fleita, and Rondón did not piece together the sequence of events at the time, it was apparent that neither the Quirozes nor Fleita were lying. Kemper Insurance Company issued the $6,043.75 check on December 29, 1998.[94] Presumably Kemper sent this check to Rondón in Venezuela for delivery to Alexi. The check would have reached Rondón in January 1999, which is why Fleita assumed that Rondón had given the Quirozes the check in January. Rondón had apparently not bothered to inform the Quirozes that a reimbursement check had arrived until February, and even then Rondón had not called them directly but had used John Acosta as his messenger. No wonder Rondón did not answer Fleita's direct question.

The Quirozes pressed Fleita about the rest of the money, and he confirmed the Quirozes' worst fears. He told the Quirozes they should be happy with the first check and forget about the rest of the expenses. Alexi told Fleita and Rondón that he and his father were not there to beg for money. He had twice provided the Cubs with all the receipts, and the medical expenses were the Cubs' responsibility. Fleita gave the same response: "You should be happy with what you got." Fleita continued by saying that major league teams always run into disgruntled players who ask for more than they deserve. Fleita seemed to be telling the Quirozes that the check would be all the Cubs would pay for "just your story." Alexi reminded Fleita and Rondón that because of the injury, his baseball career might be ruined. Fleita responded, "I don't care about your future."[95]

For Alexis Sr., Fleita's remark crossed the line, and he vented his wrath on Fleita and Rondón. Alexis Sr. attacked the Cubs for lying many times to Alexi—Rondón, Wilder, and now Fleita were liars:

> The Cubs, and especially Rondón, have promised my son many things. You have broken all your promises, and you have hurt my son. As a father, I will do everything for my son that I can. If you get in my way, then I am sorry for you. I will do everything possible to help my son. You have children. You know what a father can and will do for his son. I will fight until the end to make you take responsibility for the physical and emotional damage you have caused my boy. Stop lying to young players. Stop making false promises that you have no intention of keeping. I will fight until the end so that you don't do this to anybody else.[96]

Alexi and his father left. The time had passed for expecting the Chicago Cubs to live up to their responsibilities in connection with Alexi's injury and how the team had ruined his baseball career. The time had passed for expecting Fleita or Rondón to show any compassion or understanding about what the Cubs had done to Alexi. The time had passed for the Quirozes to be patient. The time had come to pursue justice and right.

CHAPTER TEN

THE PURSUIT OF JUSTICE
GOES TERRIBLY WRONG

IN HIS RELATIONSHIP WITH THE CHICAGO CUBS, Alexi Quiroz had been lied to, cheated, subjected to degrading treatment, and had suffered an injury that ended his baseball career because the Cubs had not provided him with proper medical treatment. To add insult to injury, the Cubs had not paid all his medical expenses, and Oneri Fleita had accused Alexi of lying about what happened to him. Alexi wanted the Cubs to live up to their responsibilities, both for the medical expenses incurred but also for their negligence in the Dominican academy that destroyed any career in baseball Alexi might have enjoyed. Alexi knew the way he had been treated was not right.[1]

In Mesa, Alexi had seen how the Cubs treated American players. What had happened to him would never, Alexi believed, have happened to players in the United States. Alexi wanted to pursue his claims against the Cubs and achieve some measure of justice in his case, but he also wanted his case to ensure that what had happened to him would not happen to future Venezuelan baseball prospects. He wanted to fight the discriminatory treatment he saw the Cubs inflict on Latin ballplayers. His fight for justice would be about more than his and his family's physical, mental, and financial suffering.[2]

Alexi's determination to pursue justice in his case was unusual for a Latin player wronged by a Major League Baseball team. Many players with stories like Alexi's want justice for themselves and others, but they rarely get far. Their lack of experience and lack of money usually mean that the kind of stonewalling and obstruction the Cubs displayed with the Quirozes works—the problem goes away, and it is back to business as usual for the teams. There was, however, one big problem with Alexi's noble aims: He had no idea about how to pursue justice against the Cubs. Alexi remembered the advice he had gotten from Sandy Alomar Sr. when he was in Mesa. Alomar advised Alexi to "get a lawyer" to help him recover the salary he lost during the 1997 baseball season. Perhaps Alexi needed to go to the United States and find a lawyer who would pursue his claims against the Chicago Cubs. After all, lawyers are trained to pursue justice for their clients. Perhaps an American lawyer would be the weapon that Alexi needed to make the Chicago Cubs take responsibility for what happened to him. So, on March 21, 1999, Alexi went to Mesa, Arizona, to hunt for a lawyer who would champion his claims against the Chicago Cubs.[3]

In Mesa, Alexi hooked up with Magdelena Schwartz, whom he had briefly met during his previous trip to Arizona. Schwartz ran a community services center for Latins and was well connected with the Latin community in Mesa. She would be a good source of contacts, information, and advice. Alexi felt comfortable with Schwartz because she was a Christian woman whom Alexi believed he could trust. He and his family had trusted people with the Chicago Cubs too much, so trusting people was no longer easy for Alexi.[4]

Using Schwartz's house as his base of operations, Alexi began contacting lawyers in Mesa. His strategy was to sit down with the Mesa phone book and call law firms. Alexi did not speak English, so he needed to find law firms that had people fluent in Spanish. Schwartz had some advice about what law firms had Spanish-language abilities, but not as much advice as Alexi had hoped. He called about ten law firms in Mesa and managed to convey the essence of his story to someone at each of the firms. Only two of the ten followed up—Day, Kavanaugh & Blommel and Taylor & Associates.[5] Day, Kavanaugh & Blommel sent Alexi a prospective client questionnaire, which Alexi completed on March 24, 1999, but never returned to the law firm.[6] The reason he did not return the questionnaire was the response he got from Taylor & Associates, which called Alexi back and set up a meeting for 2:30 P.M. on March 25th at its office in Mesa.[7] Taylor & Associates advertised themselves as "injury and disability law-yers" who represented injured workers all over the state of Arizona.[8] The firm began in 1975 "and has grown over the years to better represent our clients with caring and experienced attorneys and staff."[9] All work by the firm "is handled on a 'contingency fee' basis, that is, on a percentage of the benefits recov-ered."[10] In addition to their work on behalf of injured workers, Taylor & Asso-ciates' caring approach to its clients "extends to the many abandoned cats that have become part of our family over the years, and when you're in our offices, you will probably meet several of our feline friends in our reception areas."[11]

On the afternoon of March 25, 1999, Alexi waited, with some cats, in the reception room of the Mesa office of Taylor & Associates. He was met by a legal assistant to Roger Schwartz, one of the principal attorneys for the firm, who talked in Spanish with Alexi about his case[12] and had Alexi complete a number of documents.[13] Alexi was not exactly sure what he was signing, and he did not recall the assistant explaining the documents to him. He remem-bered that the only thing she explained to him was Taylor & Associates' con-tingency fee arrangement. If Alexi recovered nothing from the Cubs, then

Taylor & Associates collected nothing. But if Alexi got anything from the Cubs through Taylor & Associates' representation, the firm would take 25 percent of the recovery.[14] None of the documents Alexi signed were in Spanish or had Spanish translations, but Taylor & Associates provided Alexi with a full set of the documents he signed and sent him copies of these documents on March 29, 1999, along with a cover letter indicating that the firm had filed workers' compensation papers on Alexi's behalf with the Industrial Commission of Arizona.[15]

Even though Alexi now had lawyers on his side, he did not understand anything about his legal case. He had no idea what he signed with Taylor & Associates, nor did he understand workers' compensation claims or the law supporting the workers' compensation process.[16] Alexi did not understand that filing a workers' compensation claim would mean that he could not sue the Cubs for their negligent treatment of him in the Dominican Republic.[17] Although Alexi did not know what a tort was, he wanted to sue the Cubs and force them to take full responsibility for what they had done to him.[18] The impact of filing a workers' compensation claim on a possible tort suit is something Alexi did not understand until later in his pursuit of justice. But then it was too late.

During his first week in Arizona, Alexi also had his first contact with the Major League Baseball Commissioner's Office about his case. Alexi believed that the Commissioner's Office would have some kind of formal complaint process which he could access,[19,20] and on March 30, 1999, he called Roy Krasik, director of operations for Major League Baseball, at the Commissioner's Office in New York. Instead of talking to Krasik, Alexi was referred to Juan Lara. Alexi told Lara his story and told Lara that he had documents to support his story. Lara asked Alexi to send him copies of the documents, after which he would investigate the matter. The conversation ended.

Alexi was not sure Lara had taken him seriously. To Alexi, Lara's tone during their conversation was perfunctory, as if Lara dealt with these kinds of complaints all the time. Alexi got the impression that Lara was simply going through the motions and was not interested in his case. Alexi believed that Lara just wanted him to get lost, so he decided not to send the documents to Lara yet.[21]

After hiring Taylor & Associates, Alexi accompanied Schwartz on a trip she made to a Latin community center in Phoenix. While at the center, Alexi met a doctor, Dennis Goldberg, who said he worked with injured workers in workers' compensation cases and took an interest in Alexi's case. Goldberg also gave Alexi the name of a lawyer in Phoenix whom Goldberg recommended Alexi speak with about his case. Alexi called the lawyer and made an appointment to see him the next day.[22]

Schwartz drove Alexi back to Phoenix the next day to meet with the lawyer.[23] Alexi was not sure why he was going to talk with another lawyer, but Goldberg and Schwartz thought the meeting was a good idea. But what the

Phoenix lawyer said hit Alexi hard and shook his confidence in his hiring of Taylor & Associates. The lawyer said that Alexi did not need lawyers to file a workers' compensation claim. A claim could be made without lawyers, and lawyers should enter the picture only if Alexi was not satisfied with the outcome of the workers' compensation process.[24] The meeting with the lawyer was brief but it was to have a profound impact on Alexi's thinking and his pursuit of justice.

The meeting with the Phoenix lawyer confused Alexi. He thought he needed lawyers to pursue his claims, and so he hired lawyers. But then another lawyer told him he did not need lawyers. But could he pursue his claims without out a lawyer? Alexi did not speak English or understand the workers' compensation process. He had come to Arizona determined to pursue justice against the Cubs. Now, after only a few days in Arizona, Alexi started to feel lost, and a feeling of unease began to follow Alexi around, which soon turned into full-blown panic.[25]

On March 28th or 29th, Schwartz told Alexi that she had made an appointment for him to talk to a firm of private investigators (SRISA)[26] about his case. Alexi was not sure how Schwartz had contact with private investigators, but however they met, SRISA took an interest in Alexi's case when Schwartz told them about it. On March 30, 1999, Alexi told the whole story to two Spanish-speaking investigators from SRISA, and they were inspired.

"You have an easy case," they told Alexi, "and you don't need lawyers to win because they're just out for your money."[27] Did this confirm what the Phoenix lawyer had told him? Was Taylor & Associates simply out for 25 percent of the money that was rightfully his? The SRISA sales pitch had, however, only just begun.

The SRISA representatives told Alexi he should fire his lawyers and hire their firm, which had lawyers of its own (presumably ones not just interested in the client's money). With such an easy case and such an experienced team, SRISA could get big results in three months. How big? The private investigators told Alexi they would contact the president of the Chicago Cubs and ask for $75 million. SRISA would settle for nothing less than $50 million. These numbers made Alexi's head spin.

But the sales pitch was not finished yet. The private investigators said it was imperative that Alexi be seen by a physician who specialized in sports injuries. SRISA would pay for all Alexi's expenses while it handled his case, and he would not have to reimburse SRISA for such expenses. SRISA would handle his case, expenses and all, in return for 40 percent of any monies recovered from the Cubs. They had a contract ready for Alexi to sign.[28]

Alexi was now in an emotional quagmire. He was not sure about SRISA and its promises. These private investigators talked about numbers that Alexi had not contemplated. Not settle for anything less than $50 million? Was it really as easy as SRISA said it would be? Alexi had no idea. He felt confused and uncertain. Alexi wanted to talk to his father, but he could not reach his father in Venezuela. What should he do? He talked privately with Schwartz. She was not sure, but she thought it might be a good idea for him to go with SRISA. But . . . was this really a good idea? Agonizing even as he did so, Alexi signed the contract.[29] This signature would prove to be a turning point in Alexi's pursuit of justice.

On March 31, 1999, in keeping with the agreement with SRISA, Alexi called Taylor & Associates and told them to drop the case. "Why?" Taylor & Associates asked. Alexi then lied to Taylor & Associates; he told them he had to return to Venezuela.[30]

Taylor & Associates filed a letter dated April 1, 1999, with the Industrial Commission of Arizona informing it that "[p]er client's request, Taylor & Associates will no longer be representing Mr. Quiroz in the aforementioned claim."[31] The letter was copied to Alexi and to Kemper Insurance,[32] which was the carrier for the Chicago Cubs' workers' compensation insurance. But Taylor & Associates called Alexi to find out why he terminated their services. Alexi agreed to meet a Taylor & Associates' lawyer at a Denny's restaurant in Mesa to talk about the case and why he changed his mind.[33]

With Alexi sitting uncomfortably in the booth at Denny's, the lawyer[34] told him that the Managing Partner instructed her to find out why Alexi had terminated his relationship with Taylor & Associates. He had obviously not returned home, as he had said he was earlier on the telephone. The lawyer wanted Alexi to tell her his concerns about Taylor & Associates. If he had any problems, she was sure Taylor & Associates could resolve them. They spoke in Spanish, and the lawyer presented Alexi with a document in Spanish for rehiring Taylor & Associates. Alexi did not want to tell her the truth about what he had done with SRISA because he was still unsure about that arrangement. And so one lie led to another.[35]

Alexi told the lawyer he was unhappy with Taylor & Associates because they had not kept in contact with him by telephone after he signed documents on March 25th. Alexi did not mention that on March 29th, Taylor & Associates had sent him copies of all documents he had signed and that they had filed on his behalf. From these documents he knew, with Schwartz's translation help, that Taylor & Associates was pursuing his claim. The lawyer explained the workers' compensation process to Alexi, indicating that Taylor & Associates would be in contact when necessary. Alexi, of course, had nothing more to say because he really had no complaints about Taylor & Associates. Yes, he would have preferred if they had explained the documents he signed. Yes, the Phoenix lawyer's comments that "you don't need a lawyer" raised the fear that Taylor & Associates was only out for money. But Alexi did not raise these thoughts because he knew they were not behind the termination of the relationship.

The lawyer left Denny's without Alexi's signature. Alexi left Denny's feeling that he was into something over his head. "Everything will be all right in the end," Alexi remembered his father telling him earlier. Once again, Alexi had the sinking feeling that his father might not be right. Worse was an awareness that Alexi was perhaps digging a hole for himself through his signing with SRISA and his lying to Taylor & Associates. Do heroes lie in the pursuit of justice and right?[36]

Ironically, the vice Alexi accused Taylor & Associates of exhibiting, not calling him to inform him of the progress of the case, became Alexi's first concern with SRISA. After March 30th, Alexi left messages with SRISA, but SRISA did not return his calls until April 15th.[37] During this time, Alexi received a letter from the Claims Division of the Industrial Commission of Arizona[38] informing him that "[y]our employer's insurance carrier has been notified of your claim. The insurance carrier has 21 days to determine if it will accept or deny your claim."[39] Alexi was surprised when Schwartz translated the letter because he believed that his workers' compensation claim ended when he fired Taylor & Associates. Perhaps the Phoenix lawyer was right. Maybe he did not need a lawyer to pursue his claims against the Chicago Cubs. Then again, Alexi still did not have a clue about his claim before the Industrial Commission of Arizona.[40]

Finally, on April 15th, Alexi managed to speak with a representative of SRISA, who told Alexi that SRISA's first objective was to get the Cubs to pay for all of Alexi's medical expenses. This surprised Alexi because what the Cubs still owed him for his family's out-of-pocket medical expenses was not between $50 and $75 million. It was more like $3,000, which SRISA must have known because Alexi had given SRISA copies of all the receipts. Alexi was not interested only in reimbursement for his family's out-of-pocket expenditures; there were bigger issues he wanted the Cubs to face, such as taking responsibility for mistreating him and ruining his baseball career. Alexi believed that SRISA would focus on getting the Cubs to take responsibility for these things. So why would SRISA focus on smaller amounts of money when its 40 percent fee should encourage it to go after the big issues? Alexi's confusion deepened.[41]

The SRISA representative told Alexi that she called Kemper Insurance to pursue getting all medical expenses reimbursed and lost salary paid. She said Kemper replied that it had no records on Alexis Quiroz. When she pointed out that Kemper had previously sent Alexi a check, Kemper responded that the Cubs ordered it to cut and send that check, but it did not have any other records on Alexis Quiroz. The SRISA representative told Alexi she sent copies of all the medical receipts to Kemper.[42]

The SRISA rep also told Alexi she had called Patti Kargakis at the Cubs' facility in Mesa to get copies of Alexi's contracts, and she had referred the inquiry to Jim Hendry at the Cubs' headquarters in Chicago.[43] When the SRISA rep called Hendry, she was referred to Oneri Fleita. The rep told Alexi that Fleita said the Quiroz case was a "dead issue" and that she should not call back. None of this surprised Alexi. He had seen and heard enough from Fleita and the Cubs to believe this episode.[44]

The SRISA rep also told Alexi that she wanted to interview other Cubs' players to get more information for his case. She and Alexi went to the hotel where the Mesa Cubs stayed, and Alexi found and talked to Mariano Medina, Juan Piñero, Ibrahim Navarro, and Renny Paredes (the SRISA rep waited in the car). Alexi convinced the players to meet the SRISA rep. They crammed into her car, and she drove around explaining why she wanted to interview them. They told her and Alexi that they were still active players and that being interviewed under these circumstances might jeopardize their futures. They declined to be interviewed.

Back at the hotel, Alexi met with the players (except Navarro) privately. They told Alexi that they knew what he had gone through and that what had happened to him was wrong, but they could not get involved. Their dreams of making it to *las Grandes Ligas* were still alive. Alexi understood all too well what drove these players, and he respected their decision. He would have probably done the same thing.[45]

Despite this activity by SRISA, Alexi again became concerned when SRISA did not call him or return his phone calls. In addition, on April 15th Alexi had moved out of Schwartz's house into a small apartment. He did so because SRISA had promised to pay his expenses in Mesa while it investigated his case, but Alexi started paying rent himself because he could not reach anyone at SRISA to arrange payment of his rent. Alexi began to lose his patience with SRISA.

He talked with Schwartz about his concerns, and Schwartz advised him to be patient. "These things take time," she said. Alexi realized that if he fired SRISA, he would have to start over again because then he would be without any help. He realized that he did not know what to do and that he needed help. Rather than terminate his contract with SRISA, Alexi decided to grit his teeth and see the matter through to the end.[46] The end would come in a manner that Alexi never anticipated.

Just down the street from Alexi's new apartment lived Judy Smith, who was Magdelena Schwartz's sister, and her husband Brett. The Smiths had met Alexi at Schwartz's house, and Alexi had told Brett and Judy about his mistreatment by the Cubs. Alexi struck up a friendship with the Smiths, and when he moved into his apartment down the street from where the Smiths were renting, Alexi became a frequent visitor to the Smiths' apartment. Brett and his wife could see the deepening level of Alexi's frustrations. Brett Smith sensed that Alexi did not know what he was doing and that Alexi was scared. But the Smiths were also struck by Alexi's determination to see justice done in his case. Alexi believed that the Smiths were kind people he could trust.[47]

On April 21st, SRISA called Alexi and told him it wanted to have a press conference on April 30th, during which it would publicly present Alexi's story. SRISA told Alexi that it would send out flyers announcing the press conference, and it would contact newspapers, including the *Chicago Tribune*, and TV stations so they would cover the event. SRISA also told Alexi that it made an appointment for him to see Dr. Stuart Kozinn at the Scottsdale Musculoskeletal Institute in Scottsdale, Arizona. Alexi did not know anything about press conferences, but he was more at ease because at least SRISA was doing something about his case—the press conference and the medical appointment.[48]

SRISA apparently had concerns of its own concerning Alexi and his case. SRISA sat down with Alexi on April 25th to sign a new contract with terms more precise and comprehensive than the original contract. Under the new contract, SRISA would receive 30 percent of (1) all medical reimbursement payments from any party, including Kemper Insurance; (2) all wages lost and workers' compensation payments, including from Kemper Insurance; and (3) any disability claim settlement paid by Kemper Insurance.[49] The new Agreement for Services also provided that SRISA would get 40 percent of any settlement from the Chicago Cubs,[50] and 10 percent of any payments made to Alexi for public appearances or interviews, including television, newspaper, magazines, or movies.[51] The new contract also provided that SRISA "will pay for all expenses (i.e., travel, airfare, hotel, court fees, office services) as deemed necessary."[52] If Alexi terminated the contract before settlement with the Cubs was reached, Alexi would have to pay SRISA the sum of $65 for each hour SRISA spent on his case since March 30, 1999 (the date of the original contract) *plus* all costs incurred by SRISA in providing their services.[53] This new contract term created a significant disincentive for Alexi to terminate the agreement prior to SRISA's completing its investigation and representation of Alexi. Perhaps SRISA sensed that Alexi might fire them given his unhappiness with its performance to date and wanted protection if Alexi moved in this direction.

At the same time, SRISA had Alexi execute a document authorizing SRISA to access his medical records.[54] At the bottom of this document, SRISA typed in the following: "Under no conditions or circumstances will we provide legal advice. If an attorney is needed the agency will provide counsel services at additional costs as they occur."[55] Then immediately following this was the handwritten statement, "Unless otherwise indicated in Contract," which was initialed by an SRISA rep and Alexi.[56] Alexi, of course, did not know what this document said, but the disclaimer about providing legal services contrasted with what SRISA told Alexi in their first meeting—that it had lawyers on staff.

SRISA was having Alexi practice for the press conference. His diary entries for April 25th, 26th, and 28th are filled with bullet points for the press conference that laid out his story.[57] Alexi would speak in Spanish, and SRISA would translate for the large crowd it expected to come to the press conference. Alexi was not skilled in public speaking, so he practiced what SRISA wanted him to say. Maybe the press conference would be the event that turned Alexi's pursuit of justice from a confusing, frustrating, and doubt-ridden endeavor into an effort that would force the Chicago Cubs to take responsibility for what had happened to him.[58]

The Cubs gave Alexi additional provocation for exposing their treatment of him. Oneri Fleita of the Cubs told SRISA that the Cubs had already reimbursed Quiroz, and that players today always ask for more than they deserve. He said Alexi's story was a lie and that Alexi had nothing more coming from the Cubs.[59] More provocation came before the press conference. Alexi received a letter dated April 28, 1999, from Kemper Insurance informing him that his claim against the Cubs had been accepted by Kemper Insurance but that "[n]o compensation [will be] paid because no time was lost from work in excess of seven (7) days attributable to this injury."[60] As Schwartz translated, Alexi's confusion rose. How could this be? How could this letter say that "no time was lost from work in excess of seven (7) days attributable to this injury?" He had spent seven months in rehabilitation. His entire baseball career had been ruined. Desperate for an answer, Alexi called Kemper Insurance with Schwartz's help to ask what the letter meant. Kemper said that the Chicago Cubs had informed them that Alexi had not lost more than seven days of work because of the injury, which is why it denied his claim. For Alexi, this letter represented the latest outrage from the Cubs. Well, the press conference would be payback time.[61]

On April 27th, SRISA issued its press release. The text is reprinted in full below:

Press Release
FORMER CHICAGO CUBS MINOR LEAGUE PLAYER ALEXIS QUIROZ ACCUSES CHICAGO CUBS OF POOR PLAYER MANAGEMENT & MEDICAL NEGLECT.

A press conference will be held on Friday April 30, 1999 at 11:00am at the Mesa Community Center, 201 N. Center St., Mesa, Arizona, U.S.A. (602) 644–2178.

Alexis Quiroz accuses the Chicago Cubs Organization of failing to provide appropriate medical care following an injury during a baseball game in the Dominican Republic in the summer of 1998. The team trainer and other persons attempted to put his shoulder back in place by using their foot while Alexis laid on a mattress on the floor of a room that looked like a "storeroom."

Alexis was never provided copies of any contracts he signed. He was told he would be receiving a $4,000.00 signing bonus but when the check arrived it was for $6,000.00. Alexis' father was told by Mr. Alberto Rondon (Chicago Cubs Rep. in Venezuela/Dominican Republic) that they were to cash this check and give him $2,000.00.

Chicago Cubs Administrative Offices have refused to meet with Alexis to review his concern. Mr. Oneri Fleita of the Chicago Cubs office states "This is a dead issue."

Alexis has paid all expenses for medical and travel to the United States. He is concerned that Latin American prospective players understand their right to be treated professionally[,] expediently and with equal treatment as any player in the minor leagues in the United States.

Alexis Quiroz has requested that the U.S. Embassy of Venezuela look into the matter.[62]

SRISA also prepared a fact sheet for the press conference that contained more details of Alexi's story, including:

- The deplorable living conditions in the Cubs' Dominican academy during the 1996 Summer League season.
- Lineups for games during the 1996 Summer League season being drafted by Julio Valdez's twelve-year-old son.
- Valdez's warnings to the Venezuelan players about complaining about the poor living conditions in the Dominican Summer League.
- The failure of the Chicago Cubs to give Alexi a written release letter in 1997.
- The experience with David Wilder at the Mesa facility in October 1997.
- The fact that Alexi's family had to pay for all his medical expenses.[63]

The fact sheet also contained information related to SRISA's efforts to deal with Kemper Insurance and the Chicago Cubs on behalf of Alexi. The fact sheet said that, despite Kemper's asking for copies of medical receipts and promising to pay all medical and rehabilitation expenses, "[f]ollow up calls up to 4/30/99 have failed to get a response from anyone at Kemper."[64] As for the Cubs, the fact sheet said that calls were made to Patti Kargakis, Jim Hendry, and Oneri Fleita and that Kargakis referred SRISA to Hendry, who did not return the call.[65] When Fleita returned the call, he told SRISA that the Quiroz situation was a "dead issue."[66]

The fact sheet also contained interesting statements about Alexi's pursuit for justice. First, it claimed that Alexi "is asking for compensation of approximately $35,000 in expenses to include: lost wages, medical bill reimbursement, travel expenses, retainer fees for professional services. Also to have all rehabilitation services covered."[67] Alexi did not know what this fact sheet said, SRISA did not explain to him what was in it, and SRISA never translated it into Spanish. To this day, Alexi does not understand how SRISA came up with the $35,000 figure.[68]

Second, the fact sheet said that Alexi "is currently consulting an attorney and will file suit for an amount not disclosed at this time."[69] But Alexi was not "currently consulting an attorney." He fired his attorneys on SRISA's advice, and SRISA's new contract with him stated that SRISA was not providing legal advice.[70]

Third, the fact sheet said that Alexi "is planning to establish a foundation to educate and assist Venezuelan prospective athletes around the world of professional athletics. It is his hope to establish or improve player management guidelines for major league team operation in other countries."[71] Alexi had spoken to SRISA about his desire to use his case to make sure no other Venezuelan baseball player suffered what he did.[72] This part of the fact sheet is consistent with the press release's statement that Alexi "is concerned that Latin American prospective players understand their right to be treated professionally . . . and with equal treatment as any player in the minor leagues in the United States."[73] Alexi saw himself pursuing justice not for himself but for others, and making sure that abuses he suffered were stopped before major league teams ruined more careers and lives. Having seen the difference between the treatment enjoyed by American players and the treatment in the Dominican Republic at the hands of the Cubs, Alexi saw clearly that he and others were victims of intentional discrimination by the Chicago Cubs. Alexi knew from his experience at the Oakland A's facility in the Dominican Republic that major league teams could, if they wanted, provide Latin players with decent, humane living conditions and treatment.[74]

When Alexi arrived at the Mesa Community Center for the press conference on April 30th, he knew immediately something was wrong. The only people in the room when Alexi arrived were the head of SRISA and one of his employees, Magdelena Schwartz, Dr. Goldberg and a physician colleague, and a friend of Schwartz's. Otherwise, a small sea of empty chairs faced Alexi. This was not what he anticipated. This would not advance his pursuit of justice. This was embarrassing.

"It's a little early," the SRISA reps reassured Alexi. An hour later, it was too late to deny that the press conference was a colossal failure. Alexi stared in disbelief at the empty chairs. Nobody came. Nobody. The SRISA reps wondered whether the Chicago Cubs had sabotaged the press conference. Despite the shroud of failure that descended on the people in the room, the head of SRISA tried to cheer Alexi up. "Don't worry," he said to Alexi, "we can say it was a really big success. Because nobody came, nobody will know otherwise."[75]

The disastrous press conference confirmed Alexi's misgivings about SRISA. After the press conference, Alexi did not hear anything from SRISA except to confirm his appointment with Dr. Kozinn in Scottsdale for May 3rd. Schwartz again encouraged Alexi to be patient, but Alexi's nerves had frayed by this point, and he lost his patience. A month had passed since SRISA told Alexi he had an easy case, worth no less than $50 million. The press conference had indicated that his was not such an easy case. What exactly was SRISA doing about his case other than planning disastrous press conferences?[76]

On May 3rd, Alexi traveled to Scottsdale with an SRISA rep to be examined by Dr. Stuart Kozinn. Dr. Kozinn confirmed what Alexi already realized—that he would never play professional baseball again. In his medical report, Dr. Kozinn wrote:

> This patient is a 20-year-old baseball player with a chief complaint of severe left shoulder injury while playing baseball in August of 1998. This was an industrial injury, because he was employed by the Chicago Cubs organization on a minor league team and suffered an injury during the game. . . . It seems that he ended up having the surgery in Venezuela by an orthopedic surgeon who did a modified Bristow type procedure, moving the coracoid process over to the anterior glenoid. This certainly cured his dislocation problem, but has left him with a rather significant frozen shoulder and loss of motion in the shoulder. The patient has difficulty getting the arm up more than 45 degrees. He certainly cannot play baseball, which was his occupation because of the limitation of motion. . . . Through the interpreter, we have determined that he is not happy with the situation and feels that it really keeps him from doing all types of significant lifting work, regardless of an ability to play baseball or not. Although he would like to play baseball again if he could, I do not think that is really likely to happen with further surgery, although another surgical procedure could help him regain some range of motion of the shoulder and decrease his pain when he tries to lift the arm.[77]

Kozinn's examination revealed some additional problems that troubled Alexi. Kozinn advised that exploration with an arthroscope would be prudent to examine the intra-articular grinding occurring in his shoulder to determine whether further surgery was needed "to decrease the risk of ongoing degenerative arthritis."[78] In addition to this frightening diagnosis, Kozinn recommended a CT scan to get a better idea whether the screw and hardware implanted in the surgery in Venezuela might be causing problems.[79] After exploratory arthroscopy and a CT scan, Dr. Kozinn suggested "diagnostic surgical athroscopy with lysis of adhesions and then probable open reconstruction of the shoulder with a capsular shift type procedure."[80] Dr. Kozinn was blunt with Alexi about the likely outcome of these treatment options. Kozinn wrote: "The patient understands that no guarantee of success can be made, that complications could occur, it could even be made worse, neurovascular compromise can occur with scar tissue involvement."[81]

Degenerative arthritis. Open surgical reconstruction of the shoulder. Possible neurovascular damage. Would the Chicago Cubs now realize how badly Alexi had been injured? Dr. Kozinn wrote in the treatment section of his report that Alexi's "industrial carrier should cover" the further medical and surgical procedures that Alexi needed,[82] and he copied the medical report to the "Industrial Carrier," Kemper Insurance.[83] As of the beginning of May 1999, it would not be possible for the Chicago Cubs to deny the extent of the injury that Alexi had suffered. But Alexi knew that the Cubs already understood the extent of his injury; they had simply refused to take responsibility for it.

Shortly after Alexi's depressing examination by Dr. Kozinn, he managed to get an SRISA rep on the phone to find out how the case was progressing. In disbelief Alexi heard the rep tell him that SRISA had no money to do anything on the case. She said SRISA had already spent too much on the case and it had nothing left to spend. Further, she added, SRISA did not promise him anything specific in terms of results.

Alexi could not believe what he heard. Had the press conference disaster forced SRISA to cut it losses and dump Alexi's case? Did this mean that SRISA would not pay for Alexi's expenses he incurred in Mesa, such as his apartment rent? When Alexi reminded SRISA that it had promised to pay for his expenses in Mesa while it worked on his case, the rep denied that SRISA had made such a promise. The telephone conversation ended with an obvious gulf between Alexi and SRISA, and Alexi did not have to wait long before his relationship with SRISA collapsed.[84]

The very next morning, May 6th, SRISA called Alexi to tell him that it wanted to terminate their relationship. Alexi was thunderstruck. What came next devastated Alexi. SRISA told Alexi that, upon termination of the contract, Alexi would owe it $7,000 for all the expenses SRISA had incurred in investigating his case. In shock, Alexi began to panic. Seven thousand dollars? For what? Neither Alexi nor his family had that kind of money. The pursuit of justice had just descended into another nightmare. The doubts Alexi harbored about signing with SRISA now became demons that tormented him. How had he gotten into this mess? How was he going to get out?[85]

Scared, Alexi called his father. Alexis Sr. tried to calm his son down. He saw no other way than to travel to Arizona to help his son extricate himself from this latest calamity.[86] On May 9, 1999, Alexis Sr. arrived in Arizona. On May 11th, Alexi, his father, and representatives of SRISA had a meeting. The SRISA reps said that the firm no longer wanted to work with Alexi and that Alexi would have to pay for all the expenses the firm incurred in working on his case. Alexis Sr. replied that he did not have $7,000, but the SRISA reps repeated that Alexi was responsible for their expenses. Then Alexis Sr. caught the SRISA reps off guard by saying that the second contract Alexi signed with SRISA stated that Alexi was responsible for SRISA's expenses only if Alexi terminated the contract, and Alexi was not terminating the contract, SRISA was. So, under the contract, Alexi owed them nothing. Alexi, Alexis Sr., and Schwartz had reviewed the contract prior to the meeting.[87]

But then Alexis Sr. did something that caught Alexi off guard. Instead of following up the lawyerly analysis of the contract with the negotiating weapon of silence, Alexis Sr. said that, in fairness, SRISA had worked for Alexi and that he and Alexi would pay them something toward the expenses they incurred. Alexi was furious at his father. But Alexis Sr. was trying to play fair and he thought that paying something was the honorable thing to do. This gesture provided the opening SRISA needed to save face. While complaining about all the pressure Alexi placed on them, the SRISA reps agreed to continue with the case. Alexis Sr. wrote SRISA a $1,000 check at the end of the meeting to offset some of its expenses.[88]

On May 13, 1999, Kemper Insurance issued a $1,650.91 check to Alexis Quiroz for reimbursement of medical expenses related to his injury.[89] While this check still did not fully reimburse the Quirozes for expenses incurred in connection with Alexi's injury, Alexi was convinced that the second check would never have been sent had he not pursued his claims in Arizona. But that pursuit brought him other problems. Kemper sent the check to SRISA rather than to Alexi.[90] Alexis Sr. told SRISA to take $1,000 from the check as a payment toward expenses SRISA had incurred working for Alexi.[91] On May 19, 1999, SRISA issued a handwritten receipt to the Quirozes for the $1,000 check Alexis Sr. had written on May 11th and for $1,000 to be taken from the Kemper Insurance check, with $650 to be returned to Alexi as soon as the check had cleared.[92] The Quirozes never received the $650 from SRISA.[93]

On May 21st, Alexis Sr. returned to Venezuela. He thought he left his son behind with a situation that Alexi could manage and see through to an acceptable end.[94] This turned out to be wishful thinking. The relationship between Alexi and SRISA quickly deteriorated again. On June 2, 1999, Alexi met with a representative of SRISA, who told him that the most SRISA could get for Alexi was between $35,000 and $40,000. Alexi argued that this was not what SRISA promised it could recover. The rep responded that, when SRISA first took up the case, it believed that it could recover big bucks. But now, after working on the case since the end of March, SRISA was convinced that Alexi's case would yield only a small recovery. Alexi refused to believe it. "I'm not going to settle for that amount," he told SRISA. "I would prefer to fight on alone."[95]

This response is probably what SRISA wanted, because it then told Alexi that if he wanted to terminate the relationship, he would have to pay them for the expenses incurred. SRISA showed Alexi a file full of papers that it said were expense receipts, but it did not let Alexi look at them. Given that he did not read English, it would not have mattered if he had looked at the papers. Alexi replied that he did not have $7,000, and besides, he and his father had already paid SRISA $2,000 for expenses. SRISA agreed that $5,000 was the proper amount, but this hardly changed the fact that neither Alexi nor his father had $5,000. Alexi promised to give SRISA the security deposit on his Mesa apartment, and he told SRISA he would try to pay the money over time. Was the nightmare ever going to end?[96]

Alexi had reached rock bottom. He had just about lost hope that his pursuit of justice would lead anywhere. He had nobody assisting him in his pursuit of justice now that the relationship with SRISA had collapsed. He moved out of his Mesa apartment and went to stay with Brett and Judy Smith. Without any idea about what to do next, Alexi unexpectedly received an idea from the Smiths. One night, Alexi tagged along with Brett and Judy to the closing on the house the Smiths had just purchased. After the closing, Brett introduced Alexi to his real estate agent, who listened to Alexi's story and said that she had the phone number of a lawyer in Chicago by the name of Steve Gleason. "Give him a call," the woman encouraged Alexi. So Alexi called Gleason, and after listening to Alexi's tale, Gleason encouraged Alexi to come to Chicago to explore the possibilities of the case in person. Alexi did not rejoice at this invitation. His optimism and determination to persevere had taken a terrible beating while he had been in Mesa.[97] Unfortunately, the terrible beating was not finished.

Alexi wanted a final meeting with SRISA to sort out the expenses issue. A meeting was scheduled for Friday, June 11th, in Schwartz's office, with Brett Smith along to accompany Alexi and translate for him. At the meeting, Alexi requested that SRISA give him a letter indicating exactly how much Alexi owed and breaking down precisely what expenses were covered in the total amount. The head of SRISA said that Alexi did not understand the situation he was in. He owed SRISA more that $5,000 for hours worked, phone calls, and other things. Alexi demanded that SRISA produce documentation to support the expenses, and angrily told the head of SRISA he would not pay until SRISA provided proof of expenditures. The head of SRISA also started to get angry.

Alexi demanded that SRISA produce a document that said exactly how much he owed. As the atmosphere in the room grew increasingly tense, the head of SRISA quickly wrote something down and handed the document to Brett Smith, who translated it for Alexi. The document stated that Alexi owed SRISA money and that SRISA would write to Kemper Insurance informing them that Alexi owed SRISA money. The document also said that Alexi had terminated the contract and that he would not contact SRISA again. Alexi refused to sign. The head of SRISA told Smith to initial the document. Alexi snatched the document out of Smith's hands.[98]

In a threatening tone, the head of SRISA approached Alexi and Smith and said "drop that letter." He said that Alexi was the one with problems, and he threatened to sue Alexi. He fumed, "Get out of my office. You'll hear from my lawyers on Monday."[99]

With this threat ringing in their ears, Alexi and Brett Smith left the meeting.

Alexi had come to Mesa to find a lawyer, a champion for his desire to achieve justice in his case. Now he was afraid that lawyers were pursuing him. As he left the office, he felt as if he was living a nightmare that simply would not end.[100]

CHAPTER ELEVEN

SEVENTH-INNING STRETCH:
CHICAGO, NEW YORK,
MARACAY

ALEXI WENT TO ARIZONA to make the Chicago Cubs live up to their responsibilities toward him and other Latin baseball players. During the disastrous experience in Mesa, Alexi did not achieve these goals. In fact, the episode was a calamity for Alexi and his cause. On the personal level, Alexi and his family lost even more money because Alexis Sr. had flown to Arizona, they had paid SRISA $1,000, and they had handed over the second check from Kemper Insurance, worth $1,650.91, to SRISA. The financial setback was even worse when the money spent by Alexi traveling to and living in Mesa from late March until June 1999 is considered.*

In terms of Alexi's larger social objective of ensuring that what had happened to him would not happen to future Venezuelan baseball players, the whole nightmare in Mesa was an embarrassment, hardly helpful to prospective Venezuelan players. Alexi's decisions and mistakes made it easier for the Chicago Cubs and everyone else to ignore him and his claims of injury, mistreatment, and discrimination. Perhaps Oneri Fleita would prove right after all. In the wake of what happened in Mesa, Alexi's case might be a "dead issue."

Before the June 11th meeting with SRISA, Alexi had decided to go to Chicago to take up Steve Gleason's invitation to talk about his case.[1] He talked with his father about the wisdom of going to Chicago to continue his pursuit of justice, and both father and son reluctantly agreed that if Alexi's cause was going anywhere, Alexi would now probably have to go to Chicago and to the Major League Baseball Commissioner's Office in New York. Despite the events in Mesa, how the Cubs had treated Alexi was wrong, and for Alexi to

---

*Alexi had, by the end of the Mesa debacle, used up the funds remaining from that portion of his signing bonus ($3,500) he and his father had deposited in the United States in 1996.

give up now would also be wrong. Alexi's family wired him some money before the June 11th meeting to facilitate his journey to Chicago and New York. This money meant a great deal to Alexi because it represented not only another financial hardship for his family but also its continuing support for and belief in him. The Quirozes remained united in trying to right the wrong done to Alexi and other Latin players by the Chicago Cubs.[2]

The ugly June 11th meeting with SRISA gave Alexi additional incentive to go to Chicago. He simply wanted to get out of Mesa as fast as he could. Brett Smith worked for an airline, and after the June 11th meeting, he told Alexi that tickets to Chicago for the next day were probably available to buy if Alexi was ready to leave Mesa. Yes, Alexi was ready to go tomorrow. On June 12, 1999, Alexi departed Mesa for Chicago.[3]

On June 14th, Alexi met in Chicago with Steven M. Gleason of the law firm Nilson, Stookal, Gleason & Caputo, Ltd. (NSGC). As fortune would have it, Gleason's secretary was from Venezuela, and she translated between Gleason and Alexi during the initial meeting and all subsequent communications with NSGC. Alexi told Gleason what had happened to him in his relationship with the Cubs and about what had happened in Mesa with the private investigators. After listening to Alexi, Gleason structured his advice in three parts.

First, Gleason said that according to what Alexi told him, the private investigators were illegally practicing law; at least they would have been illegally practicing law in Illinois. Gleason could pursue this matter with the Arizona bar and perhaps recover the monies the private investigators obtained from the Quirozes.[4]

Second, Gleason said his firm could represent Alexi in a workers' compensation claim against the Chicago Cubs, the same kind of process that Taylor & Associates had started in Arizona. Gleason told Alexi that workers' compensation claims do not produce much money for injured workers because recoveries are based on a statutory schedule. Still, Gleason thought that his firm, and his partner Marc Stookal specifically, could help Alexi through this process and recover something from the Chicago Cubs.[5]

Third, Gleason talked to Alexi about a possible tort claim against the Cubs. Gleason stressed how difficult tort litigation would be versus the easier workers' compensation process. He asked Alexi what he wanted from the Cubs: publicity to force the Cubs to take responsibility for what they had done, or money. Gleason said that if Alexi talked to the media about his case, the Cubs would be less likely to offer him much money. On the other hand, if Alexi stayed quiet, maybe the Cubs would settle for more money. Gleason said that if Alexi went public, he did not know how or whether people would react or even care. Alexi, remembering the sea of empty chairs at the press conference in late April,[6] knew Gleason was right.

"What do you want?" Gleason asked. Alexi said he wanted to be healthy again and to be able to play baseball again. But he knew that playing baseball was impossible. He wanted the Chicago Cubs to take responsibility for what had happened to Alexi and to make sure Alexi's mistreatment did not happen to other players in the future.

After Alexi finished, Gleason recommended that Alexi pursue workers' compensation. Alexi agreed and signed an Attorney Representation Agreement[7] in connection with the workers' compensation complaint.[8] After his experiences in Mesa, Alexi was not sure where his relationship with NSGC would go, but at least he entered the relationship without unrealistic expectations. His pursuit of justice would now have to be, after the mistakes in Mesa, a more humble undertaking.[9]

After meeting Gleason, Alexi called Juan Lara at the MLB Commissioner's Office. Alexi had earlier called Lara from Mesa in late March 1999, but Lara's tone of voice had discouraged Alexi from sending Lara his documents on his case. Now Alexi wanted to press the matter further with the Commissioner's Office, particularly trying to make sure that what happened to him did not happen to players for the Chicago Cubs in the future. Alexi told Lara he was coming to New York and wanted an appointment. Lara agreed to meet with Alexi when he was in New York.[10]

Alexi traveled to New York and met with Lara on June 21, 1999. Alexi was nervous about this meeting. If Lara took him seriously, the Commissioner's Office might pressure the Cubs to change their practices in Latin America and force the Cubs to take responsibility for what had happened to him. If Lara did not take him seriously, then Alexi would have run into another brick wall. Alexi did not have to wait long to discover whether his hopes for support from the Commissioner's Office would be fulfilled. When they met, Lara simply asked that Alexi leave his documents. Lara said he would look at them and call Alexi back.

Alexi felt that Lara had no interest in the case. Alexi was not satisfied with simply leaving the documents and waiting for a call, and he suspected he would be waiting forever for this phone call. At the same time, he could not force Lara to talk to him. Would the documents be enough to convince the Commissioner's Office to investigate his mistreatment? His meeting with Lara lasted only a couple of minutes.[11]

Confused and emotionally torn, Alexi left the documents with Lara and descended in the elevator. In the lobby, Alexi broke down and cried. The crying brought back bad memories. He had cried when he had been released in 1997. He had cried because of his injury and during the painful months of rehabilitation. Now the tears flowed again, in the lobby of the building housing the MLB Commissioner's Office. He tried to control his emotions and stem the tears, but anger built up inside. The physical, emotional, and financial damage that he and his family had suffered because of the Chicago Cubs was wrong. If he walked out of this building now, he would be surrendering. As badly as his fight had gone in Mesa, he would not surrender in a pool of tears. He got in the elevator to ascend once again to Juan Lara's office.[12]

Catching Lara off guard by reappearing, Alexi angrily told him about how badly the Chicago Cubs had treated him. He repeated the hardships, the pain and suffering, and the financial sacrifices that the Cubs had caused. Then Alexi turned on Lara. "All these things happened to me because of a Major League Baseball team, and all you can do is talk to me for two minutes," Alexi said. Alexi's return and angry monologue took Lara by surprise. He invited Alexi to a conference room to talk more about his case, and he called someone named George to join them. In the conference room, Alexi again went over his story as Lara took notes.

When Alexi finished, Lara told him that, unfortunately, what happened to him with the Cubs was "normal." Alexi vividly recalled this moment because he was shocked, even after what had happened to him, that someone inside the Commissioner's Office would admit that such treatment of Latin players was normal.[13]

Then Lara said something equally surprising. Lara said that, unfortunately, the Commissioner's Office could never do anything against teams that behaved in these ways because the players never sued the teams for mistreatment. The Commissioner's Office could never do anything about normal mistreatment of Latin players by major league teams? Was Lara serious?[14]

But Lara was full of surprising things to say. Lara suggested that because Alexi was suing the Cubs, perhaps the Commissioner's Office could do something, like fine the Cubs. Further, Lara told Alexi that the Cubs had breached their contracts by sending him to play in the Dominican Republic rather than in the United States, as stipulated in the contracts. The Commissioner's Office could fine the Cubs for such breaches of contract as well. Lara told Alexi that the Commissioner's Office would start an investigation. From the conference room, Lara called Roy Krasik, who was not in his office at that moment. Lara said that Krasik would be in charge of the investigation and that Krasik or Lara would be in contact with Alexi shortly. Had Alexi made a major breakthrough in his case? Alexi was not sure. "Can you put all this in writing and send it to my lawyers in Chicago?" Alexi asked. Lara said he would.[15]

Descending the elevator for the second time that day, Alexi felt better. He had had no idea what would happen when he went back to confront Lara, but the confrontation had gone better than he could have imagined. Lara did not say, as Oneri Fleita had done, "That's just your story." In fact, Lara had said that what happened to Alexi was "normal." Lara seemed to believe Alexi and did not challenge him on any issue or fact. Alexi left the building believing that Lara would pursue the case and investigate the matter. Had Alexi snatched progress from the jaws of despair?[16]

The next day, June 22nd, Alexi called Lara. Lara said that the Commissioner's Office would send a letter to the Chicago Cubs after it had completed an investigation. Lara also said that he had called Steve Gleason, but Gleason had not been in his office, so Lara had left a message. Lara thought it would be helpful if the Commissioner's Office would send a letter to Alexi's lawyers in Chicago, and Alexi agreed that this would be a positive step. Alexi called Gleason from New York to report about his meetings with Lara. Gleason agreed that a letter from the Commissioner's Office would be helpful, and that once they had such a letter the case would probably accelerate.[17]

Alexi left New York by train on June 23rd, arriving back in Chicago on June 24th. The next day, Alexi had a short meeting with Steve Gleason. Alexi wanted to know what would happen next. He did not want to be kept in the dark the way he felt he had been with the private investigators. Gleason said the workers' compensation claim could be wrapped up quickly because the firm was experienced in these matters and it knew the relevant people at Kemper Insurance. Gleason also told Alexi that he had contacted the Arizona bar about the behavior of the private investigators but had not yet heard anything back. He would let Alexi know when he heard something.[18]

A few days later, Alexi returned to Venezuela. He had been gone from home since late March, and it was now the end of June. While the trip to Chicago and New York removed some of the sting of the Mesa calamity, Alexi still came home with a great deal of sadness. His sister Carolina remarked about Alexi's more somber demeanor when she said that "he still smiles, but his smile is a long way from what it used to be; his smile is now also full of sadness."[19]

Alexi did not know what would happen with his case in Chicago or at the Commissioner's Office, but he also faced other, more important uncertainties. What was he going to do now that his baseball career was ruined? Alexi had never wanted to be anything other than a professional baseball player. Now his life's ambitions had to change. Nagging at him too was the fact that his left shoulder and arm might never regain normal movement and strength and that degenerative arthritis could haunt his future.[20]

As Alexi settled back into life in Venezuela, he read a newspaper article that reignited his passion to see justice done in his case. On July 21, 1999, on the first page of the sports section of *El Universal*, a leading Venezuelan newspaper, a story appeared about Eric Relucido. Relucido was a twenty-year-old Venezuelan baseball player whose baseball career was destroyed when the New York Yankees failed to give his shoulder injury proper medical treatment at its Venezuelan baseball academy.[21] Relucido had signed with the Yankees in 1996 and played third base for the Venezuelan Summer League team during the 1997 season. In the 1998 season, the Yankees tried Relucido as a pitcher even though Relucido had never pitched. The Yankees did not provide him with proper training on how to pitch, and early in the 1998 Venezuelan Summer League season, Relucido hurt his shoulder badly.

When he brought his injury to the attention of his Yankee coaches, they told him to find a doctor himself to get treatment. Relucido left to get treatment. His doctor in Venezuela, Dr. Germán Medina, a Venezuelan sports doctor who treated players for *Los Leones del Caracas* of the Venezuelan professional league, diagnosed Relucido with a severe rotator cuff injury and badly damaged ligaments. He ordered four weeks of rest and rehabilitation.[22]

Relucido went back to the Yankees' academy to be with the Summer League team. The Yankee coaches ordered him to start pitching again despite the doctor's orders that Relucido rehabilitate his shoulder. Relucido badly reinjured his shoulder when he started pitching again. Eventually, the Yankees released Relucido, presumably because he could no longer pitch or play baseball. Dr. Medina told *El Universal* that surgery would only help Relucido recover 45 percent of his shoulder's abilities and that "[h]is injury limits what a normal person can do, like driving a car or lifting objects."[23]

The person in charge of the Yankees' Venezuelan Summer League team, Raúl "Chingo" Ortega, told *El Universal* that he thought Relucido had left the academy to go to the dentist. Ortega was not aware of any injury to Relucido's arm. He said the Yankees' international scouting director, Gordon Blakely, ordered him to release Relucido. Ortega then told *El Universal* that once he heard the full story, he told Relucido's father to talk to the MLB Commissioner's Office. The newspaper story reported that Relucido filed lawsuits in both the United States and Venezuela against the New York Yankees for between $8 million and $25 million.[24]

The *El Universal* story on Eric Relucido hit Alexi like a revelation. Relucido's story had much in common with what had happened to Alexi: the injury, the lack of medical attention from the major league team, the team's insensitivity about the injury, the team's denial of knowledge about the injury, and the life-altering consequences for a young Latin baseball player of a major league team's mistreatment. Juan Lara of the Commissioner's Office had hit the nail on the head—what happened to Alexi was "normal." Relucido was further evidence of endemic mistreatment and discrimination against Latin baseball players by Major League Baseball teams.[25]

The *El Universal* story on Relucido reinforced this conclusion in another way. The reporter also interviewed Angel Vargas, president of the Venezuela Baseball Players Association (VBPA) and general secretary of the Confederation of Caribbean Baseball Players Associations, about the Relucido case.[26] Vargas told *El Universal* that the VBPA was very concerned about the Relucido case because it was representative of wider problems with how major league teams behaved in Latin American countries.[27] Vargas said that the VBPA was going to start visiting major league teams' academies in Venezuela to check the conditions under which more than 300 young players signed by major league teams play.[28] The Relucido case and Vargas's comments were, for Alexi, vindication of his motivation to use his case to expose the mistreatment and discrimination major league teams inflicted on Latin baseball prospects. Out of nowhere, Alexi suddenly felt as if he was no longer fighting alone but had allies who knew the truth. It was no longer "just your story"; it was a story known to a great many people angry about the behavior of Major League Baseball teams in Latin America. Alexi now had new hope.[29]

Alexi went into action. On July 22nd, he called Angel Vargas, whose name and comments Alexi had seen in the *El Universal* story on Relucido. When Vargas and Alexi agreed to meet, Alexi told Vargas his story. Even someone as familiar as Vargas with the behavior of major league teams in Latin American countries could hardly believe what he heard from Alexi. "Son, are you telling me the truth?" Vargas asked Alexi. Alexi emphatically said that he was. Alexi was not offended by Vargas's question. Vargas's question and his demeanor toward Alexi indicated that Vargas understood all too well how Alexi could be telling the truth. Vargas promised to help Alexi in whatever way he could, and he gave Alexi some names of reporters and lawyers to contact about his case.[30]

Vargas recommended that Alexi first contact a Venezuelan lawyer named Arturo J. Marcano.* Vargas told Alexi that Marcano was working on issues relating to how Major League Baseball teams operate in Latin American countries, and that Marcano had published in May 1999 with David Fidler, a law professor in the United States, an article critical of the behavior of major league teams in Latin American countries.[31,32] After publication of this article, Marcano became International Legal Advisor to the VBPA to assist Vargas and his colleagues in improving conditions for and treatment of players by major league teams.[33] Vargas believed Alexi should contact Marcano because Marcano would be interested in Alexi's story.

On August 2nd, Alexi called Marcano, who happened to be in Venezuela at the time doing research on the globalization of baseball. Just as Angel Vargas had indicated, Marcano was interested in meeting Alexi. In fact, Marcano wanted to interview Alexi for the research he and the American law professor were conducting on the globalization of baseball. On August 3rd, Marcano and Alexi met at the Sambil Mall in Caracas, where Marcano interviewed Alexi. Like Angel Vargas, Marcano was hardened to the reality of major league teams' behavior in Latin America, yet Alexi's story still astonished him.

But then Alexi handed Marcano and his collaborator a researcher's dream: a three-ring binder full of documents supporting his story—copies of contracts, pay slips, letters written by himself and his father to the Cubs, medi-

---

*It was at this point that the authors of this book first became acquainted with Alexi Quiroz and his case.

cal receipts, doctors' reports, etc. Angel Vargas would later tell us that he got many telephone calls from players who had had bad experiences with major league teams, but universally these players had not kept documents that supported their stories. Vargas believed the stories were true, but without some supporting evidence, it was hard, if not impossible, to help the players.[34] But Alexi had documents to substantiate his story.

On August 26th, Alexi called Juan Lara at the Commissioner's Office. Lara said that on August 11th, Roy Krasik had received a short letter from Steve Gleason that said:

> As you may know, this office represents Alexis Quiroz regarding claims that have arisen from an injury he suffered while playing in the Dominican Republic for the Chicago Cubs Organization. Mr. Quiroz has advise[d] me previously that he has spoken to you about his matter and that he was told by you that an investigation into his claims would be forthcoming and that I should expect to be contacted by you. Could you be so kind as to contact the undersigned so that we may discuss this matter.[35]

Lara told Alexi that Krasik had called Gleason, but that Gleason had not returned Krasik's message. Lara emphasized that Krasik wanted to talk to Gleason about Alexi's case but that Gleason had not responded.[36]

On August 30th, Alexi called Steve Gleason to get a report on where the case stood. Gleason reported that little progress had been made on his case. He had contacted the Arizona bar about the private investigators and written (on August 11th) SRISA demanding that it return Alexi's money.[37] He had written to Roy Krasik (also on August 11th) but had not heard back from Krasik or Lara. Alexi told Gleason that Lara said that Krasik had called him but that Gleason had not returned his call. Gleason repeated that he was still waiting for a call from the Commissioner's Office.

Gleason also told Alexi that the Cubs were trying to move the workers' compensation claim out of Illinois to another jurisdiction, and this issue had to be resolved before that claim could move forward. Alexi then asked about filing a tort suit, as Relucido had done, against the Cubs. Gleason's answer surprised Alexi. Gleason said that under Illinois law, Alexi could not file a workers' compensation claim *and* a tort claim against the Cubs for the same injury. A tort claim would, thus, be impossible under Illinois law. It was only at this point that Alexi understood the effect of a workers' compensation claim on other kinds of legal actions, such as tort suits.[38]

On September 10th, Alexi received a fax from Steve Gleason that contained copies of the August 11th letters from Gleason to Krasik and SRISA; an August 17th letter from one of the SRISA officers who worked with Alexi in

Mesa to Gleason informing him she was no longer with SRISA;[39] an August 18th letter from Gleason to a different officer of SRISA enclosing again the August 11th letter;[40] and a letter from Gleason to Alexi dated September 9th in which Gleason informed Alexi that the Chicago Cubs' attorneys had accepted Illinois jurisdiction in the workers' compensation case and were still considering Alexi's questions about additional surgery in the United States to improve the functioning of the injured shoulder.[41] In a phone call on October 13th, Gleason told Alexi that he still had heard nothing from the Commissioner's Office. Gleason had called Krasik, but Krasik had not returned his call. Alexi had met with Juan Lara on June 21st, and now it was mid-October. It was apparent to Alexi that the Commissioner's Office had not started an investigation. It was also apparent to Alexi that his belief in Lara's sincerity and willingness to help had been a mistake. Alexi believed that the Commissioner's Office was adopting the same approach the Cubs used—ignore the problem and it will go away. Perhaps this was the "normal" response of the Commissioner's Office to mistreatment of and discrimination against Latin American players in the Dominican Republic and Venezuela.[42]

As 1999 drew to a close, Alexi reflected on the past twelve months. The year had begun with the continuation of his painful rehabilitation process as he had tried to bring his left shoulder and arm back to some semblance of normality. In February, Alexi and his father had had their "showdown" with Rondón and Fleita in Puerto Cabello, which represented the last straw for the Quirozes. The Cubs would have to be forced to take responsibility for what had happened to Alexi, in terms of paying for all the medical expenses the family had incurred, compensating Alexi for his destroyed baseball career, and making changes to their system in the Dominican Republic and Venezuela to ensure that future players were treated properly, or at least as well as American players.[43]

The pursuit of these objectives had turned disastrous in Mesa, and Alexi knew that he could not lay the blame for the Mesa calamity entirely at the door of the Chicago Cubs. He had trusted too much and made bad decisions in circumstances he did not understand or have the ability to control. His efforts in Mesa had forced the Cubs to pay more (but not yet all) of the Quirozes' out-of-pocket medical expenses, but that money had gone into the pockets of the private investigators, and the Quirozes knew it was gone forever. The family had incurred additional financial hardship in supporting Alexi as he struggled to get the Cubs to deal with his mistreatment. While Gleason and his colleagues were moving ahead on the workers' compensation claim, Alexi felt that the larger goals of his pursuit of justice remained unfulfilled as 1999 drew to a close. Unfortunately, he also knew by the end of 1999 that the Major League Baseball Commissioner's Office cared no more about his mistreatment than did the Chicago Cubs.[44]

In September 1999, Alexi began to work on a small farm to earn some money to help his family. What he could do on the farm was limited by his shoulder injury, but he knew he had to make an effort to earn some money after everything that his family, especially his father, had done for him. Working on the farm allowed Alexi time to reflect on his future. With the cold reality staring him in the face that he had no future as a baseball player, Alexi needed to decide where he was going with his life. He was not going to drop his effort to force the Chicago Cubs to live up to their responsibilities to him and other Latin baseball players, but this could not consume his life. There were too many years ahead to let this baseball tragedy completely ruin his life.[45]

Outside influences were also helping Alexi think about his post-baseball future. His girlfriend, Elisa Pino, whom he had been dating for five years and who had supported him during the darkest moments of his ordeal with the Chicago Cubs, was dropping none-too-subtle hints about marriage. Until his injury, Alexi had never been able to separate himself from baseball. Baseball was his identity. But Elisa loved and cared for him regardless of Alexi's success or failure in baseball. His relationship with Elisa helped Alexi realize that his identity did not have to be, and should not be, determined by his ill-fated journey into professional baseball.[46]

But what direction should his career take now that baseball was dead and buried as a possibility? As he worked on the farm, reflecting on everything that had happened to him and thinking through what he would like to do with his career, his mind began, slowly, to focus on a career in law. His ordeal with the Cubs, including the ill-fated pursuit of justice in Mesa, forced him to think about the meaning of justice and law's place in it. Alexi knew he was lost when it came to all the contracts and laws that had affected his journey through professional baseball. This frustration was, strangely, mutating into curiosity about how the law worked and how legal training might assist society's pursuit of justice. As the new millennium approached, Alexi started looking around for opportunities to study law and become a lawyer.[47]

CHAPTER TWELVE

THE FINAL INNING

WHILE WORKING ON A FARM and contemplating law school helped focus Alexi's attention on his future outside baseball, being in Venezuela made it difficult to advance his case against the Chicago Cubs. Communications with Steve Gleason were difficult, and Alexi sensed that the Commissioner's Office had conveniently forgotten about his mistreatment by the Cubs. After discussions with his father, Alexi decided that another trip to Chicago and New York was needed.[1]

After his August 1999 meeting with Arturo Marcano in Caracas, Alexi stayed in frequent contact with Marcano by e-mail and telephone about his case. Marcano and Fidler invited Alexi to Bloomington, Indiana, during his trip to the United States to be interviewed in more depth for their research on the globalization of baseball. Alexi agreed.

Alexi arrived in Bloomington on January 26, 2000, and from January 26th to the 28th, Marcano and Fidler interviewed Alexi, who brought along another three-ring binder full of documents supporting his story. Alexi telephoned both Steve Gleason and the Commissioner's Office from Bloomington, confirming his appointment with Gleason but having no luck in reaching either Juan Lara or Roy Krasik at the Commissioner's Office. He left messages that he had called and would be coming to New York shortly to meet with them about his case. While Marcano and Fidler drove Alexi to the Indianapolis International Airport for his flight to New York on January 29, Alexi saw something he had never seen before—snow falling from the sky.

On January 31st, Alexi met with Roy Krasik and Juan Lara at the Commissioner's Office. One of their first questions surprised him. "Were you meeting with David Fidler?" they asked. This question struck Alexi as odd because he had not mentioned that he had been in Bloomington. Why did they want to know this? Then Alexi realized that Lara and Krasik had read Marcano and

Fidler's article criticizing Major League Baseball's behavior in Latin American countries. Alexi had read the Spanish translation of Marcano and Fidler's article by this time, and he understood why Krasik and Lara might be nervous. Alexi had not only read this article but he had also suffered much of what it criticized.[2]

Alexi pressed Krasik and Lara about what they had done with his case. Lara asked Alexi basic questions about what had happened to him, and Alexi lost his patience, interrupting Lara and emphasizing that he told them what happened back in June 1999, more than six months before. In addition, Alexi had left documents with the Commissioner's Office supporting his claims of mistreatment by the Chicago Cubs. It was, however, clear to Alexi early in the meeting that neither Krasik nor Lara had done anything about his case. With Alexi thoroughly disgusted, the meeting meandered to a useless end.[3] Alexi was not to know for a month that the meeting had not proved useless. In fact, it had provoked the Commissioner's Office to do something.

Alexi flew to Chicago from New York on February 3rd to meet with Steve Gleason. On February 4th, Gleason told him that, in connection with the workers' compensation claim, the Chicago Cubs had agreed to have a Cubs' physician examine Alexi to determine whether his shoulder required further surgery. (In workers' compensation cases, such an examination by the employer's physician is part of the process if further medical treatment might be needed.) An appointment had been scheduled for February 7th, the following Monday. Gleason told Alexi that Kemper Insurance said it had made arrangements for Alexi to stay, free of charge, in a Chicago hotel to facilitate Alexi's examination. Well, this seemed like progress.[4]

This impression vanished, however, when Alexi arrived at the designated hotel. The hotel clerk told Alexi that no one had arranged to pay for his hotel room and that he would be responsible for all expenses. Alexi, who had not budgeted to stay another weekend in Chicago, tried unsuccessfully to reach Gleason or Kemper Insurance, then tried to explain that there must be some misunderstanding. Misunderstanding or not, the hotel employee insisted, Alexi was responsible for his expenses if he stayed at the hotel. Furious at another slap in the face from the Chicago Cubs, Alexi decided to return to Venezuela.[5] He would shortly see how the Chicago Cubs interpreted this decision.

At the beginning of March 2000, Alexi received a letter dated February 22nd from Roy Krasik of the Commissioner's Office.[6] In the letter, Krasik told Alexi he had written the Cubs on January 31st "to ask their response to your allegation that you have unpaid medical bills relating to your service as a Minor League player for them in the Dominican Republic."[7] Krasik enclosed the Cubs' response to his letter for Alexi's attention.

Two things about Krasik's letter struck Alexi as curious. The first was the date on which Krasik wrote the Cubs. It was January 31st, the very day Alexi had met with Juan Lara and Krasik. For more than six months the Commissioner's Office did nothing with his case and his documents, but on the very day he appeared in New York after meeting with Marcano and Fidler, Krasik wrote a letter to the Cubs about his case.[8]

The second curious thing about the letter was that Krasik focused only on the medical expenses. Despite all the mistreatment that he described and documented for the Commissioner's Office, Krasik ignored all of them when he wrote to the Cubs.

The Cubs had responded to Krasik in a letter dated February 11, 2000, in which Jenifer Surma, manager of human resources, stated that the Cubs "have processed all bills received regarding Mr. Quiroz."[9] Krasik concluded his letter to Alexi by encouraging him to work directly with the Cubs,[10] which Alexi interpreted as "Leave us out of this."[11]

The Cubs' February 11th letter also related to Krasik their side of the hotel misunderstanding story:

> Additionally, we arranged an appointment for Mr. Quiroz to be evaluated by Orthopedist Dr. Michael Schafer on the following Monday morning, February 7 at 7:30 A.M. The additional expenses of his lay over were offered to be paid by the Cubs. Mr. Quiroz failed to appear for that appointment, and we assume he chose to return to Venezuela instead.[12]

The Cubs were pointing the finger of blame at him in connection with what happened at the hotel. In addition, the letter from the Cubs contained no acknowledgement, no recognition of how the Cubs' organization had mistreated Alexi over the entire course of their relationship. He was not just interested in money for past or future medical expenses. Did the Cubs or the Commissioner's Office not understand what his case was really about? Alexi decided these letters indicated that at least now he had the attention of both the Commissioner's Office and the Cubs, and he would take the opportunity to write a letter that would lay everything out for them in plain words.[13]

Alexi asked Marcano and Fidler to help him organize and draft his letter. They agreed as long as Alexi understood three things: First, the letter had to be *his* letter and not a letter from Marcano and Fidler; second, in helping him with this letter, they were not providing him with legal advice of any kind; and third, he had to send his finished letter to Steve Gleason for his review and possible comments *prior* to sending it to the Cubs. Alexi agreed to these conditions.

Alexi sent his finished letter in Spanish and in English (courtesy of Marcano's translation) to Steve Gleason and Marc Stookal on April 13th, giving NSGC a deadline of April 19th for comments or responses.[14] Neither Gleason nor Stookal provided any comments by April 19th, so Alexi sent the letter to officials at the Chicago Cubs, the Commissioner's Office, the Major League Baseball Players Association, Angel Vargas, and Iván González of the Venezuelan newspaper *El Mundo*.[15,16]

The letter covered the entire spectrum of mistreatment that Alexi suffered in his relationship with the Chicago Cubs, and he attached eleven annexes containing documents to support his claims.[17] Never mind that the Chicago Cubs were well aware of all this, and that the Commissioner's Office had had the story and the documents since June 1999. Alexi laid it all out so what happened to him could not be ignored.

At the beginning of the letter, Alexi put his cards on the table:

> While the Cubs have sent me two checks totaling $7,694.66 for medical expenses I and my family incurred in treating my injury, neither the Chicago Cubs nor the Major League Baseball Commissioner's Office have shown any appreciation of the larger issues raised by my mistreatment by the Chicago Cubs.
>
> My goal in raising my mistreatment with the Cubs and the Commissioner's Office has been to get the Chicago Cubs organization to take responsibility for what has happened to me. To date, I have seen no willingness on the part of any representative of the Chicago Cubs in the United States or Venezuela to take responsibility for the damage done to my career and health. Nor do I perceive that the Commissioner's Office is interested in properly investigating my mistreatment.[18]

The letter then raised the problems Alexi experienced with the Cubs that have already been described in earlier chapters of this book.

While writing the letter proved cathartic for Alexi, more immediate challenges consumed his attention. In May 2000, Alexi began his legal studies at the Universidad Bicentenaria de Aragua. Along with 800 other people, he took an entrance exam required by this school, and Alexi was among the 150 who passed and were selected to attend. Succeeding at his legal studies now became Alexi's top priority, and he turned his discipline and determination toward studying law.[19]

His case against the Cubs was never far from his mind, and his law studies began to affect how Alexi approached his pursuit of justice. On August 30, 2000, Alexi called the Commissioner's Office again, but this time was directed not to Krasik or Lara but to Louis Melendez, vice president for international baseball operations. This conversation proved enormously frustrating because Melendez was not familiar with the case and Alexi had to tell him the whole story again. Melendez replied in ways that angered Alexi. For example, after Alexi described how García had "treated" Alexi in San Cristóbal, Melendez replied that García's actions were not the fault of the Chicago Cubs but were

García's fault! But Melendez said at least one thing that made Alexi smile. After Alexi challenged Melendez on an issue, Melendez said, "Man, you're talking like a lawyer."[20]

After interviewing Alexi at the end of January, Marcano and Fidler, during the spring and summer months of 2000, twice wrote to all the officials and employees of the Chicago Cubs involved in Alexi's case to request interviews for their research,[21] and followed up the letters with telephone calls. No official or employee of the Chicago Cubs responded to the letters or telephone calls. Marcano and Fidler also twice wrote and called Roy Krasik and Juan Lara, inviting them to be interviewed about Alexi's case and the larger issues it raised about the behavior of major league teams toward Latin players. Krasik and Lara declined to be interviewed, but they passed along the interview request to Louis Melendez. Melendez wanted to see a list of the interview questions before he agreed to be interviewed,[22] and Marcano and Fidler sent him the list on September 29, 2000.[23] In a letter dated October 30, 2000, Melendez refused to be interviewed and stated how proud the Commissioner's Office was of Major League Baseball's activities in Latin America.[24]

In October 2000, interesting things began to happen in connection with Alexi's case. On October 17, 2000, Jenifer Surma of the Chicago Cubs FedExed to Alexi in Maracay, Venezuela, a $2,000 check with an undated letter which read:

Dear Alexis,

Enclosed is a $2,000.00 check to account for the discrepancy in your original signing bonus.

Sincerely,

Jenifer Surma

Cc: Louis Melendez[25]

Alexi could not believe his eyes. Completely out of the blue came a $2,000 check from the Cubs for the "discrepancy" in his 1995 signing bonus! The letter and check heartened Alexi because in his hands was an admission by the Chicago Cubs that one of its employees, Alberto Rondón, had defrauded Alexi in connection with the signing bonus. Alexi described this fraudulent behavior in his April 11th letter to the Cubs, but no one from the Cubs responded to this letter. Then, six months later, with no prior communication, a check arrived. Why now?[26]

Alexi believed that Louis Melendez must have intervened with the Cubs on this issue because Surma copied her letter to Melendez.[27] A letter about a "discrepancy" in a signing bonus paid five years before is hardly a matter on which to copy MLB's vice president for international operations, unless the

Commissioner's Office and the Cubs were engaging in damage control. After more than two years of ignoring Alexi and his mistreatment, he sensed that the Cubs and the Commissioner's Office were now worried about his case.[28]

The letter and check also angered Alexi. The terseness of Surma's letter and the euphemistic way she referred to the $2,000 Rondón swindled indicated no willingness on the part of the Cubs to confront what had happened to Alexi. Indeed, Surma's one-line letter showed no appreciation of the more important issues the Cubs' mistreatment of Alexi raised. The check was proof that the Cubs had read his April 11th letter and could not deny the larger problems Alexi was trying to force them to address. Rather than address them, Alexi believed the $2,000 check was the Cubs' attempt to buy him off so he would just go away.[29]

Steve Gleason and Marc Stookal also made progress in October 2000 in Alexi's workers' compensation case. The Cubs said they would pay for Alexi to travel from Venezuela to Chicago to be examined on October 24th by Dr. Michael Schafer, the Cubs' team physician,[30] as part of moving the workers' compensation claim forward.[31] Alexi made sure this time that all arrangements were made in advance and confirmed so he would not be expected to pay any expenses he incurred. Alexi had other plans for his trip to Chicago. He wanted to go to Wrigley Field—but not to watch a baseball game.[32]

Alexi asked Arturo Marcano to translate for him during the examination of Alexi's left shoulder and arm, and Marcano met Alexi in Chicago on October 23rd. The next day, Dr. Michael Schafer examined Alexi with Marcano present for translation purposes. After the examination was complete, Schafer said that Alexi's left shoulder had been badly damaged by the injury.[33]

Schafer also said that the lack of immediate and proper medical attention in the Dominican Republic had contributed to the extent of the damage to the shoulder. In a memorable analogy, Schafer said that not treating such a serious injury properly right away is like not giving water to a new flower.[34]

Even though the doctor had confirmed what Alexi already knew, to hear the Cubs' chief physician lay blame for the extent of his injury at the door of the Chicago Cubs surprised him and Marcano. Alexi appreciated Schafer's forthright comments. Schafer discussed with Alexi whether further surgery would help the shoulder, and Alexi determined from Schafer's diagnosis that more surgery would not help a great deal. Alexi did not want to make a decision about surgery until he talked with his father upon his return to Venezuela, but he was virtually certain at that point that he did not want to have more surgery and post-surgical rehabilitation if the results would only marginally improve his shoulder.[35]

On October 25th, Alexi went to Wrigley Field to talk with Scott Nelson and Jenifer Surma about his mistreatment by the Chicago Cubs. Alexi showed up at the Cubs' offices without making an appointment or giving Nelson or Surma any advance warning. Accompanying Alexi were Marcano and William Gutierrez, a law student doing research on the globalization of baseball.[36]

Not surprisingly, neither Scott Nelson nor Jenifer Surma could see Alexi because they were in meetings. All day. Please come back tomorrow. Alexi refused to leave until Nelson or Surma agreed to talk to him. After making a few calls, the receptionist said that Surma was out of the office and thus could not possibly meet with Alexi today. Come back tomorrow. Alexi told the receptionist that he would wait for Nelson, and so Alexi, Marcano, and Gutierrez sat down in the reception area to wait. Directly across from where they were sitting was a coffee machine.[37]

Soon a man came to get a cup of coffee. He kept looking at the three men sitting in the reception area as he poured his coffee. After the man left, Alexi said to Marcano, "That's Scott Nelson." Alexi recognized him from Nelson's brief visit to the Dominican Summer League team in 1996. Nelson was soon back at the coffee machine, again glancing in the direction of the three men. Then Nelson came again for a third cup of coffee.[38]

Suddenly, the receptionist informed Alexi that Scott Nelson was ready to see him. Alexi and Marcano decided that Gutierrez should translate for Alexi if Nelson or Surma agreed to meet because Marcano's presence might chill the discussion given how many letters he and Fidler had written to Cubs' employees requesting interviews. When Alexi and Gutierrez entered Nelson's office, Jenifer Surma was already there.[39]

Alexi proceeded to discuss with Nelson and Surma many of the problems he raised in his April 11th letter to the Cubs. The first substantive issue was Rondón's taking of the $2,000 from Alexi's signing bonus. Surma said the Cubs could not condone Rondón's behavior and that the Cubs "made good" to Alexi on this point by sending him the $2,000 check.[40]

Further, the Cubs had terminated Rondón's employment with the team. Surma said that Rondón's dismissal was a personnel matter that she could not discuss, but she assured Alexi that his complaints about Rondón's behavior—from the signing bonus to the release letter problem—factored into the decision to fire him.[41] Surma's statements revealed that the Cubs had detailed knowledge of his complaints and had relied on them in a personnel matter, but they could not be bothered to treat Alexi with respect and consideration during his ordeal with the team.

Surma continued on the topic of the release letter, telling Alexi that Patti Kargakis had a copy of Alexi's 1997 release letter in his Mesa files if he would like a copy. Nelson chimed in that a released player is automatically put into the computer so everybody knows his status. Nelson was sure this was what happened in Alexi's case, and the other teams had not looked on the computer to check Alexi's status.[42] This statement does not, of course, accord with the confusion the Cubs demonstrated when Alexi showed up in Mesa to get his release letter or with the fact that Roy Krasik at the Commissioner's Office signed Alexi's 1997 contract one month *after* Alexi had supposedly been released.

The Cubs' repeated promises to Alexi that he would play in the United States was the next issue discussed. Nelson told Alexi that the director of the minor leagues (in Alexi's case, David Wilder) can assign players wherever he wants regardless of what the player's contract says. The idea, then, that the Cubs breached Alexi's contract by sending him to the Dominican Republic and not the United States was just wrong.[43] As a matter of interpreting the Minor League Uniform Player Contract, Nelson was correct.[44] The promises broken by sending Alexi to the Dominican Republic were personal promises, not contractual ones. Nelson essentially confirmed that Rondón, Wilder, and Fleita all had made promises to Alexi and his father that were utterly worthless and that the Cubs' employees knew they were worthless but pretended otherwise.

Alexi raised the issue of Wilder's threats in 1998 to suspend him if he wanted his release letter rather than play for the Cubs in the Dominican Republic. Nelson said that he had not heard about this incident before, but major league teams suspend players who do not want to be reassigned (e.g., from Mesa to the Dominican Republic) to prevent players from quitting and then joining another team.[45] The logic of Nelson's argument was not lost on Alexi; the Cubs could terminate his employment at will, but Alexi could not terminate his employment without punishment to avoid being physically and emotionally mistreated by the Cubs in the Dominican Republic.[46]

Alexi moved to discuss the deplorable conditions at the Cubs' Dominican academy and related the behavior of Julio Valdez, including the drunken, gun-toting tirade. Nelson and Surma acted shocked and said they had never heard of this incident before. They assured Alexi that if they had heard of this kind of behavior they would have investigated immediately. Surma wanted Alexi to put the complaint in writing. Nelson agreed that Alexi should get the complaint down in writing and "Jenny would take care of it."[47]

Alexi felt disgusted by Nelson and Surma at this point.[48] The Venezuelan players had told Rondón twice about the incident, and nothing had happened. Alexis Sr. had written a letter on May 26, 1997, to David Wilder, which included a description not only of the gun incident but also Valdez's threats to "break knees with a baseball bat" if he lost his job because of complaints from the Venezuelan players.[49] No investigation had ever been started despite a written complaint. Alexi's April 11th letter to the Cubs, which Nelson and Surma had obviously read, included the following: "The Venezuelan players at the academy called Alberto Rondón to complain about these deplorable conditions. . . . Shortly thereafter, Valdez approached the Venezuelan players and threatened to 'crack our knees with a baseball bat' if he lost his job over our complaints."[50] Neither Surma nor Nelson had taken this written complaint seriously and investigated the matter. Was Valdez's behavior another "discrepancy" to Surma and Nelson? How many complaints, written or otherwise, did the Cubs as an organization need before they acted?

On the problem of the horrible living conditions at the Cubs' Dominican facility, Nelson began to argue with Alexi about the conditions, indicating he thought they were good. Alexi said he had pictures from his time in the academy in 1996. "You have pictures?" Nelson asked. Nelson then backtracked and said, yes, he did visit the academy in 1996, saw the housing quarters, and would agree that they were not in good condition. Nelson even said that the academy was substandard even by Dominican standards![51]

Nelson went on to say that he believed the problems the players experienced in the 1996 Summer League season had been corrected, but because he had not visited the academy since 1996, he would have to defer to Alexi about the conditions in 1998. "I assume the conditions are better because I have not heard any complaints from the scouts or academy directors," Nelson said. A key official for the Chicago Cubs had direct knowledge that the team's Dominican facilities were very bad in the 1996 Summer League season, and he had just *assumed* that everything had gotten better without making sure the Cubs' Latin recruits were treated humanely? Alexi assured Nelson that the living conditions in 1998 were still deplorable. Well, Nelson replied, he would talk to Oneri Fleita about Alexi's allegations. Nelson invited Alexi to submit a written complaint.[52]

The players who went to the Dominican Republic in 1995 and who had warned Alexi and the others about "Vietnam" complained to the Cubs' organization about the living conditions at the academy. Nothing happened. Alexi and his Venezuelan teammates had complained about the conditions in 1996 twice to Rondón, who told the Cubs' head office about the complaints. Nothing happened except threats of physical violence from Valdez. Alexis Sr. wrote to David Wilder in May 1997 and complained about the deplorable living conditions Alexi and the others endured in 1996.[53] Nothing happened. Alexi's April 11th letter to the Cubs, which Nelson and Surma had read, contained an entire page detailing the horrible living conditions at the academy in 1996 and 1998. Nothing happened.[54] How many complaints, written or otherwise, did the Cubs as an organization need before they acted?

Nelson was not finished explaining the Cubs' approach to living conditions in the academy. He told Alexi that Major League Baseball did not have any written standards for academies in the Dominican Republic that the Commissioner's Office applied or checked up on.[55] "Standards are different in the Dominican Republic," he continued. "I don't know what the DR standards are. I live in Chicago; it's different here than down there."[56]

The conversation next turned to the money the Cubs deducted from Alexi's paychecks while he played on the Dominican Summer League teams in 1996 and 1998. Surma handled this issue, saying that the failure to disclose the deductions was the Cubs' mistake. She blamed the Tribune, the Cubs' parent company that paid all the bills. The Tribune lost the information on the deductions, she told Alexi. The Cubs had corrected the problem, pursuant to correspondence with Roy Krasik at the Commissioner's Office (!).[57]

And what were the deductions for? Surma replied that money had been deducted from paychecks to pay for room and board.[58] In other words, the Cubs charged their players for food and housing while they played in the Dominican Summer League. Surma's explanation meant that Alexi had 45 percent of his 1996 paychecks and 35 percent of his 1998 paychecks deducted so he could live in health-threatening squalor. While Surma admitted that failing to disclose the deductions was an error by the Cubs, neither Nelson nor Surma would admit that forcing players to pay to live in such deplorable conditions was a mistake or a "discrepancy."

The final topic of the meeting was the Cubs' continued failure to pay all the medical expenses Alexi had incurred treating his injury and undergoing rehabilitation. Nelson said that, ideally, the director of the academy should take an injured player to the hospital and pay for all medical bills, but that the Cubs had no formal process for dealing with medical bills and injuries in the Dominican academy. Nelson admitted that the director of the academy was responsible for getting the player the proper medical attention.[59]

Alexi asked Nelson for his personal opinion about Valdez's behavior toward Alexi and his injury. Nelson replied that he did not have an opinion because he was not a doctor. Besides, Nelson continued, the Cubs had paid all Alexi's medical bills. Nelson added that he was an executive in Chicago who was not responsible for what happened in the foreign academies, nor was he responsible for the behavior of Cubs' scouts or academy directors in Latin America.[60] "Was anybody responsible?" Alexi wondered to himself.[61]

The meeting ended with Nelson and Surma indicating their willingness to take written complaints from Alexi about any matter.[62] Alexi had heard enough. It was time to go.

Alexi stayed in Chicago one more day and then flew back to Venezuela. He returned to his legal studies, trying to put aside the frustrations and anger the examination and meeting with Nelson and Surma had caused. The major decision he still had to make was whether to go forward with shoulder surgery, as Dr. Schafer had discussed with him. Gleason and Stookal needed the formal, written medical report from Dr. Schafer and Alexi's decision before the workers' compensation claim could proceed.[63]

The Cubs forwarded Dr. Schafer's written medical report of his examination of Alexi to Marc Stookal in early December 2000. Stookal immediately sent the report to Alexi.[64] Typically, the Cubs sent the medical report in English, so Alexi could not read it. Although Alexi was nearly certain he would not have surgery, he instructed Marc Stookal by a letter dated January 9, 2001, that he wanted the Cubs to translate the medical report into Spanish so that he could read it.[65]

On January 19, 2001, Kemper Insurance—the Cubs' workers' compensation insurance carrier—alerted Marc Stookal that it had just issued Alexis Quiroz a check for $1,219.15 for outstanding medical expenses Alexi had incurred in connection with his injury.[66] The check was vindication for Alexi's repeated assertions that the Cubs had failed to pay all the medical expenses he had incurred. Jenifer Surma asserted in her February 11, 2000, letter to Roy Krasik that the Cubs had reimbursed all Alexi's medical expenses. Scott Nelson in the October meeting with Alexi said that the Cubs had paid all his medical expenses. And then a check for more than $1,200 arrived in January 2001 to reimburse expenses incurred long ago. Alexi could only shake his head and laugh at the Cubs.[67]

Even though Dr. Schafer's medical report was two and a half pages long, it took the Chicago Cubs five months to translate it.[68] When Alexi read the translated letter in May 2001, he made his decision. No more surgery. He authorized Stookal to finish the workers' compensation case with the Cubs. The only issue now was how much money the workers' compensation process would produce for Alexi. Stookal warned Alexi repeatedly that he would not receive much because workers' compensation is determined according to a fixed statutory schedule that factors in such things as the extent of the injury and the worker's wage level at the time of injury. Stookal's law firm would also take a percentage of the recovered funds as its contingency fee, reducing Alexi's compensation.[69]

Alexi waited for Stookal to conclude the lawsuit with the Cubs. The Cubs' penchant for refusing to deal with Alexi's case continued. The Cubs' lawyers told Stookal that they could not focus on the case until the 2001 major league season was over, which pushed back any resolution until the late fall of 2001.[70] Why the Cubs' lawyers could not deal with a lawsuit sanctioned by Illinois workers' compensation law until the major league season concluded was a mystery. Alexi doubted whether American employees of the Chicago Cubs would have been told to put their workers' compensation cases on hold until the season was over.

In January 2002, the Chicago Cubs made Alexi a settlement offer in connection with his workers' compensation case.[71] The Cubs offered Alexi $30,000 to settle his claim against the team, which after deductions for attorneys' fees ($6,000) and medical records ($50) meant Alexi would receive $23,950.[72] The settlement offer was not translated into Spanish, so again Alexi and his father had to get the document translated so they could understand its terms. Stookal had repeatedly told Alexi that the workers' compensation process would not produce much money regarding his injury, so the $30,000 settlement offer did not surprise Alexi or his father.[73]

Alexi and his father reviewed the Spanish translation of the settlement offer in detail, and Alexi decided in February 2002 to reject the settlement offer. Alexi's concern was not with the amount of money offered by the Cubs. Alexi did not like other aspects of the settlement offer. What bothered both Alexi and his father were two provisions in the settlement offer that read:

> I understand that by signing this contract, I am giving up the following rights:
>
> . . .
>
> 3. My right to any further medical treatment, at the employer's expense, for the results of the injury;
>
> 4. My right to any additional benefits if any condition worsens as a result of this injury.[74]

Alexi and his father remained worried that Alexi would face more health problems in the future as a result of the injury and the mistreatment Alexi received at the hands of the Chicago Cubs.[75] Alexi did not want to sign a document that let the Cubs off the hook for the health problems and expenses he might face in the future because of the injury.[76] The next stage in the process, in which the claim would go before an arbitrator of the Illinois Industrial Commission, was unlikely to produce either more money or different terms; but Alexi was, at this stage, too uncomfortable signing a document that released the Cubs from responsibility for his injuries and mistreament.

In July 2002, Alexi learned that no progress had been made in bringing his case before an arbitrator. Tired of the long, drawn-out legal process, Alexi reluctantly agreed to sign another settlement offer from the Cubs that contained essentially the same terms as the earlier offer. Alexi's unhappiness at having to release the Cubs from future liability for his injury and mistreatment was balanced by his sense of relief that the legal ordeal was finally over.

PART III

Repairing the Global Ballpark

HUMAN RIGHTS, LABOR STANDARDS, AND MAJOR LEAGUE BASEBALL'S EXPLOITATION OF CHILDREN IN LATIN AMERICA

Three Strikes against Major League Baseball

THE TRAGIC BASEBALL STORY of Alexi Quiroz provides a disturbing glimpse into the abusive and discriminatory manner in which Major League Baseball (MLB) teams have operated in Latin American countries. In chapter 1, we quoted Latin American baseball players who argued that Latins "have taken over" and "control" the game because of the increased number of Latin major leaguers. Alexi Quiroz's story demonstrates who really controls Latin participation in baseball's minor and major leagues. Further, the Quiroz story puts a human face on the exploitative and discriminatory system through which Latin players find their way into the major leagues, which chapter 3 described.

The analysis in chapter 3 and the Quiroz story demonstrate that how Major League Baseball has built the global ballpark is unacceptable. Against overwhelming odds, Alexi fought the system because he believed that how the Cubs and the Commissioner's Office had treated him and other Latin children and young men was wrong. Alexi pursued a cause that he felt was right and just: to force the Chicago Cubs and Major League Baseball to live up to their responsibilities in the globalized game of baseball. Alexi Quiroz wants Major League Baseball to treat Latin children and young men as human beings, not as commodities.

In the globalization of baseball, Major League Baseball has created and operates a system that intentionally discriminates against Latin children and young men so the teams can access cheap sources of labor in order to make profits in North America. As chapter 3 stressed and Alexi understood, major league teams' primary focus in Latin America is getting players as young as possible, preferably under eighteen years of age. The major leagues' *target* is, therefore, Latin *children*. Major league teams handle Latin children in ways

171

that would be unthinkable and illegal in the United States and Canada. The major leagues' *strategy* is to target Latin children and discriminate against them because cheap labor enhances profits, and the major leagues' *objective* is to make money. Major League Baseball's behavior in Latin American countries results in violations of internationally recognized human rights and labor standards designed to protect children from discrimination and exploitation. When Major League Baseball practices toward Latin American ballplayers have variously been described as neocolonialism,[1] racist,[2] reminiscent of West African slave trading techniques,[3] abusive of human rights,[4] a "boatload mentality" seeking cheap commodities,[5] and like concentration camps,[6] it is time to hold Major League Baseball accountable for its behavior. When a baseball-loving kid, such as Alexi Quiroz, suffers through the degradation and disrespect meted out to him by a major league team and the Commissioner's Office, it is time to make Major League Baseball take responsibility for its globalization. When major league teams systematically engage in violations of the human rights of children and of international labor standards designed to protect children, something is wrong in and around the global ballpark. Targeting children in a discriminatory manner simply to increase profits are the three strikes against Major League Baseball's global strategy that we explore in this chapter.

Strike One: Targeting Children—The Relevance of Human Rights and Labor Standards

The United Nations Convention on the Rights of the Child (UNCRC), adopted in 1989, defines a child as "every human being below the age of eighteen years."[7] More than 190 countries have ratified this treaty, making the UNCRC the most widely ratified human rights treaty in the world.[8] The United Nations Children's Fund (UNICEF) argues that the UNCRC makes clear that "[c]hildren living in developing countries have the same rights as children in wealthy countries."[9]

The UNCRC contains rights designed, among other things, (1) to protect children from discrimination;[10] (2) to ensure that the best interests of the child shall be the primary consideration in all actions concerning children;[11] (3) to protect the right to express views freely in all matters affecting the child;[12] (4) to recognize the child's right to freedom of association;[13] (5) to protect the child from all forms of physical or mental violence, injury or abuse, neglect or mistreatment, maltreatment or exploitation by any person who has care of the child;[14] (6) to protect the child's right to the enjoyment of the highest attainable standard of health and to facilities for the treatment of illness and the rehabilitation of health;[15] (7) to ensure a standard of living adequate for the child's development;[16] (8) to further the child's right to an education;[17] and (9) to protect children from economic exploitation.[18]

International standards on labor conditions reinforce the protections for children contained in the UNCRC. For example, the International Labor Organization adopted in 1973 the Convention Concerning the Minimum Age for Admission to Employment (MAC),[19] which 110 countries have ratified.[20] The MAC commits countries to raise progressively the minimum working age with a view to the eventual abolition of child labor.[21] The MAC supports the UNCRC's definition of a child by providing that "[t]he minimum age for admission to any type of work which by its nature or the circumstances in which it is carried out is likely to jeopardize the health, safety or morals of young persons shall not be less than 18 years."[22] The MAC demonstrates that humans under the age of eighteen need special consideration and protection in the context of labor conditions.

These brief descriptions of international human rights and labor standards underscore that major league teams target children in their hunt for Latin talent. Major league teams want Latin players younger than eighteen, and chapter 3 described the lengths that major league teams go to get Latin players as young as possible. What the human rights and labor standards emphasize is that children need special protections and treatment. As the United Nations declared in 1989, "the child, by reason of his physical and mental immaturity, needs special safeguards and care. . . ."[23] International documents pronounced this position repeatedly in the twentieth century.[24] Under the age of eighteen, children need *more* not *less* care and protection. Further, the UNCRC proclaims that "children living in exceptionally difficult conditions . . . need special consideration."[25] Thus, under international human rights and labor standards, children living in developing countries—the very targets of Major League Baseball—deserve special care and protection.

The system created and operated by Major League Baseball to bring Latin children into the minor and major leagues was not, as previous parts of this book demonstrate, designed to protect children or give them the special care and attention required by international human rights and labor standards. Major League Baseball commodifies children—the "boatload mentality," "Latin players on the cheap," "quality out of quantity."

Those versed in international law may quarrel with the application of international human rights and labor standards to Major League Baseball because the treaties cited above technically apply to *governments* and not to *multinational corporations*. One of the most interesting and exciting developments in international relations in the past two decades has been the increasing application of human rights and labor standards directly against multinational corporations (MNCs) by non-governmental organizations (NGOs) and civil society groups. NGOs have shamed many MNCs into adopting "codes of conduct" for their global business to ensure that the MNCs abide by internationally recognized human rights and labor standards. Certification and compliance systems have developed to verify that MNCs are following the international standards. While these developments are not without controversy, the idea that MNCs, such as Major League Baseball teams, do not have to answer to international human rights and labor standards has little credibility today. Further, excusing a major league team from respecting human rights and labor standards for *children* because it is an MNC and not a government would, we believe, be unacceptable to most people.

Strike Two: Discrimination against Latin Children

One of the factors that drove Alexi Quiroz's effort against the Cubs was his experience playing for the Mesa Cubs in the fall of 1997. Alexi was able to compare how the Cubs treated minor league players in Mesa with the degradation he and his Latin teammates suffered at the Dominican academy in 1996. The contrast in the Cubs' treatment of minor league players in the United States and Latin America deepened when he returned to the Dominican Republic and suffered his injury and career-destroying "treatment."

Alexi's story provides a glimpse at how Major League Baseball intentionally treats Latin children less favorably than it treats amateur and minor league players in the United States. As chapter 3 described, Major League Baseball operates within a system in the United States that affords children and young men protection against exploitation. Similar protections do not constrain major league operations in the Dominican Republic and Venezuela. As Alexi's story indicates, major league teams treat Latin children in ways that would not be tolerated today in North America. In their study of Miguel Tejada's road to the major leagues, journalists Marcos Bretón and José Villegas asked, "Would it be tolerated if underprivileged Americans were treated by major league baseball the way Latinos are?"[26] In its treatment of minor league players, Major League Baseball discriminates against Latins.

The prohibition against discrimination on the basis of national origin is one of the most fundamental principles in international human rights law. The UNCRC provides, for example, that contracting parties shall ensure all rights of children in the treaty without discrimination of any kind.[27] The antidiscrimination principle also affects NGOs' activities against MNCs because NGOs often accuse MNCs of locating and operating facilities in foreign countries where wages and labor standards are lower. The MNCs treat foreign workers in poor countries less favorably than their rich-country employees in terms of working conditions. One reason NGOs advocate and monitor corporate "codes of conduct" is to harmonize MNC practices so that discrimination between workers in poor and rich countries is reduced.

Anyone familiar with the history of Major League Baseball knows that discrimination has long been a problem in the sport. African American and Latin players in the minor and major leagues in the United States have confronted discrimination and racism for decades. Other books have explored in depth these stories of racism in baseball. Chico Carrasquel, one of the most famous Latin major leaguers who played in The Show in the 1950s, recalled for us the environment he experienced:

> When I came up to play in 1950, my objective was simply to survive. We Latinos in the majors had no clout or influence. We were too few and too disoriented. We were playing in America's pastime in America. We were not always welcome. In the face of discrimination, racism, and hard times, we just wanted to hang on. Survive.[28]

Other Latin major leaguers, such as Tony Fernández and Carlos Delgado, believe that racism against Latins still exists in the major leagues today, even if the discrimination is not as bad as in the early years of Latin participation.[29] Given the historical and lingering discrimination against Latins in the major leagues, it is not hard to believe that discrimination also haunts how the major leagues bring Latin children into the minor leagues.

Discrimination against Latin major league ballplayers is today indirect and covert rather than part of the formal way teams deal with players.[30] Major League Baseball's discrimination against Latin children and young men entering into the minor leagues is, however, written directly into Major League Baseball's own rules. Analysis of the Major League Rules (MLRs) uncovers at least twelve "double standards" in which the rules on their face treat Latin players less favorably than players subjected to the North American draft. These double standards are:

- Major league teams are prohibited from signing high school players in the United States, Puerto Rico, and Canada during the period of their eligibility to participate in high school athletics (MLR 3(a)(2)). Major League Baseball accords high school students in Latin American countries no equivalent protection.
- Major league teams are prohibited from signing players in colleges in the United States, Puerto Rico, and Canada except under specific conditions (MLR 3(a)(3)). No similar protection applies in Latin American countries.
- Major league teams cannot sign players playing in American Legion youth baseball (MLR 3(a)(5)). Major League Baseball does not accord the same protections to players playing for Latin youth leagues.
- Major league rules prohibit major league teams from trying to influence a student to withdraw from high school or college (MLR 3(g)(1)). Major league teams are, however, free to try to influence Latin children and young men to leave school to play professional baseball.

- Major league rules closely regulate when tryouts for high school, college, junior college, and American Legion players may be held (MLR 3(g)(2)). Latin players are not accorded equivalent protections in connection with tryouts.
- Major league rules require major league teams to provide drafted players with (1) written notice of their selection; (2) a copy of the MLR on contracts; and (3) copies of the Minor League Uniform Player Contract completed by the major league team (MLR 4(e)(1)). No MLR exists on tendering contracts to Latin minor league players.
- If a major league team violates the above-mentioned contract-tendering rules, the player automatically becomes a free agent (MLR 4(e)(4)). Latin minor league players are not similarly protected in the tendering process.
- Major league teams must translate into Spanish major league rules on misconduct (e.g., betting on games) and post such translations in the dugout (MLR 21(g)). Major League Baseball does not, however, have a rule mandating that teams translate the Minor League Uniform Player Contract and other important documents into Spanish for use with Latin minor league players.
- Under major league rules, major league teams bear the responsibility for determining whether a player is eligible to sign (MLR 3(a)). In Latin America, major league teams are not under an express mandate to determine whether a player meets the criteria of the seventeen-year-old rule; all the teams must do is send documents on proof of age.
- Under major league rules, a player gets credited with a year of minor league service for each championship season in which the player was on the active or disabled list of a minor league club (MLR 51). However, a player's time on the active or disabled list of a minor league club in a minor league outside the United States or Canada does not count toward minor league service.*
- Major league rules contain detailed quality standards that apply to minor league facilities in the United States and Canada (MLR 58

---

*The effect of these different standards is as follows: Under the Minor League Uniform Player Contract, a minor league player is first eligible for free agency after seven years. For example, a Venezuelan begins his baseball career by playing three years in the Venezuelan or Dominican Summer Leagues, which are part of Major League Baseball's minor league system. Then the Venezuelan begins to play in the minor leagues in the United States, but the three years in the Latin Summer Leagues *does not* count toward the Venezuelan's seven-year wait for free agency eligibility. In effect, major league teams lock in Latin minor leaguers who play in the Latin Summer Leagues to a longer period of time than U.S. minor leaguers in terms of eligibility for free agency.

and Attachment 58). These detailed quality standards do not and are not applied to minor league facilities of major league teams in Latin American countries.

- If a major league team violates the MLR in signing a player, the contract shall be declared null and void and the player is a free agent (MLR 3(f)(1)). In Latin America, if a major league team violates the seventeen-year-old rule, the contract is not automatically null and void because the Commissioner has discretion whether to so declare (MLR 3(a)(1)(B)).

The discrimination against Latin players on the face of the MLRs is astonishing by itself, but the context of this discrimination needs to be emphasized. Major league teams target Latin children, and yet the MLRs contain only one rule—the seventeen-year-old rule—that affirmatively protects Latin children from major league teams' behavior. And, as chapter 3 described, major league teams have massively violated the seventeen-year-old rule over the years. The MLRs clearly express an attitude toward Latin children fundamentally at odds with international human rights and labor standards that require extra protection and care for children. The MLRs on their face and in practice provide no protection at all, let alone special protection, for Latin children recruited by major league teams. Rafael Pérez, head of MLB's new Dominican office (see more on this office below), admitted that major league teams have violated these norms and have not respected the need for special treatment for children. He said in February 2001 that "[b]aseball has been running things in Latin America in a very informal way."[31] It is no wonder sportswriters have compared Major League Baseball recruiting in the Dominican Republic and Venezuela to the lawlessness of the "Wild West."[32]

The MLRs also reveal that the discrimination against Latin children is intentional. The seventeen-year-old rule demonstrates that the Commissioner's Office can adopt rules to regulate major league teams' behavior in Latin American countries. The absence of any other protective rules, and the presence of rules that treat Latin children less favorably, are compelling evidence of a system designed to discriminate against Latin children.

The failure of the Commissioner's Office and major league teams to design a system through the MLRs to protect Latin children, as required by international human rights and labor standards, might not be so damning if the major league teams, in practice, treated Latin children the same or similarly to the way minor leaguers in North America are treated. But, as Alexi's tragic story showed, such equal or similar treatment does not occur. Not all players suffer the kind or extent of degradation and abuse Alexi Quiroz did, and Alexi did not suffer every kind of abuse (e.g., he was not signed in violation of the seventeen-year-old rule). Even Alexi experienced good treatment in the Oakland

A's facility. Experts perceive that some teams, such as the Los Angeles Dodgers and Oakland A's in the Dominican Republic and the Houston Astros and Seattle Mariners in Venezuela,[33] have adequate facilities. But keep in mind that the Los Angeles Dodgers have been one of the most notorious violators of the seventeen-year-old rule.[34] The Oakland A's had thirteen- and fourteen-year-old players at their academy when Alexi played there,[35] and the Houston Astros have historically trained very young players in their Venezuelan academy.[36] All major league teams benefit and take advantage of the environment the MLRs and the Commissioner's Office create for recruiting Latin children.

Strike Three: Exploitation of Children for Profit
Targeting Latin children and discriminating against them allow major league teams to access cheap labor in order to keep costs down and profits up. Recall the quotes from major league officials cited in chapter 3 that boasted of how cheaply their teams could sign Latin minor league players and run baseball academies in the Dominican Republic and Venezuela. These officials did not disguise the primary motives behind recruiting boatloads of children and training them as cheaply as possible. As noted earlier, historian Samuel Regalado traced this tradition of "Latin players on the cheap" from the earliest days of Latin involvement to the present day.[37] Major league teams operate like other MNCs that access cheap sources of labor in developing countries to remain competitive in lucrative markets in developed countries. As Alexi Quiroz and his family learned, baseball is a brutal global business.

Outside the insular world of Major League Baseball, what major league teams do with Latin children is called exploitation. Within the world of Major League Baseball, what they do with Latin children is called opportunity. When we reach the third strike against baseball's global strategy—exploitation of children for profit—defenders of Major League Baseball trot out the "opportunity thesis" discussed in chapter 3. Simply phrased, this thesis holds that Major League Baseball offers children opportunity, not exploitation. Use of the "opportunity thesis" is, however, disingenuous when the way the major league system for recruiting Latin children into minor league baseball is exposed. Major league teams are interested foremost in cheap labor to bolster profits, not opportunities for Latin children.

Critics of Major League Baseball's discriminatory treatment of Latin children acknowledge that major league teams offer opportunities many of these children would never otherwise see. The end (opportunity) does not justify the means (violation of international human rights and labor standards on the protection of children, including discriminatory treatment). In short, opportunity and exploitation coexist in the globalization of baseball in Latin America. International human rights and labor standards for the protection of children apply in this opportunity/exploitation context all the time everywhere in the world. Major League Baseball is no different in having to confront providing opportunity without exploiting children. The approach traditionally taken by Major League Baseball, which continues today, demonstrates that Major League Baseball prefers pious platitudes about opportunity to rationalize its intentional and systematic exploitation of Latin children for profit.

Repairs to the Global Ballpark Needed

In chapter 1, we cited the statistic that more than 40 percent of minor league players are from foreign countries. The overwhelming majority of these minor league players come from Latin American countries. In other words, nearly half of minor league players enter the major league system through a process that targets and discriminates against Latin children for the purpose of strengthening the corporate bottom line. As with so much in baseball, the statistics speak for themselves.

Despite stubborn devotion to the opportunity thesis, bad publicity and harsh, published criticism have forced MLB officials in the Commissioner's Office to acknowledge that the profitable monster they created and nurtured for decades was out of control. Like Alexi Quiroz, the problem would not go away if Major League Baseball just ignored it. Keep in mind that MLB officials and teams have known *for decades* the way the system really worked, so the sudden concern on the part of the Commissioner's Office should be viewed with a healthy dose of skepticism. We analyze below how the Commissioner's Office has responded to the recent public exposure and criticism of its systematic exploitation of Latin children.

On December 5, 2000, Major League Baseball opened an office in the Dominican Republic from which a new administrator for Latin America would oversee MLB operations in the Dominican Republic and Venezuela. The Commissioner's Office appointed Rafael Pérez to be the new Latin American Administrator.* Pérez's responsibilities are wide-ranging, but most importantly for this book include the following:

- Monitor signings by major league teams in the Dominican Republic and other Latin American countries.
- Identify and investigate illegal signings.
- Insure compliance with the seventeen-year-old rule in the Dominican Republic and other Latin American countries.
- Interact with and instruct scouts in the Dominican Republic and Latin America to ensure that they understand the signing rules.

*Mr. Pérez also declined to be interviewed for our research on this book.

- Inspect academies in the Dominican Republic and Venezuela to ensure compliance with the standards adopted by Major League Baseball.
- Make recommendations with respect to necessary improvements that may be required in the academies located in the Dominican Republic and Venezuela.[38]

While this list of responsibilities suggests that the Commissioner's Office is focusing on the problems highlighted in this book, a closer look at this new office and administrator is needed to maintain perspective on whether this effort constitutes fundamental repairs to the global ballpark.

First, the establishment of the office in the Dominican Republic confirms what critics of Major League Baseball had been arguing—that Major League Baseball's exploitative behavior in Latin American countries was out of control and had been for years. The office represents a reactive move from the Commissioner's Office in response to criticism rather than a proactive strategy it undertook on the basis of its own knowledge of the situation in Latin American countries. Like other MNCs, critics and bad publicity shamed the major leagues into reacting to their abusive behavior.

The Commissioner's Office should have been seriously engaging in the activities it assigned to the administrator long before December 2000. One 1998 quote from Sandy Alderson, then an executive with the Oakland A's, illustrates this point. In connection with a *New York Times* story about the problems with baseball recruiting in Latin America, Alderson said, "There are a whole host of abuses down there."[39] Despite open knowledge about the "whole host of abuses," the Commissioner's Office did nothing. In this light, the new office is evidence of a dereliction of duty by MLB leaders rather than an achievement that exemplifies a proud heritage of developing Latin American baseball players.

Second, Latin America is and has always been the major source of foreign baseball talent for the major leagues. Yet, despite the significance of that region to the major leagues and evidence of widely known abuses and exploitation by major league teams, the Commissioner's Office opened offices in England and Australia—those famous pipelines of major league talent—before it got around to opening an office for Latin America. While the Commissioner's Office invested resources in marketing MLB products to rich Brits and Aussies as part of its global strategy, it was not, until shamed into doing so, interested in curbing the discriminatory exploitation of children in developing countries.

Third, we understand the office in the Dominican Republic consists of Rafael Pérez and a secretary.[40] The official responsibilities of the administrator cover the entire Latin American region and involve formidable tasks. How is the administrator realistically to complete all his tasks with no staff? Does Pérez's budget mirror the size of his staff? These questions suggest that perhaps the Commissioner's Office and the major league teams do not intend for Pérez to succeed as "baseball's sheriff"[41] in Latin America and that the new office is mostly for public relations purposes.

Embarrassed again by criticism and press coverage, Major League Baseball took steps to address the exploitative system it created. The *Washington Post* reported that in 2001 Pérez "inspected all 47 training complexes in the Dominican Republic and Venezuela to establish minimum living and training standards,"[42] an indication of the urgency of this situation. After twenty years of operating baseball academies for Latin children and young men, MLB only begins to think about establishing and enforcing minimum living and training standards for these facilities in 2001 because of bad publicity? This is progress?

Pérez apparently presented the findings of his inspection to major league team owners in New York, again an indication of the seriousness of the problem. We doubt, however, that his findings will be made public because of their likely embarrassing and disturbing contents. Nor is there any indication that, after the meeting, major league team owners are now motivated to address the exploitation from which they profit.

As of this writing, the new office in the Dominican Republic has only been operating for just over one year, so perhaps it is too early to judge whether the Commissioner's Office is conducting an exercise in public relations or is serious about repairing the global ballpark. One product of the new initiative by the Commissioner's Office appears to be the translation into Spanish of the Minor League Uniform Player Contract for use in signing Latin American minor leaguers. As noted earlier in this book, the *Washington Post* reported that the summer of 2001 was the first time that major league teams had a Spanish translation of the Minor League Uniform Player Contract to use in signing children and young men who speak almost exclusively Spanish.[43]

Major league teams have recruited in Latin America for most of the twentieth century and continue to do so in the beginning years of this new century. In all these decades of signing Latin players, the summer of 2001 is the first time major league teams will use a contract the Latin players can actually read? This is progress? In other contexts, the Commissioner's Office has recognized the importance of translating contracts so that players can read them. The Winter League Agreement requires, for example, that the Winter League Uniform Player Contract "shall be printed in both the English and Spanish languages."[44]

Further, whether the Commissioner's Office requires teams to use the Spanish translation or is merely recommending it is not clear. The current Major League Rules, as noted above, do not and have never required that major league teams provide Latin players with contracts they can read. Presenting a child and his parents in the Dominican Republic with a Spanish-language version of an eight-page complicated legal agreement does not level the playing field. Many children who sign in the Dominican Republic are illiterate, as are their parents.[45]

We understand, however, that the Commissioner's Office and major league teams are distributing the Spanish translation only to scouts without instructions to give the translation to players who sign. In other words, despite the existence of an official Spanish translation of the Minor League Uniform Player Contract, the process of providing English-only contracts to Spanish-speaking children and their parents continues unchanged. This situation—involving something as simple as a translated contract—should give the reader a sense of how uninterested the Commissioner's Office is in addressing major league teams' exploitation of Latin children.

Finally, the Major League Rules should be revised to mandate that Latin players and their children be given the right by every major league team to have and evaluate the contract before signing, in the same way the MLRs give draft choices the right to examine contractual documents in advance of signing with a major league team. Much more has to be done to conform to the spirit and the letter of international human rights and labor standards than translating a complicated legal document into Spanish.

CHAPTER FOURTEEN

GLOBAL BALLPARK
REPAIR STRATEGIES

Baseball Governance in the Global Era

THE PROBLEM OF MAJOR LEAGUE BASEBALL'S BEHAVIOR toward children and young men in Latin American countries is a governance problem—controlling and regulating the exercise of power. This book argues that Major League Baseball's policies and practices in connection with Latin America represent the abuse of power and the exploitation of children. In essence, effective governance of Major League Baseball's behavior in recruiting and training Latin minor league players in Latin America does not exist. The challenge is to create a governance structure that will provide a more solid foundation for the global ballpark.

Analyzing how the major leagues are governed provides insights that can be applied to the problem of major league teams' practices in Latin America. Political scientist Mark Rosentraub characterizes governance of professional baseball in North America as a power-sharing relationship between private actors—the team owners and the Major League Baseball Players Association (MLBPA)—with little public governmental involvement in how baseball operates.[1] The owners control the number and location of baseball franchises, while the owners share governance with the MLBPA over employment matters for major league players, including contracts, salaries, and pensions.[2] Other private actors, such as the National Collegiate Athletic Association (NCAA), also play subsidiary roles in professional baseball governance in North America. The NCAA imposes rules, for example, on its member universities that regulate student-athlete contact with sports agents and professional teams (see chapter 3).

Rosentraub argues that the public sector—the government—"exercises little control over baseball."[3] A historical example of this limited governmental role would be baseball's infamous exemption from U.S. antitrust laws.[4] Government plays a larger role than Rosentraub indicates. The controversy about the application of U.S. antitrust law to Major League Baseball aside, how major league teams deal with players and with the MLBPA is disciplined by the framework of public law that supports contracts and collective bargaining between companies and unions. None of this law was created specifically to govern professional baseball, but it nonetheless plays a role in baseball governance in North America. Similarly, state laws in the United States and provincial laws in Canada regulating the behavior of sports agents also contribute to the governance structure of professional baseball in North America.

By contrast, Rosentraub argues that major league team owners "exercise unfettered international power."[5] This statement is accurate for that part of the global ballpark that includes Latin America, but not for those parts that involve Japan and Korea. As chapter 3 noted, the MLB Commissioner's Office has entered into formal agreements that structure how professional baseball talent moves back and forth across the Pacific Ocean. Major League Baseball does not have unfettered power, for example, in Japan because of the governance created by the league-to-league agreement. Further, as labor law expert William Gould argues, the existence of these MLB–Asian league agreements may give the MLBPA a say in the governance of trans-Pacific baseball relations as they relate to employment conditions.[6] Similarly, MLB and the professional leagues in Latin America have entered into the Winter League Agreement that regulates playing conditions for major and minor league players who play in the Latin Winter Leagues, as previously analyzed in chapter 3.[7]

Major League Baseball does, however, exercise nearly unfettered power in the recruiting and training of Latin children and young men in the Dominican Republic and Venezuela. The Latin children and young men recruited by major league teams are not represented by any labor union. As Rosentraub observes, "the MLBPA has no authority to deal with the working conditions for major or minor league prospects in foreign countries, even when the teams and MLB are involved in these nations. MLBPA jurisdiction is limited to players signed to MLB contracts and on the roster of a MLB team."[8]

The Venezuelan Baseball Players Association (VBPA) similarly does not have jurisdiction over Latin children and young men signed to Major League Baseball minor league contracts and who play in academies and the Summer League in Venezuela.[9] The VBPA only has jurisdiction over players under contract to Venezuelan professional teams.[10] Although Dominican players signed to Major League Baseball minor league contracts technically join the professional baseball players union in the Dominican Republic, the union itself apparently does not represent the interests of those Dominicans playing minor league ball for major league teams in the Dominican Republic.[11]

Unlike Latin major leaguers, Latin minor leaguers have no labor union to counterbalance the power and influence of the major league teams and Commissioner's Office in the Dominican Republic and Venezuela. The only remaining potential source of governance pressure to countervail MLB power is the governments of the Dominican Republic and Venezuela. The Dominican Republic passed a law in 1985 to regulate baseball academies,[12] but baseball experts believe that major league teams have ignored this law with impunity.[13] Venezuelan public law applies to many aspects of major league team behavior in that country, but, as in the Dominican Republic, major league teams routinely ignore the local rule of law in their dealings with players and coaches (see below for more on this issue).[14] Governmental involvement in governance of Major League Baseball's behavior in the Dominican Republic and Venezuela appears, therefore, to be weak.

In sum, governance of MLB's globalization in Latin America currently involves no balance of power. The remainder of this chapter explores various strategies to redistribute power and improve governance of MLB behavior in Latin American countries. The first set of strategies involves unilateral changes made by MLB in response to public but informal criticism of the existing situation: (1) restructuring MLB's global governance system, and (2) instituting an international draft. The second set of strategies stands at the opposite end of the spectrum to internal MLB reforms because they involve formal pressure on MLB from two outside sources: governments and labor unions. The third strategic possibility represents a middle road between MLB unilateral changes and pressure from outside entities — the creation of a corporate code of conduct and certification system crafted collaboratively by MLB and other affected and interested parties.

Unilateral Major League Baseball Governance Reforms

GLOBALIZING MAJOR LEAGUE BASEBALL AS AN ORGANIZATION

The establishment of an office in the Dominican Republic to oversee major league teams' behavior in Latin America represents a unilateral MLB governance reform in response to public but informal criticism. Chapter 13 discussed the inadequacy of this reform. Major League Baseball could, however, undertake more radical unilateral governance changes to deal with the problems the existing effective governance monopoly creates.

The first of these more radical reforms would be to turn MLB into a truly global international sports organization. Currently MLB's center of gravity is still North America, but the problems in Latin America and the formal agreements with professional leagues in Japan and Korea represent an internationalization of baseball governance. To globalize governance would involve turning MLB into a global sports organization, modeled after soccer's *Fédération Internationale de Football Association* (FIFA).

FIFA acts as a global umbrella organization and coordinates and regulates different national soccer associations.[15] FIFA is an example of the globalization among national sports leagues undertaken to direct the future of a globalized sport. The International Olympic Committee (IOC) is also an example of an international organization directing a global sports movement.[16]

This path would require turning MLB into a global organization with officials, representatives, and staff members from many different countries, not just North America. In addition, the globalized MLB would oversee relations between national and regional professional baseball leagues, meaning that "MLB North America" would become a subset of the larger entity rather than the main source of power. Such a broadening of MLB's governance scope would bring the less favorable treatment of Latin children and young men entering minor league baseball to the surface as Latin Americans would play a larger and more active role in MLB governance than they do today.

Leaving aside whether creating a new world order for professional baseball would be appealing, this strategy is unrealistic. Why would Major League Baseball team owners unilaterally divest themselves of the tremendous power and influence they now wield globally in professional baseball? Further, the FIFA and IOC models do not fit the baseball context well. Although baseball is actively played and followed in other parts of the world, the major leagues remain the only "big league" in global professional baseball. Other leagues around the world are not only inferior in quality but are also increasingly becoming talent feeders to the major leagues.

AN INTERNATIONAL DRAFT

While globalizing MLB as an organization is unrealistic, serious discussions have occurred involving the second MLB unilateral reform idea. The most far-reaching response that we have seen debated to deal with the dark side of the globalization of baseball is the proposal for an international draft. Sandy Alderson, executive vice president of MLB, said in November 1999 that "[t]he international draft [is a train that] has left the station. It's going to happen within 18 months."[17] (The train is a little slower than Alderson anticipated because the international draft still has not happened.) The Blue Ribbon Task Force on Baseball Economics, composed of George Will, George Mitchell, Richard Levin, and Paul Volcker, also recommended in July 2000 that all foreign players be included in an international draft.[18] Baseball pundit Bob Costas has also advocated the institution of an international draft.[19]

These and other calls for an international draft suggest that important officials and experts inside and outside MLB perceive such a draft to be a necessary remedy for some of MLB's problems. While the international draft may be intended to deal with problems that arise with recruiting Asian players,[20] Latin America is the gold mine for foreign talent, so any discussion of an international draft must occur with Latin America as the foremost concern.

We are not convinced that the Commissioner's Office and other baseball experts are interested in an international draft for reasons that relate to the major leagues' commodification of Latin children. Recall the economic reasons why the major leagues instituted the draft in the 1960s in the United States—free agency for young talent favored rich teams who could scout comprehensively and pay big signing bonuses (see chapter 3). To control salary costs and to create more competitive balance among teams, the major leagues created the draft.

With agents increasingly getting into the Latin action, the costs for signing bonuses for a very small number of Latin players are escalating. Small-market teams increasingly find it hard to compete with the richer teams for the top Latin talent. Also important in this dynamic is the competition for Cuban players who defect, take up residence in Costa Rica and other countries, and then offer their services to the highest bidder. This also favors rich, big-market teams.[21] Joe Cubas, the agent for a number of Cuban ballplayers who have left Cuba, captured this reality when he said that "[y]ou'll never see the Pittsburgh Pirates, the Milwaukee Brewers or the Minnesota Twins at one of my workouts."[22]

The solution to these economic problems is an international draft that covers only a limited number of Latin players. Alderson indicated that the international draft the Commissioner's Office has in mind would cover only a small number of players, leaving plenty of opportunity for major league teams to continue to run their academies for players not in the draft. "The draft will only apply to a few top Dominican [and presumably also Venezuelan] players," said Alderson. "They'll be 16 and 17. There'll be plenty of incentive to continue to have the development schools and programs."[23]

We hear from people involved in professional baseball in Venezuela that what the Commissioner's Office appears to have in mind is a system where each major league team gets to draft *one* player, with all other Latin players remaining free agents. This information accords with Alderson's statement about the restricted scope of any international draft. The clear intent of this kind of restricted draft is twofold—control the size of the signing bonuses of the very few Latins drafted[24] while keeping in place most of the existing "Latin players on the cheap" system of recruiting children.

Contrast Alderson's vision of a limited draft with the recommendation of the Blue Ribbon Task Force on Baseball Economics, which included *all* foreign players in the international draft. For Alderson, the train is leaving the station without many Latins on board; but others want the train to leave the station with more passengers.

Instituting an international draft might, however, have consequences perhaps not intended by the Commissioner's Office that would work to the advantage of all Latin baseball prospects. Drafted players are more likely to be represented by agents (who will not miss out on this market opportunity) and thus will get the protection that agency representation has brought to many drafted American, Canadian, and Puerto Rican players. As sports anthropologist Alan Klein observed, "If the draft is extended to Dominican [and Venezuelan] players, the immediate effect will be to drive up the cost of signing all players."[25] In addition, to avoid discrimination, the Commissioner's Office will have to apply the Major League Rules on the existing draft to the international draft (e.g., giving drafted players copies of contracts and the Major League Rules, automatic termination of a contract for teams' violations of the MLRs, etc.), affording more protection to the drafted Latin players.

These added protections may trickle down to those Latin children not drafted as the ethos of agency representation, higher signing bonuses, and full, fair disclosure of contractual terms erodes the traditional practices of discouraging agency involvement, paying paltry signing bonuses, and having kids sign contracts they cannot read and do not understand. Thus, instituting an international draft could radically transform how major league teams interact with all Latin children who dream of playing in *las Grandes Ligas.*

Instituting an international draft may also complicate labor-management relations in the major leagues. Gould predicted that "[a]ny effort to establish an international amateur draft system will trigger antitrust litigation pursuant to the Curt Flood Act."[26] In other words, the MLBPA will fight any attempt to institute an international draft without collective bargaining with the players' union.* The MLBPA will see the international draft as "vitally related" to the terms and conditions of major leaguers covered by the collective bargaining agreement.[27] If the MLBPA were to succeed in challenging MLB's right to institute the draft unilaterally, then the major league team owners would lose one of the benefits promised by the draft in the first place—controlling costs.

Finally, to date we have not seen anyone inside or outside the Commissioner's Office explain how, as a practical matter, an international draft would be implemented in either the Dominican Republic or Venezuela. Figuring out how to organize and then run an international draft in these countries would prove to be a major headache for the major leagues.

---

*Major League Baseball's proposed elimination of two teams provoked opposition from the MLBPA, indicating that a management-labor fight looms on contraction. This controversy may be one reason the Commissioner's Office does not want to pick another fight with the MLBPA on the international draft idea at this time.

Fox Guarding the Hen House

The above analyses of potential remedies for Major League Baseball's behavior in Latin America suggest that these remedies are, at the end of the day, likely not to prove attractive to major league team owners or the Commissioner's Office. But these remedies, along with the establishment of the new office in the Dominican Republic, are akin to letting the fox guard the hen house. The very institutions and people that target Latin children for discriminatory treatment to make money should not be trusted to act unilaterally in the best interests of such children. As Major League Baseball has for so long demonstrated, how the Commissioner's Office interprets the best interests of baseball is not the same as promoting the best interests of children under international human rights and labor standards.

Outside Governance Strategies

Rather than expecting Major League Baseball to put its own house in order, strategies exist for putting pressure from outside sources on MLB to improve its behavior in Latin America, namely from governments and labor unions.

Increased Governmental Regulation of Major League Baseball's Behavior

Earlier in the chapter we mentioned the failures of governmental regulation in the Dominican Republic and Venezuela. While major league teams should be condemned for flouting the rule of law in Latin American nations, the governments of these countries bear responsibility as well.[28] The problem with looking to Latin American countries for regulatory action against major league teams is not legal because these governments have jurisdiction over Major League Baseball's activities in their territories. The problem involves politics, economics, and culture. Politically and economically, Latin American countries have more pressing matters to confront than the globalization of baseball, such as poverty, foreign debt, inflation, disease, corruption, drugs, crime, and violence. It is also important to understand baseball's place in Latin American cultures.[29] Government plans to tamper with the existing system by regulating major league teams might provoke political backlash by those fearful of the government's wrecking the dreams of Latin children to play in the American big leagues.

While these arguments have force, what must be remembered is that major league teams are hunting for talent in Latin America for a reason—they need fresh, cheap baseball talent to deliver their product and to make a profit. Latin American countries have bargaining power in this relationship. Given the proven track record of Dominican and Venezuelan players in the major leagues, enforcing existing law or adopting new laws and regulations will not, in the long run, scare off major league teams.

An example was set in December 2000 when a Venezuelan labor law court found that the New York Yankees terminated the employment of Winston Acosta, a pitching coach, in violation of Venezuelan labor laws.[30] The New York Yankees had employed Acosta as a pitching coach from January 1, 1992, until July 13, 1999, when the Yankees fired him.[31] During his employment with the Yankees, Acosta earned approximately $1,000 per month.[32] Acosta began litigation against the Yankees on July 27, 1999.[33]

The Yankees were served twice with notice of the lawsuit in Venezuela. The first notice was served on Raúl Ortega, who was in charge of the Yankees' Venezuelan academy but who was subsequently fired by the Yankees. The second notice was served on Humberto Trejo, who was at the time in charge of the Yankees' activities in Venezuela. The Yankees never appeared before the Venezuelan labor court to contest Acosta's lawsuit.[34]

Under the Venezuelan Civil Code, when a properly served defendant does not appear in court, the Venezuelan court accepts the plaintiff's allegations of fact as proven. In other words, by not appearing to contest the lawsuit, the Yankees were deemed by the Venezuelan Civil Code to have accepted the factual allegations in the lawsuit. The Venezuelan labor court awarded judgment for Acosta on May 30, 2000, and ordered the Yankees to pay Acosta a total award of $6,865.30.[35]

The Yankees' representatives in Venezuela told Acosta that the Yankees were not going to pay him anything in connection with the lawsuit.[36] To this date, the Yankees have failed to pay the judgment rendered against them in Venezuelan court. The Yankees, with revenues in 2001 of $242 million and operating profit in 2001 of $40.8 million,[37] cannot be bothered to pay Winston Acosta $6,865.30 pursuant to Venezuelan law.

The New York Yankees have, in this case, showed nothing but disrespect for the rule of law in Venezuela. The team failed to appear before the Venezuelan labor court despite being properly served with notice of the lawsuit. The team refused to recognize that Venezuelan labor law, as confirmed by the decision of the Venezuelan labor court, applied to its operations in Venezuela. The team arrogantly told Acosta that he would never see any payments from the Yankees in connection with this lawsuit. It is hard for us to imagine a scenario in which a major league team knowingly and intentionally violated the rule of law in a foreign country more than the Yankees have done in the Acosta case.[38]

Like Alexi Quiroz, Winston Acosta pursued his lawsuit against the Yankees not only to enforce his rights under Venezuelan law but also to vindicate the rights of other coaches and players who have had their rights violated in the same way by other major league teams.[39] After the Acosta case was brought to the attention of the Commissioner's Office,[40] it reminded major league teams that they should obey local laws in the foreign jurisdictions in which they operate.[41] The fact that the Commissioner's Office believed that such a reminder was necessary demonstrates how bad the situation has become.

The Acosta case is also interesting because we understand from baseball people in Venezuela that the New York Yankees shut down their academy in Venezuela in the aftermath of the Acosta litigation because of the team's exposure to Venezuelan labor law. Apparently, the Oakland A's and Texas Rangers have also closed their Venezuelan academies for the same reason. These reactions from major league teams suggest that greater enforcement of local law may provoke MLB divestments or threats of divestment. In addition, these developments mean that the Dominican Republic and Venezuela have to work together to create a unified position in order to prevent major league teams from using divestment as a threat to blunt heightened enforcement of local law against them.

LABOR UNION ACTION AND SOLIDARITY

Latin children and young men signed to minor league contracts by major league teams have no labor union to represent their interests in dealings with such teams. As noted earlier, the MLBPA and the Venezuelan Baseball Players Association (VBPA) do not have jurisdiction over minor league players signed to contracts with major league teams. The Dominican professional baseball players union technically has jurisdiction but does not exercise this authority to protect and promote the interests of Dominicans on Major League Baseball's minor league teams.

Major league players have the MLBPA, and the MLBPA has revolutionized professional baseball governance in North America for purposes of management-labor relations.[42] The MLBPA has succeeded in stopping major league teams from treating players like property through such practices as the reserve clause. In his memoir, Marvin Miller—the first head of the MLBPA—characterized the MLPBA's function as "being the only force serving as a bulwark against an unregulated monopoly with antisocial tendencies."[43]

In connection with recruiting Latin American children and young men to play minor league baseball, Major League Baseball is an essentially unregulated monopoly with antisocial tendencies. Based on baseball's past history of labor-management relations, the situation in Latin America calls for the formation of a transnational labor association to protect and promote the interests of Latin children and young men who sign minor league contracts with major league teams or who play in baseball academies without contracts.[44]

While this strategy has conceptual appeal, establishing a transnational labor association to protect Latin children and young men signed to minor league contracts with major league teams would face serious obstacles. Who, for example, would initiate such an undertaking? Marvin Miller's memoir of his time as head of the MLBPA demonstrates how difficult organizing a union for major league players was.[45] Labor activism cannot be expected from Latin children and their parents. The professional players' unions in the Dominican Republic and Venezuela could attempt to extend their formal jurisdiction and activities to include Latin minor league players, but moving in this direction might not be feasible. Angel Vargas, head of the VBPA, noted that even if the VBPA represented Latin minor leaguers, the union "does not have the resources to cope with problems in the academies and Summer League in addition to all the other problems that it faces."[46]

Moreover, major league teams and the people involved in the system would vigorously oppose efforts to unionize Latin minor leaguers, and the power of this opposition cannot be underestimated. Major league teams would probably argue, for example, that the presence of the new MLB office in the Dominican Republic precludes the need for the more radical attempt to unionize Latin minor league players. Latin prospects and signees who were active in the union would probably be marked as troublemakers and face even steeper odds of making *las Grandes Ligas*. Anyone who doubts that major league teams would target union activists for punishment is ignorant of how these teams dealt with many major leaguers who served as team representatives for the MLBPA in its formative years.[47]

While formidable, these obstacles are not insurmountable. The key is finding a source of power and money that would serve as a foundation for a transnational labor union for Latin minor league players. Such a source exists in the form of the Latin players who have achieved stardom in the major leagues. Chapter 1 provided the statistics on the growing numbers of Latin major league players. The presence of so many Latin ballplayers in the major leagues means that the muscle and money exist for a transnational players association to protect and promote the interests of Latin minor league players.

What is required is that Latin major league players step up to this challenge created by the globalization of baseball. Major leaguer Tony Fernández, who is from the Dominican Republic and has been concerned about the treatment of Latin players his entire career, argued that:

> there are a lot of players who are afraid to talk in relation to the way
> they have been exploited or what they have been subjected to as a
> minority by MLB. Some of us, the players who have been in this world
> for many years and have reached the top are in a better position than
> the rest of the players from Latin America, and it is these players who
> have the responsibility of being the voice of all the rest of the players

and especially of those who cannot express what they feel, have felt, live or have lived because of the fear of losing their job. . . . We [the Latin major league players] have never worked together on this fight and that is the only way we can see results. . . .[48]

Latin legend Chico Carrasquel agreed with Fernández about the leadership role that the Latin major league players must show:

Today, the Latino superstars have the ability to tackle the problems MLB teams cause in our countries. Confronting these problems will not be easy for Latino players. Many are very grateful for the opportunities that the major leagues have given them to escape poverty and provide a good life for their families. But perhaps the time has come for all of us to confront our responsibilities.[49]

A second requirement for establishing a union to protect the interests of Latin minor league players in their dealings with major league teams is assistance and solidarity from existing baseball labor associations. While the MLBPA and the VBPA do not have jurisdiction over Latin minor league players, both unions have experience and expertise they could lend to support the contemplated transnational labor association. Angel Vargas argues that "[c]ross-border labor union solidarity is often necessary in the era of globalization to cope with the mistreatment of laborers in many fields of economic activity. We need such solidarity in the face of the globalization of baseball."[50]

The Middle Path: Collaborative Work on a Major League Baseball Code of Conduct

A middle path between relying on major league teams to improve their behavior and pushing Latin governments to regulate or establishing a new labor union can be found. This path involves crafting a collaborative process among the Commissioner's Office, baseball labor unions, national sports ministers, interested civil society groups, and individual baseball experts to fashion a code of conduct for major league teams operating in Latin America. As mentioned earlier, in other economic contexts NGOs have managed to shame MNCs into adopting corporate codes of conduct in an effort to improve their operations in developing countries.

Informal, unorganized public and private criticism shamed Major League Baseball into opening its new office in the Dominican Republic and translating the Minor League Uniform Player Contract into Spanish, but a more structured and collaborative project to draft a code of conduct would bring MLB into the cutting-edge world of melding corporate behavior, international hu-

man rights and labor standards, and involvement of civil society stakeholders.*
Moving in this direction would show that MLB has an enlightened and global
view of what is in the best interests of not only baseball but also the children
to whom Major League Baseball provides economic opportunities.

In keeping with the experience already developed on corporate codes of
conduct,[51] the collaborative effort proposed here should include a process by
which the code's implementation by major league teams can be objectively
monitored and verified. In this regard, baseball labor unions and civil society
groups could cooperate with and help the new MLB office in the Dominican
Republic to harmonize major league teams' activities in Latin America with
the requirements of international human rights and labor standards. Latin
major leaguers could also be a powerful force in moving this collaborative
project forward by providing moral and financial support, getting personally
involved in drafting or monitoring the code of conduct, and helping to rebuild
cooperatively the global ballpark from which they have received so much.

The globalization of baseball means that baseball is now not only a global
game but a global business. Major League Baseball has built a global ballpark
to maximize its ability to capture economic returns from the globalization of
baseball. As this book has argued and Alexi Quiroz's story demonstrates, the
globalization of baseball is not just about making money. It is also about justice. The globalization of baseball means that major league teams have global
responsibilities. These responsibilities include behaving with respect toward
Latin children as required by international human rights and labor standards.

The global ballpark needs radical rebuilding if Major League Baseball is
to live up to these responsibilities. As this chapter has analyzed, different strat-
egics for the rebuilding process exist. We hope our analysis and Alexi Quiroz's
story motivate people who care about the future of the game of baseball to
begin restructuring governance for Major League Baseball's activities with
respect to Latin children and young men. Only when this restructuring justly
balances the best interests of baseball and the best interests of Latin children
will the umpire's call of "Play Ball!" resonate with global equity and fairness.

---

*One possible participant in this dialogue could be the Dominican Initiative at the Center for
International Development at Harvard University. This initiative is interested in the issues raised
in our previous work and in this book. The Dominican Initiative includes a program on "Baseball and Development" that "will examine the current system of recruitment, major league baseball camps, and the Dominican leagues to see if there are areas which could be changed to
improve the lives of aspiring and unsuccessful youth in the Dominican baseball system. . . ." The
Dominican Initiative at the Center for International Development, Harvard University, at
<http://www.cid.harvard.edu/dominican/> (visited Dec. 14, 2001).

EPILOGUE

June 26, 1999

WRIGLEY FIELD. Chicago Cubs v. Philadelphia Phillies. Alexi Quiroz bought a ticket for the "standing room only" section of Wrigley Field. Alexi knew he would never play baseball in *las Grandes Ligas* because of his injury, and his experiences with the Chicago Cubs and Major League Baseball were such that no one could blame him for never watching another major league game for the rest of his life. But he went to Wrigley Field, the home of the team that had exploited him and refused to take responsibility for the damage it had inflicted on his body and his future. He bought a ticket, adding to the Cubs' gate revenues, revenues that Alexi knew would not be invested in Latin players in the Dominican Republic and Venezuela. Somehow, Alexi felt compelled to go, to watch the Cubs play. Why?

Part of the compulsion driving Alexi to watch the Cubs and Phillies play was his remaining love for the game. Not the brutal business behind the game that had transformed his childhood baseball dreams into a nightmare of exploitation and mistreatment, but the game on the field, the game itself. Roberto González Echevarría described the connection Alexi still felt toward this game as "the magic of baseball."[1]

Alexi's love for the game was deeply rooted and would not be killed by the mistreatment he suffered at the hands of the Cubs and Major League Baseball. His attendance was an act of defiance—a message to himself that his spirit had not been broken. At his core, Alexi retained, despite all that had befallen him in his tragic odyssey in the globalization of baseball, the spark of youthful hope that gave birth so long ago to the innocent desire that began his fateful journey to this midsummer moment at Wrigley Field, "Papá, I want to play baseball."

Alexi married Elisa on December 16, 2000, in Maracay, Venezuela. He continues his law studies and also, when law school permits, helps his father operate a new business Alexis Sr. started. Alexi thanks his family for all the support they gave him during his ordeal. He is eternally grateful for their belief in him and his fight for respect and justice. Alexi also thanks all those people who assisted him during his attempt to get the Chicago Cubs and the Commissioner's Office to face their responsibilities. Finally, Alexi thanks you, the reader, for taking time and energy to read about his story and the globalization of baseball.

1. The "Golden Age" of Latin American Baseball Talent in Major League Baseball

1. "Foreign-Born Players on Rise," *USA Today*, Apr. 4, 2002, sec. C, p. 4. At the beginning of the 2001 major league season, 25.3 percent of major league players had been born outside the United States (ibid.). At the start of the 2000 season, that number was 23.6 percent. Major League Baseball (MLB), "More than 23 Percent of MLB Players Born Outside of U.S.," <http://www.majorleaguebaseball.com/u/baseball/mlbcom/int/int_foreignborn_2000.htm> (posted Apr. 6, 2000) (visited May 29, 2000); MLB, "2001 Opening Day in Puerto Rico to Culminate Second 'Month of the Americas,'" Feb. 22, 2001, MLB.com News (visited July 3, 2001).

2. "Foreign-Born Players on Rise."

3. Peter Gammons, "This Year's Draft As Uncertain As Ever," ESPN.com, June 3, 2000, <http://espn.go.com/gammons/s/0603.html> (visited December 6, 2001).

4. Steve Fainaru, "The Business of Building Ballplayers," *Washington Post*, June 17, 2001, <http://www.washingtonpost.com/wp-dyn/articles/A10070-2001Jun16.html> (visited June 18, 2001). At the end of the 2001 season, 2,614 players from thirty countries were under minor league contracts. Steve Fainaru, "Baseball's Minor Infractions: In Latin America, Young Players Come at a Bargain Price," *Washington Post*, Oct. 26, 2001, sec. D, p. 1.

5. "Foreign-Born Players on Rise."

6. Angel Vargas, "The Globalization of Baseball: A Latin American Perspective," *Indiana Journal of Global Legal Studies* 8 (2000), 21, 28.

7. "Foreign-Born Players on Rise."

8. MLB press release, "MLB Honors Latin Impact in 2000 with 'Month of the Americas,'" Nov. 10, 1999; MLB, "2001 Opening Day in Puerto Rico to Culminate Second 'Month of the Americas.'"

9. MLB press release, "MLB Honors Latin Impact in 2000 with 'Month of the Americas,'" Nov. 10, 1999; MLB, "2001 Opening Day in Puerto Rico to Culminate Second 'Month of the Americas.'"

10. MLB press release, "MLB Honors Latin Impact in 2000 with 'Month of the Americas.'"

11. Ibid.

12. Ibid.

13. Ibid.

14. MLB, "2001 Opening Day in Puerto Rico to Culminate Second 'Month of the Americas.'"

15. Marcos Bretón and José Luis Villegas, *Away Games: The Life and Times of a Latin Ball Player* (New York: Simon and Schuster, 1999), 244; Evan Grant, "Viva Beisbol: The Increasing Influence of Latin Americans," *Dallas Morning News*, Mar. 27, 2000, <http://www.baseball.dallasnews.com/mlb/topnews/55469_27mlblatin.html> (visited Mar. 28, 2000).

16. Grant, "Viva Beisbol."

17. On this history, see Samuel O. Regalado, *Viva Baseball! Latin Major Leaguers and Their Special Hunger* (Urbana: University of Illinois Press, 1998); Samuel O. Regalado, "'Latin Players on the Cheap': Professional Baseball Recruitment in Latin America and the Neocolonialist Tradition," *Indiana Journal of Global Legal Studies* 8 (2000), 9.

18. "Player Register—Tony Peña," in John Thorn and Pete Palmer, eds., *Total Baseball: The Official Encyclopedia of Major League Baseball*, 4th ed. (New York: Viking Press, 1995), 1185.

19. Quoted in Grant, "Viva Beisbol."

20. "Player Register—Felipe Alou," in Thorn and Palmer, *Total Baseball*, 678.

21. Quoted in Grant, "Viva Beisbol."

22. William Shakespeare, *The Merchant of Venice*, act 2, scene 7.

2. The Globalization of Baseball

1. Gene Budig, "Baseball Has a Worldly Look," *USA Today*, June 26, 1998, sec. C, p. 6.

2. Marc Gunther, "They All Want to Be Like Mike: Led by the NBA and Global Superstar Michael Jordan, U.S. Pro Sports Leagues Are Extending Their Worldwide TV Presence All the Way from Chile to China," *Fortune*, July 21, 1997, 51.

3. Harold Seymour, *Baseball: The Early Years* (Oxford: Oxford University Press, 1960), 80.

4. Quoted in ibid.

5. Ibid., 307–308.

6. See ibid., 309, 314 (noting how "the fans came out because they liked the American's absence of rowdyism" and the American League's success in "raiding National League stars").

7. See ibid., 322–24 (discussing details of the agreement that brought the National and American Leagues together).

8. For overviews of the business of baseball, see Andrew Zimbalist, *Baseball and Billions: A Probing Look Inside the Big Business of Our National Pastime* (New York: Basic Books, 1992); David Pietrusza, "The Business of Baseball," in John Thorn and Pete Palmer, eds., *Total Baseball: The Official Encyclopedia of Major League Baseball*, 4th ed. (New York: Viking, 1995).

9. "MLB Profits and Losses," ESPN.com, Dec. 5, 2001, <http://espn.go.com/mlb/s/2001/1205/1290765.html> (visited Dec. 11, 2001).

10. Testimony of Allan H. (Bud) Selig, Commissioner of Baseball, Hearing on the Antitrust Exemption for Major League Baseball, Before the Committee on the Judiciary, U.S. House of Representatives, Dec. 6, 2001, 2001 WESTLAW 26188117.

11. Prepared Statement of MLB Commissioner Allan H. Selig, Hearing on *Baseball's Revenue Gap: Pennant for Sale?* Before the Subcommittee on Antitrust, Business Rights, and Competition of the Committee on the Judiciary, U.S. Senate, Nov. 21, 2000, S. Hrg. 106-1045, 25.

12. "MLB Profits and Losses," ESPN.com, Dec. 5, 2001.

13. Statement of Senator Mike DeWine (R-Ohio), Hearing on *Baseball's Revenue Gap: Pennant for Sale?* Before the Subcommittee on Antitrust, Business Rights, and Competition of the Committee on the Judiciary, U.S. Senate, Nov. 21, 2000, S. Hrg. 106-1045, 1.

14. Testimony of Allan H. (Bud) Selig, Commissioner of Baseball.

15. Prepared Statement of MLB Commissioner Allan H. (Bud) Selig.

16. "Broadcast Money and Gate Receipts," ESPN.com, Dec. 5, 2001, <http://espn.go.com/mlb/s/2001/1205/1290777.html> (visited Dec. 11, 2001).

17. Prepared Statement of MLB Commissioner Allan H. (Bud) Selig.

18. "Committee: MLB Teams Need Revenue Sharing Increase," *The Sporting News*, July 13, 2000, <http://www.sportingnews.com/baseball/articles/20000713/246959.html> (visited July 15, 2000).

19. See "For the Record, Major League Baseball," *USA Today*, Dec. 13, 2001, sec. C, p. 15 (breaking down 2000 and 2001 MLB players' salaries).

20. Bob Nightengale, "Rising Star at Rising Price: Texas Signs Rodríguez to Baseball's Richest Contract Ever," *Baseball Weekly*, Dec. 13, 2000, 2000 WESTLAW 10167148.

21. Associated Press, "Steinbrenner: Texas Did Baseball a Disservice," Feb. 17, 2001, WESTLAW ALLNEWSPLUS.

22. Testimony of Allan H. (Bud) Selig, Commissioner of Baseball.

23. See House Resolution 3288—Fairness in Antitrust in National Sports (FANS) Act of 2001.

24. Statement of Representative John Conyers Jr. (D-Mich.), Hearing on the Antitrust Exemption for Major League Baseball, Before the Committee of the Judiciary, U.S. House of Representatives, Dec. 6, 2001, 2001 WESTLAW 26188113.

25. See Statement of Donald M. Fehr on Behalf of the Major League Baseball Players Association, Before the Committee of the Judiciary, U.S. House of Representatives, Dec. 6, 2001, 2001 WESTLAW 2618818.

26. Leonard Koppett, "The Globalization of Baseball: Reflections of a Sports Writer," *Indiana Journal of Global Legal Studies* 8 (2000), 81.

27. MLB, "Market Development," MLB.com—International, <http://www.majorleaguebaseball.com/u/baseball/mlbcom/int/int_programs.htm> (visited May 16, 2000).

28. Quoted in Murray Chass, "McGwire Has Disdain for International Ball Games," *International Herald Tribune*, Mar. 22, 2000, 11. It is not clear what McGwire meant when he said the major leagues are "too international as it is." He was perhaps referring to the growing prominence of Latin American and other foreign baseball players in the major leagues discussed in chapter 1. In the same interview, McGwire also said, "To me, to go play worldwide doesn't turn my crank. I want to play here in America. I have nothing against anybody else in another country. The game belongs here." Quoted in ibid.

29. Quoted in "Ticket Prices at Home Provoke Martinez," USAToday.com Baseball Weekly, Mar. 16–22, 2000, <http://www.usatoday.com/sports/baseball/bbw2/v11/bbw1112.htm> (visited Dec. 11, 14, 2001).

30. Koppett, "The Globalization of Baseball: Reflections of a Sports Writer," 83.

31. MLB, "Market Development." See also "Major League Baseball's Influence Around the World," *USA Today*, Mar. 17, 2000, sec. C, p. 16 (listing the twenty-nine countries that have participated in the Envoy program).

32. MLB, "Market Development."

33. Ibid.

34. MLB Web Page, <http://www.majorleaguebaseball.com> (visited Oct. 10, 1998).

35. MLB, "Market Development."

36. Ibid.

37. Ibid.

38. Ibid.

39. MLB, "International Broadcasters," <http://www.majorleaguebaseball.com/mlbcom/int/int_broadcasting.htm> (visited May 16, 2000).

40. Quoted in Gunther, "They All Want to Be Like Mike," 52.

41. Budig, "Baseball Has a Worldly Look," sec. C, p. 6.

42. Ibid.

43. Associated Press, "Sadaharu Oh Praises Ichiro as 'Real Thing,'" ESPN.com, July 3, 2001, <http:www.espn.go.com/mlb/news/2001/0703/1221867.htm> (visited July 5, 2001).

44. Ibid.

45. Zimbalist, *Baseball and Billions*, 57–58, 79–80.

46. MLB Web Page, <http://www.majorleaguebaseball.com> (visited July 20, 1998).

47. "Major League Baseball's Influence Around the World," sec. C, p. 16.

48. MLB Web Page, <http://www.majorleaguebaseball.com> (visited July 20, 1998).

49. MLB, "International Offices," <http://www.majorleaguebaseball.com/u/baseball/mlbcom/int/int_contact.htm> (visited May 16, 2000). In fact, MLB did not open an office in Latin America until December 2000. See chapter 13.

50. Quoted in John Harper, "The International Pastime," *New York Daily News*, Mar. 27, 1997, 16.

51. Comments of Joe Kehoskie, sports agent, in "Stealing Home: The Case of Contemporary Cuban Baseball—The Dominican Comparison," <http://www.pbs.org/stealinghome/debate/dominican.html> (visited July 17, 2001). See also Steve Fainaru and Ray Sánchez, *The Duke of Havana: Baseball, Cuba, and the Search for the American Dream* (New York: Villard, 2001), 34 (noting laments of American scouts that young players in the U.S. "grow up distracted—distracted by other sports like soccer and basketball, by television, by Nintendo, by the various and sundry diversions of the richest nation in the world").

52. G. Edward White, *Creating the National Pastime: Baseball Transforms Itself* (Princeton, N.J.: Princeton University Press, 1996), 330.

53. Quoted in Harper, "The International Pastime," 16. See also Murray Chass, "Scouts Search Globe for Talent," *New York Times*, Apr. 8, 1998, sec. C, p. 3.

54. Thomas J. Fitzgerald, *Field of Dreams*, Mar. 28, 1999, <http:www.Bergen.com/Yankees/dreamstf199903284.htm> (visited May 6, 1999).

55. Roberto González Echevarría, "The Magic of Baseball," *Indiana Journal of Global Legal Studies* 8 (2000), 145, 150.

56. Ibid.

57. See generally on Cuban baseball, Roberto González Echevarría, *The Pride of Havana: A History of Cuban Baseball* (Oxford: Oxford University Press, 1999).

58. Fainaru and Sánchez, *The Duke of Havana*, 227.

59. Harper, "The International Pastime," 16.

60. The 2001 NBA draft reinforced perceptions about the basketball path from rags to riches as high school players dominated the early first-round draft choices of NBA teams.

61. Jimmy Roberts, "What Must They Be Thinking?" <http://204.202.129.20/mlb/columns/jroberts/> (visited Feb. 18, 1999).

62. Steve Fainaru, "Baseball's Minor Infractions: In Latin America, Young Players Come at a Bargain Price," *Washington Post*, Oct. 26, 2001, sec. D, p. 1.

63. Quoted in Harvey Araton, "Clemente to Sosa, and Beyond," *New York Times*, Nov. 13, 1998, sec. D, p. 1. In a PBS documentary on contemporary Cuban baseball, González Echevarría said, "I take a dim view of what the major leagues are doing in the Dominican Republic with these so-called baseball academies, where children are being signed at a very early age, and not being cared for, most of them are providing

the context for stars to emerge. If you take a hundred baseball players in those academies, . . . only one of them will play even an inning in the major leagues. The others are there as supporting cast." "Stealing Home: The Case of Contemporary Cuban Baseball—The Dominican Connection," <http://www.pbs.org/stealinghome/debate/dominican.html> (visited July 17, 2001).

64. Quoted in Marcos Bretón and José Luis Villegas, *Away Games: The Life and Times of a Latin Ball Player* (New York: Simon and Schuster, 1999), 38.

65. Fitzgerald, "Field of Dreams."

66. Angel Vargas, "The Globalization of Baseball: A Latin American Perspective," *Indiana Journal of Global Legal Studies* 8 (2000), 21, 27.

67. "Committee: MLB Teams Need Revenue Sharing Increase."

3. The Structure and Dynamics of Major League Baseball's Recruitment of Foreign Baseball Talent

1. Len Sherman, *Big League, Big Time: The Birth of the Arizona Diamondbacks, the Billion-Dollar Business of Sports, and the Power of the Media in America* (New York: Pocket Books, 1998), 211.

2. William B. Gould IV, "Baseball and Globalization: The Game Played and Heard and Watched 'Round the World (with Apologies to Soccer and Bobby Thomson)," *Indiana Journal of Global Legal Studies* 8 (2000), 85, 119.

3. Associated Press, "M's Accused of Acting Unethically," ESPN.com, Aug. 23, 2001, <http://espn.go.com/mlb/news/2001/0823/1242917.html> (visited Aug. 23, 2001).

4. "Sports Digest," *San Francisco Chronicle*, Jan. 12, 2000, sec. E, p. 6.

5. Scott M. Cwiertny, "The Need for a Worldwide Draft: Major League Baseball and Its Relationship with the Cuban Embargo and United States Foreign Policy," *Loyola of Los Angeles Entertainment Law Review* (2000), 391. These rules have, however, been challenged in court by Cuban Rolando Viera as discrimination against Cuban nationals who take up residence in the United States. See Tom Farrey, "Cuban Defector Seeks Freedom from MLB Policy," ESPN.com, May 29, 2001, <http://espn.go.com/mlb/s/2001/0529/1206578.html> (visited May 31, 2001).

6. Cwiertny, "The Need for a Worldwide Draft," 391.

7. Ibid.; Steve Fainaru and Ray Sánchez, *The Duke of Havana: Baseball, Cuba, and the Search for the American Dream* (New York: Villard, 2001), 80, 82–83, 87–88 (on the Joe Cubas plan).

8. Quoted in T. R. Sullivan, "Rangers Find Talent Shows on Latin Beat," *Fort-Worth Star Telegram*, Mar. 8, 1998, 1.

9. On the amateur draft generally, see Allan Simpson, "The Amateur Free Agent Draft," in John Thorn and Pete Palmer, eds., *Total Baseball: The Official Encyclopedia of Major League Baseball*, 4th ed. (New York: Viking, 1995), 608.

10. Ibid., 609.

11. Ibid., 608. Whether the draft today helps keep costs for new talent down is a controversial issue. Average signing bonuses for top draft choices now approach or exceed $2 million. Top draft picks have also been able to find ways to thwart the draft's objective of distributing talent evenly, as illustrated by the famous case of J. D. Drew. For discussion of the J.D. Drew case, see Gould, "Baseball and Globalization," 112.

12. Simpson, "The Amateur Free Agent Draft," 609. Lee MacPhail, who was instrumental in the dominance of the New York Yankees in the 1950s and 1960s, observed, "We won the World Series five years in a row. Kids wanted to sign with the Yankees, the most glamorous team in baseball at the time." Quoted in ibid.

13. Ibid., 608.

14. Ibid.

15. Ibid.

16. Ibid.

17. Ibid.

18. Ibid.

19. See John Thorn, "Our Game," in Thorn and Palmer, *Total Baseball*, 5, 10. Thorn notes that "the pennant domination by the three New York teams—principally the Yankees, of course—made the national pastime a rather parochial pleasure; it was hard for fans in Pittsburgh or Detroit to wax rhapsodic over a Subway Series." Ibid.

20. Simpson argues that the draft largely achieved this objective: "Payments to untried amateur players were kept in line until the late 1980s, while new meaning has been given to competitive balance." Simpson, "The Amateur Free Agent Draft," 609.

21. Major League Rule 4(e).

22. Ibid.

23. Sherman, *Big League*, 171.

24. Major League Rule 3(a).

25. Ibid.

26. Major League Rule 3(a)(5).

27. Major League Rule 3(g).

28. Simpson, "The Amateur Free Agent Draft," 609.

29. Major League Rule 3(c)(4)(D).

30. See Lionel S. Sobel, "The Regulation of Sports Agents: An Analytical Primer," *Baylor Law Review* 39 (1987), 701, 768–69. See also Glenn M. Wong, *Essentials of Amateur Sports Law*, 2nd ed. (Westport, Conn.: Praeger,1994), 303–304.

31. See Sobel, "The Regulation of Sports Agents," 724–25; and Wong, *Essentials of Amateur Sports Law*, 671. See also Linda S. Calvert Hanson, "The Florida Legislature Revisits the Regulation and Liability of Sports Agents and Student Athletes," *Stetson Law Review* 25 (1996), 1067, 1068 note 7.

32. Sherman, *Big League*, 211.

33. Gould, "Baseball and Globalization," 107.

34. Ibid., 113.

35. This description of the MLB–Japanese baseball agreement follows Gould, "Baseball and Globalization," 113–14.

36. Murray Chass, "Mariners Gain Rights to Sign Suzuki Outbidding Mets and 2 Others," *New York Times*, Nov. 10, 2000, sec. C, p. 21.

37. Gould, "Baseball and Globalization," 119.

38. Ross Newhan, "The Great Escape: America's Pastime is also Pedro Guerrero's Passport," *Los Angeles Times*, Jan. 7, 1985, WESTLAW, ALLNEWS PLUS.

39. Steve Fainaru, e-mail discussion on "The Business of Dominican Baseball," June 22, 2001, <http://discuss.washingtonpost.com/wp-srv/z-forum/01/world_fainaru 0622.htm> (visited July 25, 2001).

40. See, e.g., Samuel O. Regalado, *Viva Baseball! Latin Major Leaguers and Their Special Hunger* (Urbana: University of Illinois Press, 1998).

41. Samuel O. Regalado, "'Latin Players on the Cheap': Professional Baseball Recruitment in Latin America and the Neocolonialist Tradition," *Indiana Journal of Global Legal Studies* 8 (2000), 9.

42. See ibid.

43. Steve Fainaru, "Baseball's Minor Infractions: In Latin America, Young Players Come at a Bargain Price," *Washington Post*, Oct. 26, 2001, sec. D, p. 1.

44. We define a child as any person under the age of eighteen. For more analysis, see chapter 13.

45. Regalado, "'Latin Players on the Cheap,'" 17.

46. Quoted in Fainaru, "Baseball's Minor Infractions," sec. D, p. 1.

47. Quoted in Rich Rupprecht, "Baseball Report," *Press Democrat* (Santa Rosa, Calif.), May 4, 1997, sec. C, p. 3, available at 1997 WESTLAW 3437307.

48. Gerdvan Liendo, interview with the authors. See also Associated Press, "False Pitches Crush Latin American Youngsters' Baseball Dreams," *The Star-Ledger Newark* (N.J.), June 4, 2000, 2000 WESTLAW 21307073.

49. Major League Rule 3(a)(1)(B).

50. Rob Neyer, "Thorny Issue Has No Easy Solution," ESPN.com, Dec. 1, 1999 (visited Dec. 1, 1999).

51. Associated Press, "Lasorda Defends Dodgers' Actions," ESPN.com, Nov. 16, 1999 (visited Nov. 17, 1999).

52. Associated Press, "Dodgers Fined for Signing Young Beltre," ESPN.com, Dec. 21, 1999 (visited Dec. 22, 1999).

53. Millson reported that "[t]he leagues put a temporary embargo on signing Dominicans late in 1984 until a system was worked out. In 1986 a signing-age minimum of 17 was established." Larry Millson, *Ballpark Figures: The Blue Jays and the Business of Baseball* (Toronto: McClelland and Stewart, 1987), 226.

54. Magglio Ordonez, now with the Chicago White Sox, described his experience: "When I was 15 years old, Andrés Reiner, a scout for the Houston Astros, told me that he wanted to sign me. So I gave up high school and went to the academy. For some reason, they kept me in the academy for almost a year without telling me anything about my future." *El Universal*, Nov. 10, 1998.

55. Steve Fainaru, "Indians Are Hit with Penalties—Sanctions for Signing Underage Player Draw Mixed Reaction," *Washington Post*, Feb. 27, 2002, sec. D, p. 1. See also Steve Fainaru, "Baseball's Minor Infractions," sec. D, p. 1.

56. Ibid., sec. D, p. 6.

57. Ibid. (emphasis added).

58. Quoted in Rob Beaton, "Baseball Tightens Grip after Beltre Case," USA Today.com, Feb. 8, 2000 (visited Feb. 14, 2000).

59. Associated Press, "Lasorda Defends Dodgers' Actions."

60. Neyer, "Thorny Issue Has No Easy Solution."

61. Rob Beaton, "Braves Penalized for Illegal Signing," *USA Today*, Feb. 25, 2000, sec. A, p. 1.

62. Paul Gutierrez, "Dodger Prospect Plans an Appeal: Team Was Fined for Illegal Signing of Venezuelan Pitcher Arellan, But Retained Players' Rights," *Los Angeles Times*, Jan. 25, 2001, sec. D, p. 5.

63. Fainaru, "Baseball's Minor Infractions," sec. D, p. 1.

64. Associated Press, "False Pitches Crush Latin American Youngsters' Baseball Dreams."

65. Ibid.

66. Jayson Stark, "Age Issues Brought on by Sept. 11," ESPN.com, Feb. 23, 2002, <http://espn.go.com/mlb/columns/stark_jayson/1339359.html> (visited Mar. 2, 2002).

67. Ibid. (identifying fifteen Latin major league players determined to be older than previously thought); Mike Fish, "Latin Players Doctor Their Birth Certificates for a Chance to Play," CNNSI.com, Feb. 26, 2002, <http://sportsillustrated.cnn.com/inside_game/mike_fish/news/2002/02/26.html> (visited Mar. 4, 2002) (identifying twenty Latin major league players identified as being older than previously thought).

68. Stark, "Age Issues Brought on by Sept. 11."

69. Ibid.

70. Rod Beaton, "Age May Be Off for Hundreds in Baseball," USAToday.com, Feb. 26, 2002, <http://www.usatoday.com/sports/baseball/stories/2002-02-26-ages.htm> (visited Feb. 27, 2002).

71. Fish, "Latin Players Doctor Their Birth Certificates for a Chance to Play." See also Scott Boeck, "Players Growing Older by the Second," USAToday.com, Feb. 22, 2002, < http://usatoday.com/sports/baseball/stories/2002-02-22-age.htm > (visited Mar. 2, 2002) (quoting Neifi Perez of the Kansas City Royals as admitting "that he lied about his age because he was told as a kid that giving a false age would help him get a professional contract"); and Peter Slevin and Dave Sheinin, "An Age Old Numbers Game: Amid Visa Crackdown, Many Dominican Players Aren't As Young As Thought," *Washington Post*, Mar. 2, 2002, sec. D, p. 1 (reporting baseball and diplomatic sources arguing that for decades "many Dominicans forged identity papers lowering their ages to increase their appeal to major league scouts and managers").

72. Fish, "Latin Players Doctor Their Birth Certificates for a Chance to Play."

73. Regalado, "'Latin Players on the Cheap,'" 16.

74. Kevin Kerrane, *Dollar Sign on the Muscle: The World of Baseball Scouting* (New York: Simon & Schuster, 1989), 30.

75. Ibid.

76. Carlos Cárdenas Lares, *Venezolanos en Las Grandes Ligas*, 2nd ed. (Caracas: Fondo Editorial Cárdenas Lares, 1994), 27.

77. Regalado, "'Latin Players on the Cheap,'" 16.

78. Quoted in ibid.

79. Sammy Sosa, with Marcos Bretón, *Sosa: An Autobiography* (New York: Warner Books, 2000), 47.

80. Angel Vargas, interview with the authors.

81. Steve Fainaru, "The Business of Building Ballplayers," *Washington Post*, June 17, 2001, <http://www.washingtonpost.com/wp-dyn/articles/A10070-2001Jun16.html> (visited June 18, 2001).

82. Ibid.

83. Tim Kurkjian, "Scary? Guerrero Getting Better," ESPN.com, May 12, 2000 (visited May 16, 2000).

84. Fainaru, "The Business of Building Ballplayers."

85. Ibid.

86. Ibid.

87. Murray Chass, "Baseball's Game of Deception in the Search for Latin Talent," *New York Times*, Mar. 23, 1998, sec. A, p. 1.

88. Fainaru, "The Business of Building Ballplayers." Jose Rijo returned to pitching in the major leagues in 2001 after a six-year absence. Scott Miller, "Rijo Takes Long Road Back to Mound in Cincy," CBSSportsline.com, Aug. 19, 2001, <http://cbs.sportsline.com/b/page/pressbox/0%2C1328%2C4210366%2C00.html> (visited Mar. 28, 2002).

89. Ibid.

90. Major League Rule 3(b)(6); Fainaru, "The Business of Building Ballplayers."

91. Ross Newhan and Paul Gutierrez, "Big Leagues Invade Dominican Republic," SportingNews.com, Dec. 5, 1999, <http://sportingnews.com/baseball/articles/19991219/197866.html> (visited June 19, 2000).

92. Fainaru, "Baseball's Minor Infractions," sec. D, p. 1.

93. Ibid.

94. Ibid.

95. Ibid.

96. Rob Plummer, e-mail response dated June 18, 2001, to Steve Fainaru, "The Business of Building Ballplayers," *Washington Post*, June 17, 2001.

97. Kerrane, *Dollar Sign on the Muscle*, 27.

98. Regalado, "'Latin Players on the Cheap,'" 12.

99. Ibid., 16.

100. Chico Carrasquel, interview with the authors.

101. Sosa with Bretón, *Sosa: An Autobiography*, 49.

102. Marcos Bretón and José Luis Villegas, *Away Games: The Life and Times of a Latin Ball Player* (New York: Simon and Schuster, 1999), 67.

103. Minor League Uniform Player Contract.

104. Major League Rule 4(e).

105. "There is no actual 'meeting of the minds,' even though the terms of the bargain are reduced to writing and signed by both parties, if one of them did not in fact read or understand the written terms. . . . In modern business life there are innumerable 'standardized' contract forms, . . . prepared by one party for his recurrent use in many transactions. They may contain many provisions, often in fine print, the purpose of which is to limit his own obligations and to avoid risks that he would otherwise have to bear. He may present this to the other party, often much less well informed or advised, on the basis of 'accept this or get nothing,' well knowing that the other party does not know or understand. In these cases, the requirement of an actual 'meeting of the minds' may well be made effective against the party in the superior position." Arthur L. Corbin, *Corbin on Contracts*, vol. 1 (St. Paul: West Publishing, 1963), 479.

106. Angel Vargas, interview.

107. William Gutierrez, interview with the authors.

108. Winter League Agreement, April 21, 1998, Article IV(a)(1).

109. Major League Rule 21.

110. For basic information on the Dominican and Venezuelan Summer Leagues, see MinorLeagueBaseball.com, <http://www.minorleaguebaseball.com/pagetemplate/league_logo.asp?pageid=292> (Dominican Summer League) and <http://www.minorleaguebaseball.com/pagetemplate/league_logo.asp?pageid=357> (Venezuelan Summer League) (visited Dec. 13, 2001).

111. Quoted in Alan Schwarz, "Diamonds in the Rough," Baseball America Online (visited Dec. 9, 1999).

112. Quoted in Newhan and Gutierrez, "Big Leagues Invade Dominican Republic."

113. Schwarz, "Diamonds in the Rough."

114. Fainaru, "Baseball's Minor Infractions," sec. D, p. 1.

115. Alan M. Klein, *Sugarball: The American Game, The Dominican Dream* (New Haven, Conn.: Yale University Press, 1991), 42.

116. Quoted in Fainaru, "Baseball's Minor Infractions," sec. D, p. 1.

117. Angel Vargas, "The Globalization of Baseball: A Latin American Perspective," *Indiana Journal of Global Legal Studies* 8 (2000), 21, 29.

118. Donald M. Fehr, Executive Director and General Counsel, Major League Baseball Players Association, Comments at Symposium on Baseball in the Global Era: Economic, Legal, and Cultural Perspectives, Bloomington, Indiana, Feb. 27, 2000.

119. Anonymous, interview with the authors.

120. Luis Peñalver, interview with the authors.

121. Ibid.

122. Winter League Agreement, Apr. 21, 1998, Article IV and Attachment A.

123. Ibid., Articles V(a) and V(e).

124. Ibid., Article X(a) (incorporating MLR 18(a)).

125. Ibid., Article X(b).

126. Presidential Regulation 3450 of 1985, translated in Aaron N. Wise and Bruce S. Meyer, *International Sports Law & Business*, vol. 2 (Ardsley, N.Y.: Transnational Publishers, 1997), 889.

127. Klein, *Sugarball*, 54.

128. Associated Press, "False Pitches Crush Latin American Youngsters' Baseball Dreams."

129. Fainaru, "Baseball's Minor Infractions," sec. D, p. 1.

130. Ibid.

131. Quoted in ibid.

132. Quoted in Michael M. Oleksak and Mary Adams Oleksak, *Beisbol: Latin Americans and the Grand Old Game* (Grand Rapids, Mich.: Masters Press, 1991), 184.

133. Angel Vargas, interview.

134. Fainaru, "Baseball's Minor Infractions," sec. D, p. 1.

135. Ibid.

136. For information on the top ten highest-paid Latin major league players in 2001, see "Special Report: The Highest Paid Latino Players in Major League Baseball (2001 Data)," <http://latinosportslegends.com/Latinos_highest_paid_in_baseball-2001.htm> (visited Dec. 13, 2001).

137. Klein, *Sugarball*, 62–103.

138. See Dave Hoekstra, "A Land of Hope, Dreams: Cubs Seek Untapped Talent in the Dominican Republic," *Chicago Sun-Times*, Feb. 29, 1988, 12 (noting efforts by the Chicago Cubs to rid prospects of parasites and to provide them with good nutrition); and Regalado, *Viva Baseball*, 201–202 (quoting Ralph Avila of the Los Angeles Dodgers, who stated that "the Dodgers promise three meals a day, a bed, a physical examination, any necessary dental work, prescription drugs and vitamins, classes in Spanish, an English teacher, transportation to and from the ball park and free laundry").

139. Regalado notes that the baseball academies "became temporary sanctuaries from poverty" for young persons in the Dominican Republic. Regalado, *Viva Baseball*, 201.

140. T. R. Reinman, "Getting to First Base: Latins Have Earned Their Place in Major Leagues," *San Diego Union-Tribune*, July 9, 1991, sec. D, p. 1.

141. Quoted in Jack Wilkinson, "Baseball Dreamers: The Road to Turner Field," *Atlanta Journal-Constitution*, Aug. 16, 1998, sec. E, p. 1.

142. Whether creatine is safe for use as a nutritional sports supplement by persons under the age of eighteen is controversial. In the August 2001 issue of the peer-reviewed scientific journal *Pediatrics*, researchers published the findings of the first study of creatine use in children and recommended that creatine use by children under eighteen should be discouraged until its safety in this population can be established. See Jordan D. Metzl, Eric Small, Steven R. Levine, and Jeffrey C. Gershel, "Creatine Use among Young Athletes," *Pediatrics* 108 (2001), 421. Other scientists criticized the findings of this study. See Richard B. Kreider, "Creatine Concerns & Link to Steroid Abuse Unfounded," *Pediatrics Online*, Aug. 11, 2001, <http://www.pediatrics.org/cgi/eletters/108/2/421> (visited Dec. 11, 2001) and Douglas S. Kalman, "Creatine Knowledge to Date," *Pediatrics Online*, Aug. 23, 2001, <http://www.pediatrics.org/cgi/eletters/108/2/421> (visited Dec. 11, 2001).

4. "Papá, I Want to Play Baseball!"

1. Alexi Quiroz, interview with the authors; Alexis Quiroz Sr., interview with the authors.

2. "Player Register," in John Thorn and Pete Palmer, eds., *Total Baseball: The Official Encyclopedia of Major League Baseball*, 4th ed. (New York: Viking, 1995), 796.

3. Alexi Quiroz, interview.

4. Ibid.; Alexis Quiroz Sr., interview.

5. Alexis Quiroz Sr., interview.

6. Ibid.; Alexi Quiroz, interview.

7. Alexi Quiroz, interview.

8. Alexis Quiroz Sr., interview.

9. Alexi Quiroz, interview.

10. Ibid.; Alexis Quiroz Sr., interview.

11. Alexi Quiroz, interview.

12. "There's not a kid in the Caribbean who reaches his 14th birthday without being seen by the major-league teams." Milton Jamail, quoted in Rich Rupprecht, "Baseball Report," *Press Democrat* (Santa Rosa, Calif.), May 4, 1997, sec. C, p. 3, available at 1997 WESTLAW 3437307.

13. Angel Vargas, interview with the authors.

14. Ibid.

15. Alexi Quiroz, interview.

16. Alexis Quiroz Sr., interview.

17. Ibid.

18. Alexi Quiroz, interview.

19. Ibid.

20. Ibid.

21. Angel Vargas, interview; Gerdvan Liendo, interview with the authors.

22. Alexi Quiroz, interview.

23. Ibid.

24. Alexis Quiroz Sr., interview.

25. Alexi Quiroz, interview.

26. Angel Vargas, interview.

27. Alexi Quiroz, interview.

28. Ibid.

29. Ibid.

30. Ibid.

31. Ibid.

32. Ibid.

33. Ibid.

34. Ibid.

35. Ibid.

36. Ibid.

37. Ibid.; Alexis Quiroz Sr., interview.

38. Alexi Quiroz, interview.

39. Ibid.

40. Ibid.

41. Ibid.

42. Ibid.

43. Ibid.
44. Ibid.
45. Ibid.
46. Ibid.; Alexis Quiroz Sr., interview.
47. Alexi Quiroz, interview.
48. Ibid.; Alexis Quiroz Sr., interview.
49. Alexi Quiroz, interview.
50. Ibid.; Alexis Quiroz Sr., interview.
51. Alexi Quiroz, interview.
52. Ibid.; Alexis Quiroz Sr., interview.
53. Alexi Quiroz, interview; Alexis Quiroz Sr., interview.
54. Alexi Quiroz, interview.
55. Alexis Quiroz Sr., interview; Alexi Quiroz, interview.
56. Alexis Quiroz Sr., interview.
57. Ibid.
58. Alexi Quiroz, interview.
59. Ibid.
60. Alexis Quiroz Sr., interview; Alexi Quiroz, interview.
61. Alexis Quiroz Sr., interview.
62. Alexi Quiroz, interview.
63. Ibid.; Alexis Quiroz Sr., interview.
64. Other players signed by Alberto Rondón on behalf of the Chicago Cubs also told us that they were presented with contracts in English they could not read. Carlos Jaragüi, Eleazar Medina, and Reinaldo Padilla, interviews with the authors.
65. Alexi Quiroz, interview; Alexis Quiroz Sr., interview.
66. Alexi Quiroz, interview.
67. Alexis Quiroz Sr., interview.
68. Carolina Quiroz, interview with the authors.
69. Alexi Quiroz, interview; Alexis Quiroz Sr., interview.
70. Alexi Quiroz, interview; Alexis Quiroz Sr., interview. Other players signed by Rondón on behalf of the Cubs also did not receive copies of their contracts. Carlos Jaragüi, Eleazar Medina, and Reinaldo Padilla, interviews.

5. Going to Vietnam

1. Alexi Quiroz, interview with the authors.
2. Ibid.
3. Ibid.; Alexis Quiroz Sr., interview with the authors.
4. Alexi Quiroz, interview; Alexis Quiroz Sr., interview.
5. Check receipt dated February 14, 1996, for $6,000 from the Chicago Cubs to Alexis Quiroz.
6. Alexi Quiroz, interview; Alexis Quiroz Sr., interview.
7. Alexi Quiroz, interview; Alexis Quiroz Sr., interview.
8. Alexi Quiroz, interview; Alexis Quiroz Sr., interview.
9. Alexi Quiroz, interview; Alexis Quiroz Sr., interview.
10. Much later in the story, Alexi raised the issue of the $2,000 with Rubén Amaro of the Chicago Cubs in Mesa, Arizona. Amaro first wanted to know whether Alexi had actually received his signing bonus, suggesting perhaps that non-payment of the bonus might itself be a problem with the Cubs. Then Amaro told Alexi that the $2,000 was

probably some way the Cubs were trying to avoid paying taxes. Whether this was evasion of U.S. or Venezuelan tax laws Amaro did not indicate. Alexi Quiroz, interview.

11. Alexi Quiroz, interview; Alexis Quiroz Sr., interview.

12. Alexi Quiroz, interview.

13. Minor League Uniform Player Contract dated October 5, 1995, between Alexis Quiroz and the Chicago Cubs, Addendum B.

14. Angel Vargas, interview with the authors.

15. Major League Rule 3(j): *"Gift for Securing Employment Forbidden.* No scout . . . of any Major or Minor League Club . . . shall demand or receive any money or other valuable consideration, whether gratuitous or otherwise, for or because of services rendered, or to be rendered, or supposed to have been rendered, in securing employment of any person with any Major or Minor League Club. Such money or other valuable consideration shall be returned immediately upon its receipt, and if not returned, the Commissioner may impose such penalties . . . as the Commissioner may deem proper."

16. Alexi Quiroz, interview; Alexis Quiroz Sr., interview.

17. Alexi Quiroz, interview.

18. Ibid.

19. Ibid.

20. Ibid.

21. Ibid. Carlos Jaragüi, who attended the Cubs' Dominican academy during the 1995 Summer League season, confirmed from his firsthand experience what Alexi and the other new signees were being told by the veterans. Jaragüi told us that before his trip to the Dominican Republic in 1995, the Cubs told him the house was nice and that he would eat well. "This," concluded Jaragüi after his experience in 1995, "was a lie." Carlos Jaragüi, interview.

22. Alexi Quiroz, interview.

23. Ibid.

24. Ibid.

25. Ibid.

26. Ibid.; Alexis Quiroz Sr., interview; Carolina Quiroz, interview with the authors.

27. Alexi Quiroz, interview; Alexis Quiroz Sr., interview; Carolina Quiroz, interview.

28. Carolina Quiroz, interview.

29. Alexi Quiroz, interview.

30. Ibid.; Pictures taken by Alexis Quiroz of the house serving as the living quarters for the Cubs' Summer League team in Santana, Dominican Republic.

31. Alexi Quiroz, interview.

32. Reinaldo Padilla, interview with the authors.

33. Alexi Quiroz, interview; Pictures taken by Alexis Quiroz of the house serving as the living quarters for the Cubs' Summer League team in Santana, Dominican Republic.

34. Alexi Quiroz, interview.

35. Ibid.

36. Ibid.; Reinaldo Padilla, interview.

37. Alexi Quiroz, interview.

38. Ibid.; Reinaldo Padilla, interview.

39. Alexi Quiroz, interview; Reinaldo Padilla, interview. Carlos Jaragüi also reported the same problems with water in the house during the 1995 Summer League season. Carlos Jaragüi, interview with the authors.

40. Alexi Quiroz, interview.

41. Ibid.; Reinaldo Padilla, interview.

42. Alexi Quiroz, interview; Reinaldo Padilla, interview.

43. Alexi Quiroz, interview; Reinaldo Padilla, interview.

44. Alexi Quiroz, interview; Reinaldo Padilla, interview.

45. Alexi Quiroz, interview.

46. Ibid.

47. Carlos Jaragüi, interview.

48. Alexi Quiroz, interview.

49. Ibid. Carlos Jaragüi did the same thing in 1995. Carlos Jaragüi, interview.

50. Alexi Quiroz, interview; Reinaldo Padilla, interview.

51. Alexi Quiroz, interview. Carlos Jaragüi described the hygienic conditions in the house down the street where he was served meals as "disgusting and totally unacceptable." Carlos Jaragüi, interview.

52. Alexi Quiroz, interview.

53. Ibid. During the 1995 Summer League season, breakfast consisted of *mondongo*, a heavy, greasy soup made from cow stomach. Carlos Jaragüi, interview.

54. Alexi Quiroz, interview.

55. Ibid.

56. Alexi Quiroz, interview; Reinaldo Padilla, interview. Carlos Jaragüi reported never having milk or vegetables during his 1995 stay at the Cubs' academy. Carlos Jaragüi, interview.

57. Anonymous, interview with the authors.

58. Alexi Quiroz, interview; Reinaldo Padilla, interview.

59. Alexi Quiroz, interview; Reinaldo Padilla, interview.

60. Alexi Quiroz, interview; Reinaldo Padilla, interview.

61. Alexi Quiroz, interview.

62. Reinaldo Padilla, interview; Alexi Quiroz, interview.

63. Reinaldo Padilla, interview; Alexi Quiroz, interview.

64. "Player Register—Julio Valdez," in John Thorn and Pete Palmer, eds., *Total Baseball: The Official Encyclopedia of Major League Baseball*, 4th ed. (New York: Viking, 1995), 1347.

65. Alexi Quiroz, interview.

66. Reinaldo Padilla, interview; Alexi Quiroz, interview.

67. Alexi Quiroz, interview.

68. Reinaldo Padilla, interview.

69. Ibid.; Alexi Quiroz, interview.

70. Alexi Quiroz, interview.

71. Reinaldo Padilla, interview.

72. Alexi Quiroz, interview.

73. Reinaldo Padilla, interview.

74. Alexi Quiroz, interview.

75. Alexi Quiroz, Reinaldo Padilla, and Carlos Jaragüi, interviews.

76. Alexi Quiroz, interview.

77. Reinaldo Padilla, interview; Alexi Quiroz, interview.

78. Reinaldo Padilla, interview; Alexi Quiroz, interview.

79. Minor League Uniform Player Contract dated October 5, 1995, between Alexis Quiroz and the Chicago Cubs, Addendum C-1.

80. Alexi Quiroz, interview.

81. Ibid.

82. Paycheck stub for Alexis Quiroz dated June 14, 1996 ($237.50); paycheck stub for Alexis Quiroz dated June 28, 1996 ($237.50); paycheck stub for Alexis Quiroz dated July 18, 1996 ($237.50); paycheck stub for Alexis Quiroz dated August 12, 1996 ($237.50); paycheck stub for Alexis Quiroz dated August 16, 1996 ($237.50).

83. Alexi Quiroz, interview.

84. Ibid.

85. Elisa Pino, interview with the authors.

86. Ibid.

87. Alexi Quiroz, interview.

88. Reinaldo Padilla, interview.

89. Ibid.; Alexi Quiroz, interview.

90. Alexi Quiroz, interview.

91. Once, after a game against the Oakland A's team, Alexi and his teammates watched the A's players eat a proper sack lunch and drink Gatorade. Alexi Quiroz, interview. Alexi would in 1997 again get to compare how the Cubs and A's treated their Dominican Summer League and academy players. See chapter 6.

92. Alexi Quiroz, Reinaldo Padilla, and Carlos Jaragüi, interviews.

93. Alexi Quiroz, Reinaldo Padilla, and Carlos Jaragüi, interviews.

94. Chicago Cubs, 1998 Information Guide 273, 277 (1998). Carlos Jaragüi also attributed his difficulties during the 1995 Summer League season to his poor treatment by the Cubs. Carlos Jaragüi, interview. Jaragüi's 1995 Summer League numbers were:

AVG	G	AB	R	H	2B	3B	HR	RBI	BB	SO	SB	E
.204	32	93	14	19	2	0	1	6	15	22	0	11

Chicago Cubs, 1996 Information Guide 256 (1996).

95. Alexi Quiroz, interview.

96. Alexi Quiroz, Reinaldo Padilla, and Carlos Jaragüi, interview.

97. Alexi Quiroz, interview.

98. Ibid.

99. Ibid.; Reinaldo Padilla, interview.

100. Alexis Quiroz Sr., interview; Alexi Quiroz, interview.

101. Alexi Quiroz, interview.

102. Carlos Jaragüi, interview.

103. Alexi Quiroz, interview.

104. Ibid.; Alexis Quiroz Sr., interview.

105. Alexi Quiroz, interview.

106. Alexis Quiroz Sr., interview.

107. Ibid.; Alexi Quiroz, interview.

108. Alexi Quiroz, interview.

109. Ibid.

6. In Baseball Purgatory

1. Alexi Quiroz, interview with the authors.

2. Ibid.

3. Ibid.

4. Ibid.

5. Ibid.
6. Ibid.
7. Carolina Quiroz, interview with the authors.
8. Alexi Quiroz, interview.
9. Ibid.
10. Ibid.; Alexis Quiroz Sr., interview with the authors.
11. Alexi Quiroz, interview. Carlos Jaragüi and Jairo Rebollaro played the 1995 and 1996 minor league seasons for the Cubs Dominican Summer League team. Chicago Cubs, *1996 Information Guide* (Chicago: Chicago Cubs, 1996), 256, 271 (listing stats of Jaragüi and Rebollaro).
12. Alexi Quiroz, interview.
13. Ibid.
14. Ibid.
15. Ibid.
16. Ibid.
17. Ibid.
18. Ibid.; Alexis Quiroz Sr., interview.
19. Alexis Quiroz Sr., interview; Alexi Quiroz, interview.
20. Alexis Quiroz Sr., interview.
21. Alexi Quiroz, interview.
22. Ibid.
23. Ibid.; Alexis Quiroz Sr., interview.
24. Minor League Uniform Player Contract, paragraph XIX.
25. Memorandum dated February 28, 1997, from David Wilder to Alexis Quiroz.
26. Minor League Uniform Player Contract, paragraph VI.
27. Minor League Uniform Player Contract dated October 5, 1995, between the Chicago Cubs and Alexis Quiroz, Addendum A.
28. Minor League Uniform Player Contract, paragraph VI.
29. Alexi Quiroz, interview; Alexis Quiroz Sr., interview.
30. Alexi Quiroz, interview; Alexis Quiroz Sr., interview.
31. Minor League Uniform Player Contract between the Chicago Cubs and Alexis Quiroz, Addendum C-97–1.
32., David Wilder to Alexis Quiroz, memorandum dated February 28, 1997.
33. Alexi Quiroz, interview.
34. Ibid.
35. Minor League Uniform Player Contract between the Chicago Cubs and Alexis Quiroz, Addendum C-97–1.
36. Alexi Quiroz, interview; Alexis Quiroz Sr., interview.
37. Alexi Quiroz, interview.
38. Ibid.; Alexis Quiroz Sr., interview.
39. Alexis Quiroz Sr. to David Wilder, May 26, 1997.
40. Ibid.
41. Ibid.
42. Alexi Quiroz, interview; Alexis Quiroz Sr., interview; Certified mail receipt for letter to David Wilder.
43. Alexi Quiroz, interview; Alexis Quiroz Sr., interview.
44. Alexi Quiroz, interview.
45. Ibid.
46. Ibid.
47. Ibid.

48. Ibid.

49. Ibid.

50. Ibid.

51. Ibid.

52. Ibid.

53. David Rawnsley, "Globetrotters: Over the Years, Baseball Has Spread All Over the World," *Baseball America,* July 8, 1999, <http://www.majorleaguebaseball.com/1999/allstar/news/rawnsley178.htm> (visited July 15, 2000).

54. Alexi Quiroz, interview.

55. Ibid.

56. Ibid.

57. Ibid.

58. Ibid.

59. Ibid.

60. Alexis Quiroz Sr., interview.

61. Juan Quiroz, interview; Alexi Quiroz, interview.

62. Juan Quiroz, interview; Alexi Quiroz, interview.

63. Juan Quiroz, interview; Alexi Quiroz, interview.

7. The Mesa Miracle

1. Alexi Quiroz, interview with the authors.

2. Ibid.; Juan Quiroz, interview with the authors.

3. Alexi Quiroz, interview; Juan Quiroz, interview.

4. Alexi Quiroz, interview; Juan Quiroz, interview.

5. "Player Register—Sandy Alomar Sr.," in John Thorn and Pete Palmer, eds., *Total Baseball: The Official Encyclopedia of Major League Baseball,* 4th ed. (New York: Viking, 1995), 678.

6. Alexi Quiroz, interview; Juan Quiroz, interview.

7. "Player Register—Jesús Marcano Trillo," in *Total Baseball,* 1341–42.

8. Alomar could have been referring to the Minor League Reserve List that MLB teams must file with the Commissioner's Office under Major League Rule 2(a).

9. Alexi Quiroz, interview; Juan Quiroz, interview.

10. Alexi Quiroz, interview; Juan Quiroz, interview.

11. Alexi was going to play in what is called the "instructional league" that major league teams hold for minor league players in the fall after the minor league season has concluded. The instructional league involves more than rookie players, so the level of competition is higher than in a rookie league.

12. Alexi Quiroz, interview; Juan Quiroz, interview.

13. Alexi Quiroz, interview; Juan Quiroz, interview.

14. At first Wilder said that he had not fired anybody. A few days later he admits that the Cubs had released Alexi. Why did he change his mind? Here is our theory: Wilder may not have known that Alexi had been told he was released. After all, Wilder did not sign or send a written release letter. Perhaps Wilder checked with Fleita, Rondón, and Valdez about Alexi's situation and learned that they had released Alexi. The Cubs faced, however, a problem because Alexi did not get the required release letter. Technically, Alexi had been under contract for 1997, and the Cubs were in breach of contract for not playing and paying him during the minor league season. To avoid this contractual liability, Wilder had to say that Alexi had been released in April even though the Cubs had not released him under the terms of the contract.

15. Alexi Quiroz, interview; "Vinny Castilla—Statistics," ESPN.com, <http://espn.go.com/mlb/profiles/stats/batting/4746.html> (visited Dec. 7, 2001).

16. Alexi Quiroz, interview.

17. Todd Noel, a right-handed pitcher, was the Cubs' first-round draft choice in 1996, was traded in 1998 to the Florida Marlins, and now plays in the farm system of the New York Yankees. Outfielder Diego Rico played college baseball at the University of Arizona and played in the Cubs farm system through the 2000 season, where he was a member of the Cubs' Daytona minor league team. Rico played in 2001 for the Yuma Bullfrogs of the independent Western Baseball League. Matt Mauck played in the Cubs' minor league system through the 2000 season, where he played first base with the Cubs' Lansing, Michigan, farm club. In 2001, Mauck played college football as a backup quarterback for Louisiana State University.

18. Alexi Quiroz, interview.

19. Ibid.

20. Ibid.

21. Major League Rule 56(g)(5)(f). *"Trainer and Medical Supplies.* The Major League Club shall provide to the Minor League Club a trainer for the championship season and all reasonable medical supplies for use by such trainer. The Major League Club shall be responsible for the entire cost of the trainer's salary and benefits. . . ."

22. Alexi Quiroz, Carlos Jaragüi, and Eleazar Medina, interviews with the authors.

23. "Player Register—Rubén Amaro," in Thorn and Palmer, *Total Baseball,* 680–81.

24. Alexi Quiroz, interview.

25. Ibid.

26. Ibid.

27. Minor League Uniform Player Contract dated October 14, 1997, between the Chicago Cubs and Alexis Quiroz, Addendum C-98–1.

28. Ibid.

29. Alexi Quiroz, interview.

30. Ibid.

8. The Dominican Disaster

1. Alexi Quiroz, interview with the authors; Newspaper clippings and Internet sites of *Los Cardenales de Lara,* 1997–1998 Winter League season.

2. Alexi Quiroz, interview.

3. Ibid.

4. Ibid.

5. Ibid.

6. Ibid.

7. Ibid.; Juan Quiroz, interview with the authors.

8. Alexi Quiroz, interview.

9. Ibid.

10. Ibid.; Juan Quiroz, interview.

11. Alexi Quiroz, interview.

12. Ibid.

13. Ibid.

14. Ibid.

15. Ibid.

16. Ibid.

17. Receipt from Super 8 Motel, Mesa, Arizona.

18. Alexi Quiroz, interview.

19. Ibid.

20. Ibid.

21. Alexis Quiroz Sr., interview with the authors.

22. Ibid.

23. Alexi Quiroz, Reinaldo Padilla, and Eleazar Medina, interviews with the authors.

24. "Here in Venezuela, I would say that the living conditions in the academies are not only bad, they are inhumane. Sometimes the location of the academies is very dangerous. Last year a player was almost killed when he was walking to where the players lived and someone tried to steal his watch and shot him. This is a consequence of putting those players where they should not be, risking their lives." Angel Vargas, interview with the authors. Vargas is the president of the Venezuelan Baseball Players Association.

25. Alexi Quiroz, interview.

26. Alexi Quiroz, Reinaldo Padilla, and Eleazar Medina, interviews.

27. Alexi Quiroz, Reinaldo Padilla, and Eleazar Medina, interviews.

28. Alexi Quiroz, interview.

29. Ibid.

30. Alexi Quiroz, Reinaldo Padilla, and Eleazar Medina, interviews.

31. Paycheck stub dated July 10, 1998, from the Chicago Cubs to Alexis Quiroz for $660 for two pay periods of $330 each; paycheck stub dated July 24, 1998, from the Chicago Cubs to Alexis Quiroz for $330.

32. Alexi Quiroz, interview.

33. Minor League Uniform Player Contract dated October 14, 1997, between the Chicago Cubs and Alexis Quiroz, Addendum C-98-1.

34. Not all the players at the Cubs' academy had problems with Julio Valdez. Eleazar Medina played for the Cubs' Dominican Summer League team in 1998 with Alexi. Medina told us that he had no problems with Valdez because he never paid any attention to what Valdez said. Medina was bothered, however, by Valdez's treatment of Alexi. Eleazar Medina, interview. Reinaldo Padilla, another 1998 Summer League player whom we interviewed, also bristled at Valdez's treatment of Alexi. Reinaldo Padilla, interview.

35. Alexi Quiroz, interview.

36. Reinaldo Padilla, interview.

37. Ibid.; Eleazar Medina, interview.

38. Reinaldo Padilla, Eleazar Medina, and Alexi Quiroz, interviews.

39. Reinaldo Padilla, Eleazar Medina, and Alexi Quiroz, interviews.

40. Reinaldo Padilla, interview; Eleazar Medina, interview.

41. Alexi Quiroz, interview.

42. Reinaldo Padilla, Eleazar Medina, and Alexi Quiroz, interviews.

43. Reinaldo Padilla, Eleazar Medina, and Alexi Quiroz, interviews.

44. Alexi Quiroz, interview.

45. Prescriptions dated June 20, 1998, from Dr. William E. Mejía to Alexis Quiroz.

46. Receipt dated June 20, 1998, from Farmacia Ortíz Báez for prescriptions for Alexis Quiroz.

47. Alexi Quiroz, interview.

48. Reinaldo Padilla, Eleazar Medina, and Alexi Quiroz, interviews.

49. Alexi Quiroz, interview.

50. Ibid.

51. Ibid.; Eleazar Medina, interview. By this point in the 1998 Summer League season, the Cubs had released Reinaldo Padilla. Aviso de Disposición dated May 20, 1998, from the Chicago Cubs to Reinaldo Padilla.

52. Alexi Quiroz, interview; Eleazar Medina, interview.

53. Alexi Quiroz, interview; Eleazar Medina, interview.

54. Alexi Quiroz, interview.

55. Ibid.

56. Ibid.

57. Ibid.

58. Ibid.

59. Ibid.

60. Hospital y Centro Sanitario Juan Pablo Piño to Alexis Quiroz, note dated July 25, 1998, referring him to an orthopedic doctor for treatment of a luxation [signature illegible].

61. Alexi Quiroz, interview.

62. Ibid.

63. Ibid.; Eleazar Medina, interview.

64. Alexi Quiroz, interview.

65. Ibid.; Eleazar Medina, interview.

66. Alexis Quiroz Sr., interview; Alexi Quiroz, interview.

67. Alexi Quiroz, interview.

68. Eleazar Medina, interview.

69. Alexi Quiroz, interview.

70. Ibid.

71. Ibid.; Alexis Quiroz Sr., interview.

72. Alexi Quiroz, interview.

73. Eleazar Medina, interview.

74. Alexi Quiroz, interview.

75. Ibid.

76. Alexi had X-rays taken at the hospital in San Cristóbal by García, but Alexi did not have the X-rays. It appears that Chuchúa brought the X-rays back to Valdez on July 25th and that Valdez FedExed the X-rays to a Greg Keuter at the Cubs' facility in Mesa, Arizona. The date on which the FedEx package was sent is not very clear on the sender's copy, but it looks as if it says "7-27-98." Julio Valdez to Greg Keuter in Mesa, Arizona, FedEx receipt dated July 27, 1998.

77. Hospital Nuestra Señora de Regla, Baní to Alexis Quiroz, receipts (#s 0081 and 0083) dated July 27, 1998.

78. Alexi Quiroz, interview.

79. Grupo Médico Baní, C. x A. Departamento de Rayos X to Alexis Quiroz, receipts (#s 2243 and 2246) dated July 27, 1998.

80. Alexi Quiroz, interview.

81. Ibid.; Alexis Quiroz Sr., interview.

82. Alexi Quiroz, interview.

83. Dr. Miranda of the Centro Médico Regional to Alexis Quiroz, Factura de Emergencia (#013939) dated July 27, 1998.

84. Alexi Quiroz, interview.

85. Ibid.; Alexis Quiroz Sr., interview.

86. Alexi Quiroz, interview; Eleazar Medina, interview.

87. Alexi Quiroz, interview.

88. Ibid.

89. Taxi cab receipt (#1141) dated July 28, 1998, from Vasopetaxis for transporting Alexis Quiroz from Nizao to Santo Domingo.

90. Tickets dated July 28, 1998, for Copa Airlines from Santo Domingo to Panama City, and for Antillean Airlines from Panama City to Caracas.

91. Alexi Quiroz, interview.

92. Carolina Quiroz, interview with the authors.

9. "That's Just Your Story"

1. Dr. José Luis Caicedo to Alexis Quiroz, receipt dated July 29, 1998.

2. Alexi Quiroz, interview with the authors.

3. Dr. José Luis Caicedo to Alexis Quiroz, medical report dated October 15, 1999.

4. Ibid. See also Dr. José Luis Caicedo to Alexis Quiroz, medical report dated November 27, 1998, and Dr. José Luis Caicedo to Alexis Quiroz, medical report dated March 18, 1999.

5. Dr. José Luis Caicedo to Alexis Quiroz, medical report dated October 15, 1999.

6. Farmacia Granada to Alexis Quiroz, receipt (#10912) dated July 29, 1998; Farmacia "Vargas Maracay" C.A. to Alexis Quiroz, receipt (#0214) dated July 29, 1998.

7. Alexi Quiroz, interview.

8. Ibid.

9. Dr. Gilberto Ojeda to Alexis Quiroz, medical report dated August 3, 1998.

10. Ibid.

11. Dr. Marisela Torcat of the Instituto de Resonancia Magnética "La Florida" to Alexis Quiroz, medical diagnosis dated July 31, 1998.

12. Dr. Gilberto Ojeda to Alexis Quiroz, medical report dated August 3, 1998.

13. Ibid.

14. Alexi Quiroz, interview.

15. Ibid.

16. Alexis Quiroz Sr., interview with the authors.

17. NYLCare Health Plans PPO Member Identification Card for Alexis Quiroz, Group #10838.

18. Alexi Quiroz, interview; Alexis Quiroz Sr., interview.

19. Alexis Quiroz Sr., interview.

20. Ibid.

21. Ibid.

22. Ibid.

23. Ibid.

24. Ibid.

25. Chicago Cubs to "whom it may concern," August 11, 1998.

26. Alexis Quiroz Sr., interview.

27. Dr. Gilberto Ojeda, medical report dated August 18, 1998 [English translation dated August 24, 1998].

28. Ibid.

29. Alexi Quiroz, interview.

30. Dr. Mario Ricardo Páez Plazola to Alexis Quiroz, receipt (#1165) dated August 24, 1998; Dr. Mario Ricardo Páez Plazola to Alexis Quiroz, medical report dated November 30, 1998.

31. Dr. Mario Ricardo Páez Plazola to Alexis Quiroz, receipt (#1165) dated August 24, 1998; Dr. Mario Ricardo Páez Plazola to Alexis Quiroz, medical report dated November 30, 1998.

32. Alexi Quiroz, Carolina Quiroz, and Alcira Castellanos, interviews with the authors.

33. Alexi Quiroz, interview.

34. Alexi Quiroz, Carolina Quiroz, and Alcira Castellanos, interviews.

35. Medical expenses list dated August 24, 1998, prepared by Alexis Quiroz and signed by Alberto Rondón.

36. Ibid.; Alexi Quiroz, interview.

37. Alexi Quiroz, interview.

38. Alexi Quiroz to the Chicago Cubs, August 3, 1998.

39. Alexis Quiroz Sr. to the Chicago Cubs, August 3, 1998.

40. Ibid.

41. Ibid.

42. Ibid.

43. Alexis Quiroz Sr. to the Chicago Cubs, August 24, 1998.

44. Ibid.

45. Ibid.

46. Ibid.

47. Ibid.

48. Alexi Quiroz, interview; Alexis Quiroz Sr., interview.

49. Alexi Quiroz, interview.

50. Alexis Quiroz Sr. to the Chicago Cubs, August 24, 1998.

51. Alexi Quiroz, interview.

52. Ibid.

53. Alexis Quiroz Sr., interview.

54. Alexi Quiroz, interview.

55. Ibid.

56. Ibid.

57. Carolina Quiroz, interview; Alcira Castellanos, interview.

58. Alexi Quiroz, interview.

59. David Wilder of the Chicago Cubs to Alexis Quiroz, October 8, 1998.

60. Alexi Quiroz, interview; Alexis Quiroz Sr., interview.

61. David Wilder of the Chicago Cubs to Alexis Quiroz, October 8, 1998.

62. Minor League Uniform Player Contract, paragraphs VIII and XIX.C.

63. Ibid., paragraph VIII.

64. David Wilder of the Chicago Cubs to Alexis Quiroz, October 8, 1998.

65. Alexi Quiroz, interview.

66. Minor League Uniform Player Contract, paragraph VI.A.

67. Minor League Uniform Player Contract dated October 14, 1997, between the Chicago Cubs and Alexis Quiroz, Addendum A.

68. Ibid.

69. David Wilder of the Chicago Cubs to Alexis Quiroz, October 8, 1998.

70. Ibid.

71. Alexi Quiroz, interview; Alexis Quiroz Sr., interview.

72. If the Quirozes had been able to look at and analyze the Minor League Uniform Player Contract, their fears might have deepened. Paragraph VIII.C of the Uniform Player Contract states as follows: "Club shall also pay all of Player's necessary and reasonable hospital and medical expenses incurred *during the term of this Minor League*

Uniform Player Contract by reason of said disability . . ." (emphasis added). Did this provision mean that any expenses Alexi incurred in connection with his rehabilitation and any future surgery that might be needed after October 15, 1998, would not be paid by the Chicago Cubs? Alexi was less than two months into his seven- to nine-month rehabilitation when he received the termination letter. Alexi would have more expenses related to the injury after October 15, 1998, not to mention that his baseball career had been ruined by what had happened in the Dominican Republic. Were the Cubs really off the financial hook to the Quirozes after October 15, 1998?

73. Alexi Quiroz, interview; Alexis Quiroz Sr., interview.
74. Alexi Quiroz, interview; Alexis Quiroz Sr., interview.
75. Alexi Quiroz, interview; Alexis Quiroz Sr., interview.
76. Alexi Quiroz, interview; Alexis Quiroz Sr., interview.
77. Alexi Quiroz, interview; Alexis Quiroz Sr., interview.
78. Alexi Quiroz, interview; Alexis Quiroz Sr., interview.
79. Alexi Quiroz, interview; Alexis Quiroz Sr., interview.
80. Alexi Quiroz, interview.
81. Ibid.
82. Chicago Cubs to Alexis Quiroz, check dated December 29, 1998, for $6,043.75.
83. Alexi Quiroz, interview; Alexis Quiroz Sr., interview.
84. In a May 2000 letter to Nilson, Stookal, Gleason & Caputo (see chapter 11), Alexi broke down his out-of-pocket medical expenses related to his injury. The following table contains the relevant information:

Alexi Quiroz's Injury-Related Expenses	Amount in US $
Medical Expenses in the Dominican Republic	$126.46
Medical Expenses in Venezuela	$7,692.60
Expense of Changing Ticket from the Dominican Republic to Venezuela after the Injury	$169
Expenses of Traveling from Maracay to Valencia and Back for Rehabilitation (Monday through Friday for seven months)	$946
TOTAL	$8,934.06

85. Alexi Quiroz, interview; Alexis Quiroz Sr., interview.
86. Alexi Quiroz, interview; Alexis Quiroz Sr., interview.
87. Alexi Quiroz, interview.
88. Ibid.
89. Ibid.
90. Alexi Quiroz, interview; Alexis Quiroz Sr., interview.
91. Alexi Quiroz, interview; Alexis Quiroz Sr., interview.
92. Alexi Quiroz, interview; Alexis Quiroz Sr., interview.
93. Alexi Quiroz, interview; Alexis Quiroz Sr., interview.
94. Chicago Cubs to Alexis Quiroz, check dated December 29, 1998 for $6,043.75.
95. Alexi Quiroz, interview; Alexis Quiroz Sr., interview.
96. Alexis Quiroz Sr., interview; Alexi Quiroz, interview.

10. The Pursuit of Justice Goes Terribly Wrong

1. Alexi Quiroz, interview with the authors.
2. Ibid.

3. Ibid.
4. Ibid.
5. Ibid.
6. Day, Kavanaugh & Blommel client questionnaire completed on March 24, 1999, by Alexis Quiroz.
7. Alexi Quiroz, interview.
8. Taylor & Associates Brochure.
9. Ibid.
10. Ibid.
11. Ibid.
12. Alexi Quiroz, interview with the authors.
13. On March 25, 1999, Alexi signed the following documents: (1) Worker's Report of Injury for the Industrial Commission of Arizona; (2) Employment Agreement between Taylor & Associates and Alexi; (3) Notice of Representation, in which Alexi notifies the Industrial Commission of Arizona that he has retained the services of Taylor & Associates with respect to his workers' compensation claim; (4) Special Power of Attorney, appointing Taylor & Associates "to receive and negotiate all workers' compensation checks issued to me" including the power "to deduct the fee agreed upon, together with any advances and case costs and return the net amount to me"; and (5) Medical Authorization, authorizing any medical provider to give copies of all records to Taylor & Associates.
14. Alexi Quiroz, interview. The Employment Agreement states that Taylor & Associates may withhold 25 percent of all workers' compensation benefits generated by the firm's efforts *and* may deduct from any benefits recovered "all necessary costs incurred in this case." Employment Agreement dated March 25, 1999, between Taylor & Associates and Alexis Quiroz. Alexi had, thus, agreed to pay Taylor & Associates 25 percent of any benefits *plus* expenses, not just the 25 percent Alexi recalls being told by the legal assistant.
15. Roger A. Schwartz of Taylor & Associates to Alexis Quiroz, March 29, 1999.
16. Alexi Quiroz, interview.
17. Arthur Larsen, *Workers' Compensation Law: Cases, Materials, and Text*, 2nd ed. (New York: Matthew Bender, 1992), 1–2.
18. Alexi Quiroz, interview.
19. Although Alexi was not aware of it, the Minor League Uniform Player Contract contains a provision about disputes between the team and player. Paragraph XX.B provides that in case of a dispute, "the decision of Club regarding the dispute or claim shall be subject exclusively to Player's right of appeal to the Commissioner which Player may exercise by filing a written, itemized, and detailed appeal form with the Commissioner within 120 days of the maturity of the claim. The decision of the Commissioner shall be final and binding and the Player agrees and understands that the decision of the Commissioner may not be challenged in any federal or state court or any other tribunal." Minor League Uniform Player Contract, paragraph XX.B.
20. Alexi did not contact the Major League Baseball Players Association (MLBPA) about his case. Making such contact never occurred to him. It would not, however, have mattered if he had contacted the MLBPA because it only represents major leaguers, not players who have only played in the minor leagues. It is our understanding that the Major League Rules, which cover both the major and minor leagues, do not provide minor leaguers with a grievance process similar to the one made available to major leaguers in Article XI of the Basic Agreement between Major League Baseball and the MLBPA. See Basic Agreement dated January 1, 1997, between the American

League of Professional Baseball Clubs and the National League of Professional Base-ball Clubs and the Major League Baseball Players Association, Article XI—Grievance Procedure.

21. Alexi Quiroz, interview. Given that the Minor League Uniform Player Con-tract specifically directs a minor league player with a dispute with his team to the Commissioner's Office, Lara's perfunctory response is surprising. If the team has not satisfactorily dealt with the dispute, the contract sends the player to the Commissioner's Office and prevents the player from taking action under the contract in a court of law.

22. Alexi Quiroz, interview.

23. We contacted the lawyer Alexi said he and Schwartz talked to in Phoenix, but the lawyer had no written record of this meeting or any personal recollections about it.

24. Alexi Quiroz, interview.

25. Ibid.

26. Despite attempts to contact the firm and all the officers and employees in-volved in Alexi's case, we could not locate the firm or any of the persons involved in this story. We were told by others involved in Alexi's Mesa story that the firm disap-peared shortly after Alexi left Mesa. Thus, we were unable to contact them about our research or successfully make a request for interviews.

27. Alexi Quiroz, interview.

28. Ibid.

29. Ibid. The Agreement for Services signed by Alexi and SRISA provides that SRISA agreed to investigate Alexi's "case on personal injury pertaining to employment with the Chicago Cubs and affiliated minor league teams." Alexi agreed to pay SRISA 40 percent of monies recovered through the investigation. Expenses and associated costs of the investigation were included in the 40 percent recovery fee. No retainer or deposit from Alexi was required. SRISA's services were to commence that day, March 30, 1999.

30. Alexi Quiroz, interview.

31. Taylor & Associates to the Industrial Commission of Arizona, April 1, 1999.

32. Ibid.

33. Ibid. This meeting took place on April 16, 1999.

34. The lawyer who met Alexi at the Denny's restaurant no longer works for Tay-lor & Associates, and we were unable to locate her to request an interview.

35. Alexi Quiroz, interview.

36. Ibid.

37. Ibid.

38. Industrial Commission of Arizona to Alexis Quiroz, April 8, 1999.

39. Ibid.

40. Alexi Quiroz, interview.

41. Ibid.

42. Ibid.

43. The Cubs eventually sent Alexi copies of all his contracts after this inquiry by SRISA. Ibid.

44. Ibid.

45. Ibid.

46. Ibid.

47. Ibid.

48. Ibid.

49. Agreement for Services dated April 25, 1999, between SRISA and Alexis Quiroz.

50. Ibid.

51. Ibid.

52. Ibid.

53. Ibid.

54. This form is dated April 12, 1999, but it appears to have been executed on April 25, 1999, along with the new Agreement for Services because it contains at the bottom the handwritten statement, "Unless otherwise indicated in contract," which is initialed by Alexi and an SRISA rep, who also signed the new contract on behalf of SRISA. The form dated April 12, 1999, is signed by a different person on behalf of SRISA.

55. Ibid.

56. Ibid.

57. Alexi Quiroz, interview.

58. Ibid.

59. Ibid.

60. Kemper Insurance to Alexis Quiroz, Notice of Claim Status dated April 28, 1999. Major League Rule 2(h)(1)(A) states that the minimum period of time a minor league player may be on the regular disabled list is seven consecutive days. But this rule obviously does not explain or justify the Cubs' claim that Alexi lost no more than seven days because of his injury.

61. Alexi Quiroz, interview.

62. Press release dated April 27, 1999, issued by SRISA.

63. Fact sheet—press conference Alexis Quiroz, issued by SRISA (undated).

64. Ibid.

65. Ibid.

66. Ibid.

67. Ibid.

68. Alexi Quiroz, interview.

69. Fact sheet—press conference Alexis Quiroz, issued by SRISA (undated).

70. Alexi's diary entry for April 30th, three days later, says that on Monday, May 3rd, he was supposed to talk with a lawyer. Alexi and an SRISA rep apparently met a lawyer on May 20th, who told them his work would cost around $40,000. The lawyer's services were not retained. Alexi Quiroz, interview.

71. Fact sheet—press conference Alexis Quiroz, issued by SRISA (undated).

72. Alexi Quiroz, interview.

73. Press release dated April 27, 1999, issued by SRISA.

74. Alexi Quiroz, interview.

75. Ibid.

76. Ibid.

77. New Patient Visit Report dated May 3, 1999, for Alexis Quiroz by Stuart C. Kozinn, M.D.

78. Ibid.

79. Ibid.

80. Ibid.

81. Ibid.

82. Ibid.

83. Ibid.

84. Alexi Quiroz, interview.

85. Ibid.

86. Alexis Quiroz Sr., interview with the authors.

87. Ibid.; Alexi Quiroz, interview.

88. Alexis Quiroz Sr., interview; Alexi Quiroz, interview.

89. Kemper Insurance to Alexis Quiroz, check for $1,650.91 dated May 13, 1999.

90. Alexi Quiroz, interview.

91. Alexis Quiroz Sr., interview; Alexi Quiroz, interview.

92. SRISA to Alexis Quiroz, receipt for $2,650.91, promising return of $650.91, dated May 19, 1999.

93. Alexi Quiroz, interview.

94. Alexis Quiroz Sr., interview.

95. Alexi Quiroz, interview.

96. Ibid.

97. Ibid.

98. Ibid.

99. Ibid.

100. Ibid.

11. Seventh-Inning Stretch: Chicago, New York, Maracay

1. Alexi Quiroz, interview with the authors.

2. Ibid.; Alexis Quiroz Sr., interview with the authors.

3. Alexi Quiroz, interview.

4. Ibid.

5. Ibid.

6. Ibid.

7. Attorney Representation Agreement dated June 14, 1999, between Nilson, Stookal, Gleason & Caputo, Ltd. and Alexis Quiroz.

8. Alexi did not understand, even at this point in his case, that by filing a workers' compensation claim he was giving up his right to sue the Cubs in tort. His misunderstanding becomes apparent later in this chapter.

9. Alexi Quiroz, interview.

10. Ibid.

11. Ibid.

12. Ibid.

13. Ibid.

14. Ibid.

15. Ibid.

16. Ibid.

17. Ibid.

18. Ibid.

19. Carolina Quiroz, interview..

20. Alexi Quiroz, interview.

21. Carlos Figueroa Ruiz, "Demanda a los Yanquis: Novato venezolano reclama sus derechos," *El Universal*, July 21, 1999, sec. 3, p. 1.

22. Ibid.

23. Ibid.

24. Ibid.

25. Alexi Quiroz, interview.

26. Ruiz, "Demanda a los Yanquis," sec. 3, p. 1.

27. Ibid.

28. Ibid.

29. Alexi Quiroz, interview.

30. Ibid.; Angel Vargas, interview with the authors.

31. Alexi Quiroz, interview; Angel Vargas, interview.

32. Arturo J. Marcano and David P. Fidler, "The Globalization of Baseball: Major League Baseball and the Mistreatment of Latin American Baseball Talent," *Indiana Journal of Global Legal Studies* 6 (1999), 511. This article was reviewed in *Foreign Policy* (Spring 2000), 184–85.

33. Angel Vargas, interview.

34. Ibid.

35. Steven M. Gleason to Roy Krasik, August 11, 1999.

36. Ibid.; Alexi Quiroz, interview.

37. Steven M. Gleason to SRISA, August 11, 1999. Gleason's letter included the following: "I contacted the State Bar of Arizona and have received its opinion regarding the unlicensed practice of law. Its opinion supports a position that your organization engaged in the unlicensed practice of law and any claimed agreement you may have had with Alexis Quiroz would be void as a matter of law. Please forward said funds to us immediately."

38. Alexi Quiroz, interview.

39. Former SRISA officer to Steven M. Gleason, August 17, 1999.

40. Steven M. Gleason to SRISA officer, August 18, 1999.

41. Steven M. Gleason to Alexis Quiroz, September 9, 1999. Alexi's questions about possible future surgery stem from the diagnosis and advice given by Dr. Stuart Kozinn in Scottsdale in May 1999. New Patient Visit Report dated May 3, 1999, for Alexis Quiroz by Stuart C. Kozinn, M.D.

42. Alexi Quiroz, interview.

43. Ibid.

44. Ibid.

45. Ibid.

46. Ibid.

47. Ibid.

12. The Final Inning

1. Alexi Quiroz, interview with the authors; Alexis Quiroz Sr., interview with the authors.

2. Alexi Quiroz, interview.

3. Ibid.

4. Ibid.

5. Ibid.

6. Roy Krasik to Alexis Quiroz, February 22, 2000.

7. Ibid.

8. Alexi Quiroz, interview.

9. Jenifer Surma to Roy Krasik, February 11, 2000.

10. Roy Krasik to Alexis Quiroz, February 22, 2000.

11. Alexi Quiroz, interview.

12. Jenifer Surma to Roy Krasik, February 11, 2000.

13. Alexi Quiroz, interview.

14. Alexis Quiroz to Steven M. Gleason, April 11, 2000.

15. Alexis Quiroz to Jenifer Surma, April 11, 2000, mailed on April 19, 2000.

16. In March 2000, Iván González of *El Mundo* became interested in Alexi's story and was preparing to do a story about his case. The story appeared in *El Mundo* on July 26, 2000. Iván González, "Beisbol organizado maltrata a los peloteros," *El Mundo*, July 26, 2000. See also Juan de Dios Espinoza, "The Ninth Inning," *El Siglo*, July 26, 2000, 14.

17. Alexis Quiroz to Jenifer Surma, April 11, 2000, mailed on April 19, 2000.

18. Ibid.

19. Alexi Quiroz, interview.

20. Ibid.

21. See the Letters and Correspondence section of the bibliography for the list of these interview request letters.

22. Louis Melendez to David Fidler, facsimile dated July 24, 2000.

23. Arturo J. Marcano and David P. Fidler to Louis Melendez, memorandum dated September 29, 2000.

24. Louis Melendez to David Fidler, October 30, 2000.

25. Jenifer Surma to Alexis Quiroz, undated letter (sent in October 2000) enclosing $2,000 check.

26. Alexi Quiroz, interview.

27. Jenifer Surma to Alexis Quiroz, undated letter (sent in October 2000) enclosing $2,000 check.

28. Alexi Quiroz, interview.

29. Ibid.

30. Marcano and Fidler had written on May 18, 2000, to Schafer and Dr. Stephen Adams to request an interview in connection with Alexi's case and specifically to interview them "about the medical and training staff the Chicago Cubs make available to players in the academy in the Dominican Republic. You are the team physicians (Chicago Cubs Front Office Personnel, <http:www.cubs.com/season/personnel>), and the young players who play in the Dominican Summer League season are members of the Chicago Cubs organization who deserve the same medical treatment as young American players get from the Cubs in the United States. We would like to understand how a young player like Mr. Quiroz with a serious injury could be treated in the manner that he was by the Chicago Cubs in the Dominican Republic." Although neither Schafer nor Adams responded to this interview request, Schafer mentions the correspondence in his written medical report to Oneri Fleita.

31. Alexi Quiroz, interview.

32. Ibid.

33. Ibid.

34. Ibid. Not surprisingly, Schafer's written medical report dated October 24, 2000, and addressed to Oneri Fleita does not include his comments to Alexi about the responsibility the Cubs bear for the mistreatment Alexi suffered after the injury in the Dominican Republic. Dr. Michael Schafer to Oneri Fleita, medical report dated October 24, 2000. The Cubs did not deliver the written medical report to Gleason and Stookal until early December 2000.

35. Alexi Quiroz, interview.

36. Gutierrez conducted research in Puerto Rico and the Dominican Republic from June through August 2000 on various aspects of the globalization of baseball. His faculty supervisor in the research was David Fidler. Marcano and Fidler thought Alexi's visit to Wrigley Field might be educational for Gutierrez, and Alexi invited him to come along as well.

37. Alexi Quiroz, interview; William Gutierrez, interview with the authors.

38. Alexi Quiroz, interview; William Gutierrez, interview.

39. Alexi Quiroz, interview; William Gutierrez, interview.

40. Alexi Quiroz, interview; William Gutierrez, interview.

41. Alexi Quiroz, interview; William Gutierrez, interview.

42. Alexi Quiroz, interview; William Gutierrez, interview.

43. Alexi Quiroz, interview; William Gutierrez, interview.

44. In their June 21, 1999, meeting, Juan Lara told Alexi that the Cubs breached their contract with him by sending him to the Dominican Republic rather than the United States. A close reading of the Minor League Uniform Player Contract demonstrates that Nelson was right. The nature of minor league baseball also requires that the directors of minor league operations have flexibility to assign players to fill requirements, both anticipated and unforeseen.

45. Alexi Quiroz, interview; William Gutierrez, interview.

46. Alexi Quiroz, interview.

47. Alexi Quiroz, interview; William Gutierrez, interview.

48. Alexi Quiroz, interview.

49. Alexis Quiroz Sr. to David Wilder, May 26, 1997.

50. Alexis Quiroz to Jenifer Surma, April 11, 2000.

51. Alexi Quiroz, interview; William Gutierrez, interview.

52. Alexi Quiroz, interview; William Gutierrez, interview.

53. Alexis Quiroz Sr. to David Wilder, May 26, 1997.

54. Alexis Quiroz to Jenifer Surma, April 11, 2000. William Gutierrez visited the Cubs' academy in the Dominican Republic in the summer of 2000. Julio Valdez refused to let Gutierrez see the players' living quarters. Valdez eventually had Gutierrez escorted away from the academy's grounds. William Gutierrez, interview. We understand that the Cubs have recently built a new facility in Nizao.

55. In a May 2000 document explaining the responsibilities of the new administrator for Latin America created by the Commissioner's Office, the following duty is specified: "Inspect academies in the Dominican Republic and Latin America to ensure compliance with the standards adopted by Major League Baseball." Part III analyzes the new office of administrator for Latin America.

56. Alexi Quiroz, interview; William Gutierrez, interview.

57. Alexi Quiroz, interview; William Gutierrez, interview.

58. Alexi Quiroz, interview; William Gutierrez, interview.

59. Alexi Quiroz, interview; William Gutierrez, interview.

60. Alexi Quiroz, interview; William Gutierrez, interview.

61. Alexi Quiroz, interview.

62. Alexi Quiroz, interview; William Gutierrez, interview.

63. Alexi Quiroz, interview.

64. Marc Stookal to Alexis Quiroz, December 4, 2000.

65. Alexis Quiroz to Marc Stookal, January 9, 2000.

66. Kemper Insurance to Marc Stookal, facsimile dated January 19, 2001; Kemper Insurance to Alexis Quiroz, check for $1,219.15 dated January 19, 2001; Marc Stookal to Alexis Quiroz, January 23, 2001.

67. Alexi Quiroz, interview.

68. Ibid.

69. Ibid.

70. Ibid.

71. Illinois Industrial Commission Settlement Contract Lump Sum Petition and Order, Case 99#WC 31919, Alexis Quiroz v. Chicago National League Ball Club.

72. Ibid.

73. Alexi Quiroz, interview; Alexis Quiroz Sr., interview.

74. Illinois Industrial Commission Settlement Contract Lump Sum Petition and Order, Case 99#WC 31919, Alexis Quiroz v. Chicago National League Ball Club.

75. Alexi Quiroz, interview; Alexis Quiroz Sr., interview.

76. Alexi Quiroz, interview.

13. Human Rights, Labor Standards, and Major League Baseball's Exploitation of Children in Latin America

1. Alan M. Klein, *Sugarball: The American Game, The Dominican Dream* (New Haven, Conn.: Yale University Press, 1991), 42; Samuel O. Regalado, "'Latin Players on the Cheap': Professional Baseball Recruitment in Latin America and the Neocolonialist Tradition," *Indiana Journal of Global Legal Studies* 8 (2000), 9.

2. Tony Fernández, interview with the authors; Chico Carrasquel, interview with the authors; "'Latente' racismo en las Mayores," *Meridiano*, Oct. 10, 2000 (interview with Carlos Delgado about latent racism in the major leagues); Samuel O. Regalado, *Viva Baseball! Latin Major Leaguers and Their Special Hunger* (Urbana: University of Illinois Press, 1998).

3. Klein, *Sugarball*, 42.

4. Tony Fernández, interview; Arturo J. Marcano and David P. Fidler, "The Globalization of Baseball: Major League Baseball and the Mistreatment of Latin American Baseball Talent," *Indiana Journal of Global Legal Studies* 6 (1999), 511.

5. Marcos Bretón and José Luis Villegas, *Away Games: The Life and Times of a Latin Ball Player* (New York: Simon and Schuster, 1999); Angel Vargas, "The Globalization of Baseball: A Latin American Perspective," *Indiana Journal of Global Legal Studies* 8 (2000), 21; Roberto González Echevarría, quoted in Harvey Araton, "Clemente to Sosa, and Beyond," *New York Times*, Nov. 13, 1998, sec. D., p. 1.

6. Papi Bisono, former Dominican Baseball Commission, quoted in Klein, *Sugarball*, 54.

7. United Nations Convention on the Rights of the Child, Nov. 20, 1989, Article 1.

8. United Nations Children's Fund (UNICEF), "Convention on the Rights of the Child," <http://www.unicef.org/crc/crc.htm> (visited June 23, 2001).

9. Ibid.

10. UNCRC, Article 2.1.

11. Ibid., Article 3.1.

12. Ibid., Article 12.1 and 13.1.

13. Ibid., Article 15.1.

14. Ibid., Article 19.1.

15. Ibid., Article 24.1.

16. Ibid., Article 27.1.

17. Ibid., Article 28.1.

18. Ibid., Article 32.1.

19. International Labor Organization (ILO) Convention No. 138 Concerning Minimum Age for Admission to Employment (MAC), June 26, 1973.

20. ILO Web Page, <http://ilolex.ilo.ch:1567/english/convdisp1.htm> (visited June 23, 2001).

21. MAC, Article 1.

22. MAC, Article 3.1.

23. United Nations General Assembly Declaration on the Rights of the Child, Nov. 20, 1989, Preamble.

24. The UNCRC states in its Preamble:

> The need to extend particular care to the child has been stated in the Geneva Declaration of the Rights of the Child of 1924 and in the Declaration of the Rights of the Child adopted by the General Assembly on 20 November 1959, and recognized in the Universal Declaration of Human Rights, in the International Covenant on Civil and Political Rights (in particular in Articles 23 and 24), in the International Covenant on Economic, Social, and Cultural Rights (in particular in Article 10) and in the statutes and relevant instruments of specialized agencies and international organizations concerned with the welfare of children.

25. UNCRC, Preamble.

26. Bretón and Villegas, *Away Games*, 48.

27. UNCRC, Article 2.1.

28. Chico Carrasquel, interview.

29. Tony Fernández, interview; "'Latente' racismo en las Mayores."

30. "'Latente' racismo en las Mayores."

31. Paul Gutierrez, "League Keeps Eye on Activities," LATimes.com, Feb. 27, 2001, <http://www.latimes.com/sports/mlb/20010227/000017574.html> (visited Feb. 27, 2001).

32. Ibid.

33. Vargas, "The Globalization of Baseball," 30.

34. The Los Angeles Dodgers have also violated MLB rules on not recruiting baseball players in Cuba. See Steve Fainaru and Ray Sánchez, *The Duke of Havana: Baseball, Cuba, and the Search for the American Dream* (New York: Villard, 2001), 228 (reporting violations of MLB rules on Cuban recruiting by the Los Angeles Dodgers in the cases of Juan Carlos Díaz and Josue Pérez).

35. Alexi Quiroz, interview with the authors.

36. Steve Fainaru, "Baseball's Minor Infractions: In Latin America, Young Players Come at a Bargain Price," *Washington Post*, Oct. 26, 2001, sec. D, p. 1.

37. Regalado, "'Latin Players on the Cheap,'" 9–20.

38. MLB Commissioner's Office, List of Administrator's Responsibilities, dated May 2000; Louis Melendez to Angel Vargas, August 8, 2000 (explaining the nature of the administrator's duties).

39. Quoted in Murray Chass, "Baseball's Game of Deception in the Search for Latin American Talent," *New York Times*, Mar. 23, 1998, sec. A, p. 1.

40. Gutierrez, "League Keeps Eye on Activities" (noting that MLB's new Dominican office is a "two-person" office).

41. Paul Gutierrez, "Foreign Allegiance," *Los Angeles Times*, Feb. 27, 2001, 2001 WESTLAW 2464975 (describing Pérez as "baseball's sheriff on the island" of the Dominican Republic).

42. Fainaru, "Baseball's Minor Infractions," sec. D, p. 1.

43. Steve Fainaru, "The Business of Building Ballplayers," *Washington Post*, June 17, 2001, <http://www.washingtonpost.com/wp-dyn/articles/A10070-2001Jun16.html> (visited June 18, 2001).

44. Winter League Agreement, April 21, 1998, Article IV (a)(1).

45. See Fainaru, "The Business of Building Ballplayers (describing how Enrique Soto taught an illiterate Dominican child how to write his name so he could sign a contract).

14. Global Ballpark Repair Strategies

1. Mark S. Rosentraub, "Governing Sports in the Global Era: A Political Economy of Major League Baseball and Its Stakeholders," *Indiana Journal of Global Legal Studies* 8 (2000), 121, 137.

2. Ibid.

3. Ibid.

4. Baseball's antitrust exemption is explored in detail in William B. Gould IV, "Baseball and Globalization: The Game Played and Heard and Watched 'Round the World (With Apologies to Soccer and Bobby Thomson)," *Indiana Journal of Global Legal Studies* 8 (2000), 85.

5. Rosentraub, "Governing Sports in the Global Era," 137.

6. Gould, "Baseball and Globalization," 113–16 (discussing implications of U.S.– Japanese agreement for labor relations in MLB).

7. Winter League Agreement, April 21, 1998.

8. Rosentraub, "Governing Sports in the Global Era," 137.

9. Angel Vargas, "The Globalization of Baseball: A Latin American Perspective," *Indiana Journal of Global Legal Studies* 8 (2000), 21, 31.

10. Ibid.

11. William Gutierrez, interview with the authors.

12. Presidential Regulation 3450 of 1985, translated in Aaron N. Wise and Bruce S. Meyer, *International Sports Law & Business*, vol. 2 (Ardsley, N.Y.: Transnational Publishers, Inc., 1997), 889.

13. Vargas, "The Globalization of Baseball," 34, n. 25 ("I do not believe that this law has been effectively implemented or enforced by the Dominican government"); Arturo J. Marcano and David P. Fidler, "The Globalization of Baseball: Major League Baseball and the Mistreatment of Latin American Baseball Talent," *Indiana Journal of Global Legal Studies* 6 (1999), 511, 540 (mentioning that all the authors could elicit from people about the Dominican law was laughter).

14. Vargas, "The Globalization of Baseball," 31–32 (discussing how major league teams violate a host of Venezuelan laws).

15. FIFA, "Inside FIFA: For the Good of the Game," <http://www.fifa.com/fgg/index_E.html> (visited June 23, 2001).

16. IOC, <http://www.olympic.org> (visited June 23, 2001).

17. Quoted in Peter Gammons, "O'Dowd Reshapes Disorganized Rockies," ESPN.com, Nov. 20, 1999 (visited Nov. 22, 1999).

18. "Committee: MLB Teams Need Revenue Sharing Increase," *The Sporting News*, July 13, 2000, <http://www.sportingnews.com/baseball/articles/20000713/246959.html> (visited July 15, 2000).

19. Bob Costas, *Fair Ball: A Fan's Case for Baseball* (New York: Broadway Books, 2000), 161.

20. Gould, "Baseball and Globalization," 116.

21. See Steve Fainaru and Ray Sánchez, *The Duke of Havana: Baseball, Cuba, and the Search for the American Dream* (New York: Villard, 2001), 229.

22. Ibid.

23. Quoted in Gammons, "O'Dowd Reshapes Disorganized Rockies."

24. See Associated Press, "Worst Teams Would Draft Players from Best Teams," ESPN.com, Dec. 25, 2000 (visited Dec. 26, 2000) (noting that major league team owners were contemplating an international draft to "eliminate much of the ability of Cuban defectors and young Dominican stars to command huge signing bonuses").

25. Alan M. Klein, *Sugarball: The American Game, The Dominican Dream* (New Haven, Conn.: Yale University Press, 1991), 61.

26. Gould, "Baseball and Globalization," 116.

27. Ibid.

28. Angel Vargas argued, for example, that "[s]couts, MLB teams, MLB academies, and agents must be better regulated by governments." Vargas, "The Globalization of Baseball," 34. Vargas could have added *buscones* and *dirigentes* to his list.

29. Rob Ruck, "Baseball in the Caribbean," in John Thorn and Pete Palmer, eds., *Total Baseball: The Official Encyclopedia of Major League Baseball*, 4th ed. (New York: Viking, 1995), 560, 564. Ruck observed in connection with baseball in the Caribbean that:

> Knitting a common cultural fabric, serving as a vent to social and political tensions, and offering a vehicle not only for individual mobility but collective social affirmation, baseball indeed has been more than a game. . . . [Baseball] has become a catalyst to national cohesion and consciousness for the region in its troubled evolution this century.

Ibid. See also Klein, *Sugarball*, 1 ("In the Dominican Republic baseball has a place all out of proportion to the normal one of sport in society. There is nothing comparable to it in the United States, nothing as central, as dearly held as baseball is for Dominicans").

30. Nelson Contreras, "Yankees perdió demanda," *El Mundo*, Dec. 16, 2000, 14.

31. Venezuelan Court Documents on the Acosta Case; Arturo J. Marcano and David P. Fidler to Louis Melendez, March 26, 2001.

32. Venezuelan Court Documents on the Acosta Case; Arturo J. Marcano and David P. Fidler to Louis Melendez, March 26, 2001.

33. Venezuelan Court Documents on the Acosta Case; Arturo J. Marcano and David P. Fidler to Louis Melendez, March 26, 2001.

34. Venezuelan Court Documents on the Acosta Case; Arturo J. Marcano and David P. Fidler to Louis Melendez, March 26, 2001.

35. Venezuelan Court Documents on the Acosta Case; Arturo J. Marcano and David P. Fidler to Louis Melendez, March 26, 2001.

36. Winston Acosta, interview with the authors; David P. Fidler to Louis Melendez, February 10, 2001; Arturo J. Marcano and David P. Fidler to Louis Melendez, March 26, 2001.

37. "MLB Profits and Losses," ESPN.com, Dec. 5, 2001, <http://espn.go.com/mlb/s/2001/1205/1290765.html> (visited Dec. 11, 2001).

38. We wrote to the New York Yankees about the Winston Acosta case but received no reply. Arturo J. Marcano and David P. Fidler to Brian Cashman, March 26, 2001.

39. Contreras, "Yankees perdió demanda," 14; Winston Acosta, interview.

40. Arturo J. Marcano and David P. Fidler to Louis Melendez, December 20, 2000.

41. Louis Melendez to David P. Fidler, January 22, 2001.

42. John Helyar, *Lords of the Realm: The Real History of Baseball* (New York: Ballantine, 1994); Marvin Miller, *A Whole Different Ballgame* (New York: Birch Lane Press, 1991).

43. Miller, *A Whole Different Ballgame*, 413.

44. Marcano and Fidler, "The Globalization of Baseball," 575–76.

45. Miller, *A Whole Different Ballgame*.

46. Vargas, "The Globalization of Baseball," 31.

47. Miller, *A Whole Different Ballgame*, 163, 165, 196–97, 206, 303, 304.

48. Tony Fernández, interview with the authors.

49. Chico Carrasquel, interview with the authors.

50. Vargas, "The Globalization of Baseball," 35.

51. See Gary Gereffi, Ronie Garcia-Johnson, and Erika Sasser, "The NGO-Industrial Complex," *Foreign Policy* (August 2001), 56.

Epilogue

1. Roberto González Echevarría, "The Magic of Baseball," *Indiana Journal of Global Legal Studies* 8 (2000), 145.

Articles from Periodicals and Newspapers

Araton, Harvey. "Clemente to Sosa, and Beyond." *New York Times*, Nov. 13, 1998, sec. D, p. 1.

Associated Press. "False Pitches Crush Latin American Youngsters' Baseball Dreams." *The Star-Ledger Newark* (N.J.), June 4, 2000, 2000 WESTLAW 21307073.

Associated Press. "Steinbrenner: Texas Did Baseball a Disservice." Feb. 17, 2001, WESTLAW ALLNEWSPLUS.

Beaton, Rod. "Braves Penalized for Illegal Signing." *USA Today*, Feb. 25, 2000, sec. A, p. 1.

Budig, Gene. "Baseball Has a Worldly Look." *USA Today*, June 26, 1998, sec. C, p. 6.

Calvert Hanson, Linda S. "The Florida Legislature Revisits the Regulation and Liability of Sports Agents and Student Athletes." *Stetson Law Review* 25 (1996), 1067.

Chass, Murray. "Baseball's Game of Deception in the Search for Latin Talent." *New York Times*, Mar. 23, 1998, sec. A, p. 1.

———. "Mariners Gain Rights to Sign Suzuki Outbidding Mets and 2 Others." *New York Times*, Nov. 10, 2000, sec. C, p. 21.

———. "McGwire Has Disdain for International Ball Games." *International Herald Tribune*, Mar. 22, 2000, 11.

———. "Scouts Search Globe for Talent." *New York Times*, Apr. 8, 1998, sec. C, p. 3.

"Committee: MLB Teams Need Revenue Sharing Increase." *The Sporting News*, July 13, 2000, <http://www.sportingnews.com/baseball/articles/20000713/246959. html> (visited July 15, 2000).

Contreras, Nelson. "Yankees perdió demanda." *El Mundo*, Dec. 16, 2000, 14.

Cwiertny, Scott M. "The Need for a Worldwide Draft: Major League Baseball and Its Relationship with the Cuban Embargo and United States Foreign Policy." *Loyola of Los Angeles Entertainment Law Review* (2000), 391.

Espinoza, Juan de Dios. "The Ninth Inning." *El Siglo*, July 26, 2000, 14.

Fainaru, Steve. "Baseball's Minor Infractions: In Latin America, Young Players Come at a Bargain Price." *Washington Post*, Oct. 26, 2001, sec. D, p. 1.

———. "The Business of Building Ballplayers." *Washington Post*, June 17, 2001, http://www.washingtonpost.com/wp-dyn/articles/A10070-2001Jun16.html (visited June 18, 2001).

———. "Indians Are Hit with Penalties—Sanctions for Signing Underage Player Draw Mixed Reaction." *Washington Post*, Feb. 27, 2002, sec. D, p. 1.

———. "Scout Returns Money: Dominican Player Gets Part of Signing Bonus." *Washington Post*, July 11, 2001, sec. D, p. 1.

Figueroa Ruiz, Carlos. "Demanda a los Yanquis: Novato venezolano reclama sus derechos." *El Universal*, July 21, 1999, sec. 3, p. 1.

"For the Record, Major League Baseball." *USA Today*, Dec. 13, 2001, sec. C, p. 15.

"Foreign-Born Players on Rise." *USA Today*, Apr. 4, 2002, sec. C, p. 4.

Gereffi, Gary, Ronie Garcia-Johnson, and Erika Sasser. "The NGO-Industrial Complex." *Foreign Policy*, Aug. 2001, 56.

González Echevarría, Roberto. "The Magic of Baseball." *Indiana Journal of Global Legal Studies* 8 (2000), 145.

González, Iván. "Beisbol organizado maltrata a los peloteros." *El Mundo*, July 26, 2000.

Gould, William B. IV. "Baseball and Globalization: The Game Played and Heard and Watched 'Round the World (with Apologies to Soccer and Bobby Thomson)." *Indiana Journal of Global Legal Studies* 8 (2000), 85.

Grant, Evan. "Viva Beisbol: The Increasing Influence of Latin Americans." *Dallas Morning News*, Mar. 27, 2000, <http://www.baseball.dallasnews.com/mlb/topnews/55469_27mlblatin.html> (visited Mar. 28, 2000).

Gunther, Marc. "They All Want to Be Like Mike: Led by the NBA and Global Superstar Michael Jordan, U.S. Pro Sports Leagues Are Extending Their Worldwide TV Presence All the Way from Chile to China." *Fortune*, July 21, 1997, 51.

Gutierrez, Paul. "Dodger Prospect Plans an Appeal: Team Was Fined for Illegal Signing of Venezuelan Pitcher Arellan, But Retained Players' Rights." *Los Angeles Times*, Jan. 25, 2001, sec. D, p. 5.

———. "Foreign Allegiance: Despite the Beltre Controversy, the Dodger Baseball Camp in the Dominican Republic Remains Open." *Los Angeles Times*, Feb. 27, 2001, 2001 WESTLAW 2464975.

———. "League Keeps Eye on Activities." LATimes.com, Feb. 27, 2001, <http://www.latimes.com/sports/mlb/20010227/000017574.html> (visited Feb. 27, 2001).

Harper, John. "The International Pastime." *New York Daily News*, Mar. 27, 1997, 16.

Hoekstra, Dave. "A Land of Hope, Dreams: Cubs Seek Untapped Talent in the Dominican Republic." *Chicago Sun-Times*, Feb. 29, 1988, 12.

Koppett, Leonard. "The Globalization of Baseball: Reflections of a Sports Writer." *Indiana Journal of Global Legal Studies* 8 (2000), 81.

"'Latente' racismo en las Mayores." *Meridiano*, Oct. 10, 2000, 4.

Marcano, Arturo J., and David P. Fidler. "The Globalization of Baseball: Major League Baseball and the Mistreatment of Latin American Baseball Talent." *Indiana Journal of Global Legal Studies* 6 (1999), 511.

McCray, Douglas. "Global Newsstand: Indiana Journal of Global Legal Studies." *Foreign Policy* (Spring 2000), 184.

Metzl, Jordan D., Eric Small, Steven R. Levine, and Jeffrey C. Gershel. "Creatine Use among Young Athletes." *Pediatrics* 108 (2001), 421.

Newhan, Ross. "The Great Escape: America's Pastime Is Also Pedro Guerrero's Passport." *Los Angeles Times*, Jan. 7, 1985, WESTLAW, ALLNEWSPLUS.

Nightengale, Bob. "Rising Star at Rising Price: Texas Signs Rodriguez to Baseball's Richest Contract Ever." *Baseball Weekly*, Dec. 13, 2000, 2000 WESTLAW 10167148.

Rawnsley, David. "Globetrotters: Over the Years, Baseball Has Spread All over the World." *Baseball America*, July 8, 1999, posted at http://www.majorleaguebaseball.com/1999/allstar/news/rawnsley178.htm (visited July 15, 2000).

Regalado, Samuel O. "'Latin Players on the Cheap': Professional Baseball Recruitment in Latin America and the Neocolonialist Tradition." *Indiana Journal of Global Legal Studies* 8 (2000), 9.

Reinman, T. R. "Getting to First Base: Latins Have Earned Their Place in Major Leagues." *San Diego Union-Tribune*, July 9, 1991, sec. D, p. 1.

Rosentraub, Mark S. "Governing Sports in the Global Era: A Political Economy of Major League Baseball and Its Stakeholders." *Indiana Journal of Global Legal Studies* 8 (2000), 121.

Rupprecht, Rich. "Baseball Report." *Press Democrat* (Santa Rosa, Calif.), May 4, 1997, sec. C, p. 3, 1997 WESTLAW 3437307.

Slevin, Peter, and Dave Sheinin. "An Age Old Numbers Game: Amid Visa Crackdown, Many Dominican Players Aren't As Young As Thought." *Washington Post*, Mar. 2, 2002, sec. D, p. 1.

Sobel, Lionel S. "The Regulation of Sports Agents: An Analytical Primer." 39 *Baylor Law Review* 701 (1987).

"Sports Digest." *San Francisco Chronicle*, Jan. 12, 2000, sec. E, p. 6.

Sullivan, T. R. "Rangers Find Talent Shows on Latin Beat." *Fort-Worth Star Telegram*, Mar. 8, 1998, 1.

Vargas, Angel. "The Globalization of Baseball: A Latin American Perspective." *Indiana Journal of Global Legal Studies* 8 (2000), 21.

Wilkinson, Jack. "Baseball Dreamers: The Road to Turner Field." *Atlanta Journal-Constitution*, Aug. 16, 1998, sec. E, p. 1.

Books and Chapters in Books

Bjarkman, Peter C. *Baseball with a Latin Beat: A History of the Latin American Game.* Jefferson, N.C.: MacFarland & Company, 1994.

Bretón, Marcos, and José Luis Villegas. *Away Games: The Life and Times of a Latin Ball Player.* New York: Simon and Schuster, 1999.

Cárdenas Lares, Carlos. *Venezolanos en Las Grandes Ligas.* 2nd ed. Caracas: Fondo Editorial Cárdenas Lares, 1994.

Chicago Cubs Media Guide 1996. Chicago: Chicago Cubs, 1996.

Chicago Cubs Media Guide 1998. Chicago: Chicago Cubs, 1998.

Corbin, Arthur L. *Corbin on Contracts.* St. Paul: West Publishing, 1963.

Costas, Bob. *Fair Ball: A Fan's Case for Baseball.* New York: Broadway Books, 2000.

Fainaru, Steve, and Ray Sánchez. *The Duke of Havana: Baseball, Cuba, and the Search for the American Dream.* New York: Villard, 2001.

González Echevarría, Roberto. *The Pride of Havana: A History of Cuban Baseball.* Oxford: Oxford University Press, 1999.

Helyar, John. *Lords of the Realm: The Real History of Baseball.* New York: Ballantine, 1994.

International Sports Law & Business. Edited by A. N. Wise and B. S. Meyer. Ardsley, N.Y.: Transnational Publishers, 1997.

Kerrane, Kevin. *Dollar Sign on the Muscle: The World of Baseball Scouting.* New York: Simon & Schuster, 1989.

Klein, Alan M. *Sugarball: The American Game, The Dominican Dream.* New Haven, Conn.: Yale University Press, 1991.

Larsen, Arthur. *Workers' Compensation Law: Cases, Materials, and Text,* 2nd ed. New York: Matthew Bender, 1992.

Miller, Marvin. *A Whole Different Ballgame: The Sport and Business of Baseball.* New York: Birch Lane Press, 1991.

Millson, Larry. *Ballpark Figures: The Blue Jays and the Business of Baseball.* Toronto: McClelland and Stewart, 1987.

Oleksak, Michael M., and Mary Adams Oleksak. *Beisbol: Latin Americans and the Grand Old Game.* Grand Rapids, Mich.: Masters Press, 1991.

Pietrusza, David. "The Business of Baseball." In *Total Baseball: The Official Encyclo-pedia of Major League Baseball,* 4th ed. Edited by John Thorn and Pete Palmer. New York: Viking, 1995, 588.

Regalado, Samuel O. *Viva Baseball! Latin Major Leaguers and Their Special Hunger.* Urbana: University of Illinois Press, 1998.

Ruck, Rob. "Baseball in the Caribbean." In *Total Baseball: The Official Encyclopedia of Major League Baseball,* 4th ed. Edited by John Thorn and Pete Palmer. New York: Viking, 1995, 560.

Seymour, Harold. *Baseball: The Early Years.* Oxford: Oxford University Press, 1960.

Sherman, Len. *Big League, Big Time: The Birth of the Arizona Diamondbacks, the Billion-Dollar Business of Sports, and the Power of the Media in America.* New York: Pocket Books, 1998.

Simpson, Allan. "The Amateur Free Agent Draft." In *Total Baseball: The Official En-cyclopedia of Major League Baseball,* 4th ed. Edited by John Thorn and Pete Palmer. New York: Viking, 1995, 608.

Sosa, Sammy (with Marcos Bretón). *Sosa: An Autobiography.* New York: Warner Books, 2000.

Thorn, John. "Our Game." In *Total Baseball: The Official Encyclopedia of Major League Baseball,* 4th ed. Edited by John Thorn and Pete Palmer. New York: Vi-king, 1995, 5.

Thorn, John, and Pete Palmer, with Michael Gershman, eds. *Total Baseball: The Official Encyclopedia of Major League Baseball.* 4th ed. New York: Viking, 1995.

White, G. Edward. *Creating the National Pastime: Baseball Transforms Itself.* Prince-ton, N.J.: Princeton University Press, 1996.

Wong, Glenn M. *Essentials of Amateur Sports Law,* 2nd ed. Westport, Conn.: Praeger, 1994.

Zimbalist, Andrew. *Baseball and Billions: A Probing Look Inside the Big Business of Our National Pastime.* New York: Basic Books, 1992.

Contracts and Other Legal Documents

Aviso de Disposición dated May 20, 1998, from the Chicago Cubs to Reinaldo Padilla.

Agreement for Services dated March 30, 1999, between SRISA and Alexis Quiroz.

Agreement for Services dated April 25, 1999, between SRISA and Alexis Quiroz.

Attorney Representation Agreement dated June [14], 1999, for Workers' Compensation/ Occupational Disease between Nilson, Stookal, Gleason & Caputo, Ltd. and Alexis Quiroz.

Basic Agreement dated January 1, 1997, between Major League Baseball and the Ma-jor League Baseball Players Association.

Dominican Republic Presidential Regulation 3450 of 1985, translated in Aaron N. Wise and Bruce S. Meyer, eds., *International Sports Law & Business,* vol. 2, 889. Ards-ley, N.Y.: Transnational Publishers, 1997.

Employment Agreement dated March 25, 1999, between Taylor & Associates and Alexis Quiroz.

Illinois Industrial Commission Settlement Contract Lump Sum Petition and Order, Case 99#WC 31919, Alexis Quiroz v. Chicago National League Ball Club.

International Labor Organization (ILO) Convention No. 138 Concerning Minimum Age for Admission to Employment, June 26, 1973.

Major League Rules, July 1999.

Medical Authorization [dated March 25, 1999] completed by Alexis Quiroz in favor of Taylor & Associates.

Medical release form dated April 12, 1999, executed by Alexis Quiroz in favor of SRISA.

Minor League Uniform Player Contract dated October 5, 1995, between the Chicago Cubs and Alexis Quiroz.

Minor League Uniform Player Contract dated April 1, 1997, between the Chicago Cubs and Alexis Quiroz.

Minor League Uniform Player Contract dated October 14, 1997, between the Chicago Cubs and Alexis Quiroz.

Notice of Claim Status dated April 28, 1999, from Kemper Insurance to Alexis Quiroz.

Notice of Representation dated March 25, 1999, completed by Alexis Quiroz in favor of Taylor & Associates.

Special Power of Attorney dated March 25, 1999, completed by Alexis Quiroz in favor of Taylor & Associates.

United Nations Convention on the Rights of the Child, Nov. 20, 1989.

United Nations General Assembly Declaration on the Rights of the Child, Nov. 20, 1989.

Venezuelan Court Documents on the Winston Acosta Case.

Winter League Agreement dated April 21, 1998, between the National League of Professional Baseball Clubs, the American League of Professional Baseball Clubs, Liga Venezolana Baseball Professional, Liga de Beisbol Professional de Puerto Rico, Inc, Liga Dominicana de Baseball Profesional, Liga Mejicana del Pacífico, and the Confederation of Caribbean Professional Baseball Leagues.

Worker's Report of Injury for the Industrial Commission of Arizona dated March 25, 1999, from Alexis Quiroz.

Internet Web Pages and Sites

"2001 MLB Profits and Losses." ESPN.com, Dec. 5, 2001, <http://espn.go.com/mlb/s/2001/1205/1290765.html> (visited Dec. 11, 2001).

Associated Press. "Lasorda Defends Dodgers' Actions." ESPN.com, Nov. 16, 1999 (visited Nov. 17, 1999).

———. "Dodgers Fined for Signing Young Beltre." ESPN.com, Dec. 21, 1999 (visited Dec. 22, 1999).

———. "M's Accused of Acting Unethically." ESPN.com, Aug. 23, 2001, <http://espn.go.com/mlb/news/2001/0823/1242917.html> (visited Aug. 23, 2001).

———. "Sadaharu Oh Praises Ichiro as 'Real Thing.'" ESPN.com, July 3, 2001, <http:www.espn.go.com/mlb/news/2001/0703/1221867.htm> (visited July 5, 2001).

———. "Worst Teams Would Draft Players From Best Teams." ESPN.com, Dec. 25, 2000 (visited Dec. 26, 2000).

Beaton, Rod. "Age May Be Off for Hundreds in Baseball." USAToday.com, Feb. 26, 2002, <http://www.usatoday.com/sports/baseball/stories/2002-02-26-ages.htm> (visited Feb. 27, 2002).

———. "Baseball Tightens Grip after Beltre Case." USA Today.com, Feb. 8, 2000 (visited Feb. 14, 2000).

Boeck, Scott. "Players Growing Older by the Second." USAToday.com, Feb. 22, 2002, <http://usatoday.com/sports/baseball/stories/2002-02-22-age.htm> (visited Mar. 2, 2002).

238   BIBLIOGRAPHY

"Broadcast Money and Gate Receipts." ESPN.com, Dec. 5, 2001, <http://espn.go.com/mlb/s/2001/1205/1290777.html> (visited Dec. 11, 2001).

Fainaru, Steve. E-Mail Discussion on "The Business of Dominican Baseball." June 22, 2001, <http://discuss.washingtonpost.com/wp-srv/zforum/01/world_fainaru0622.htm> (visited July 25, 2001).

Farrey, Tom. "Cuban Defector Seeks Freedom from MLB Policy." ESPN.com, May 29, 2001, <http://espn.go.com/mlb/s/2001/0529/1206578.html> (visited May 31, 2001).

FIFA. "Inside FIFA: For the Good of the Game." <http://www.fifa.com/fgg/index_E.html> (visited June 23, 2001).

Fish, Mike. "Latin Players Doctor Their Birth Certificates for a Chance to Play." CNNSI.com, Feb. 26, 2002, <http://sportsillustrated.cnn.com/inside_game/mike_fish/news/2002/02/26.html> (visited Mar. 4, 2002).

Fitzgerald, Thomas J. "Field of Dreams." Mar. 28, 1999, <http://www.Bergen.com/Yankees/dreamstf199903284.htm>.

Gammons, Peter. "O'Dowd Reshapes Disorganized Rockies." ESPN.com, Nov. 20, 1999 (visited Nov. 22, 1999).

———. "This Year's Draft As Uncertain As Ever." ESPN.com, June 3, 2000, <http://espn.go.com/gammons/s/0603.html>.

International Labor Organization Web Page. <http://ilolex.ilo.ch:1567/english/convdisp1.htm> (visited June 23, 2001).

International Olympic Committee. <http://www.olympic.org> (visited June 23, 2001).

Kalman, Douglas S. "Creatine Knowledge to Date." *Pediatrics Online*, Aug. 23, 2001, <http://www.pediatrics.org/cgi/eletters/108/2/421> (visited Dec. 11, 2001).

Kreider, Richard B. "Creatine Concerns & Link to Steroid Abuse Unfounded." *Pediatrics Online*, Aug. 11, 2001, <http://www.pediatrics.org/cgi/eletters/108/2/421> (visited Dec. 11, 2001).

Kurkjian, Tim. "Scary? Guerrero Getting Better." ESPN.com, May 12, 2000 (visited May 16, 2000).

Major League Baseball Web Page. <http://www.majorleaguebaseball.com> (visited Oct. 10, 1998).

———. "2001 Opening Day in Puerto Rico to Culminate Second 'Month of the Americas.'" Feb. 22, 2001, MLB.com News (visited July 3, 2001).

———. "International Broadcasters." <http://www.majorleaguebaseball.com/mlbcom/int/int_broadcasting.htm> (visited May 16, 2000).

———. "More than 23 Percent of MLB Players Born Outside of U.S.." <http://www.majorleaguebaseball.com/u/baseball/mlbcom/int/int_foreignborn_2000.htm> (posted Apr. 6, 2000)(visited May 29, 2000).

Miller, Scott. "Rijo Takes Long Road Back to Mound in Cincy." CBSSportsline.com, Aug. 19, 2001, <http://cbs.sportsline.com/b/page/pressbox/0%2C1328%2C4210366%2C00.html> (visited Mar. 28, 2002).

MinorLeagueBaseball.com. <http://www.minorleaguebaseball.com/pagetemplate/league_logo.asp?pageid=292> (Dominican Summer League) and <http://www.minorleaguebaseball.com/pagetemplate/league_logo.asp?pageid=357> (Venezuelan Summer League) (visited Dec. 13, 2001).

Newhan, Ross, and Paul Gutierrez. "Big Leagues Invade Dominican Republic." SportingNews.com, Dec. 5, 1999, <http://sportingnews.com/baseball/articles/19991219/197866.html> (visited June 19, 2000).

Neyer, Rob. "Thorny Issue Has No Easy Solution." ESPN.com, Dec. 1, 1999 (visited Dec. 1, 1999).

Plaschke, Bill. "Game is Really Off Its Rocker." LATimes.com, Jan. 7, 2000 (visited Jan. 7, 2000).

Rawnsley, David. "Ready or Not, International Draft Is on the Way." Baseball America Online (visited Dec. 1, 1999).

Roberts, Jimmy. "What Must They Be Thinking?" <http://204.202.129.20/mlb/columns/jroberts/> (visited Feb. 18, 1999).

Schwarz, Alan. "Diamonds in the Rough." Baseball America Online (visited Dec. 9, 1999).

"Special Report: The Highest Paid Latino Players in Major League Baseball (2001 Data)." <http://latinosportslegends.com/Latinos_highest_paid_in_baseball-2001.htm> (visited Dec. 13, 2001).

Stark, Jayson. "Age Issues Brought on by Sept. 11." ESPN.com, Feb. 23, 2002, <http://espn.go.com/mlb/columns/stark_jayson/1339359.html> (visited Mar. 2, 2002).

"Stealing Home: The Case of Contemporary Cuban Baseball—The Dominican Comparison." <http://www.pbs.org/stealinghome/debate/dominican.html> (visited July 17, 2001).

"Ticket Prices at Home Provoke Martinez." USAToday.com Baseball Weekly, Mar. 16–22, 2000, <http://www.usatoday.com/sports/baseball/bbw2/v11/bbw1112.htm> (visited Dec. 11, 14, 2001).

UNICEF. Convention on the Rights of the Child, <http://www.unicef.org/crc/crc.htm> (visited June 23, 2001).

United Nations Economic and Social Council, Commission on Human Rights, Sub-Commission on Prevention of Discrimination and Protection of Minorities, Working Group on Contemporary Forms of Slavery, 23rd Sess., Forced Labour on Sugar Cane Plantations in the Dominican Republic, May 1998, <http://www.antislavery.org/archive/submission/submission1998-05Dominican.htm> (visited Aug. 23, 2001).

Interviews with the Authors (in alphabetical order)

Anonymous, Jan. 2000.
Anonymous, Jan. 2000.
Anonymous, May 2000.
Winston Acosta, Aug. 2000–March 2001.
Chico Carrasquel, May 2000.
Alcira Castellanos, Aug. 2000.
Juan Escalante, Jan. 2000.
Tony Fernández, Aug. 1999.
William Gutierrez, July 2000–July 2001.
Carlos Jaragüi, Mar. 2000.
Gerdvan Liendo, June 2000.
Eleazar Medina, Mar. 2000.
Reinaldo Padilla, Mar. 2000.
Luis Peñalver, Apr. 2001.
Elisa Pino, Aug. 2000.
Alexi Quiroz, Aug. 1999–July 2002 (which includes a diary Alexi kept during his attempt to become a professional baseball player in the United States).
Alexis Quiroz Sr., Apr. 2000–July 2002.
Carolina Quiroz, Aug. 2000.
Juan Quiroz, Apr. 2000.

Ebenecer López Ruyol, Feb. 2000.
Angel Vargas, Aug. 1999–Mar. 2002.

Letters and Correspondence (in chronological order)

Memorandum dated February 28, 1997, from David Wilder to Alexis Quiroz (re: contract and Addendum C for 1997 minor league season).

Letter dated May 26, 1997, from Alexis Quiroz Sr. to David Wilder (re: Cubs' mistreatment of Alexis Quiroz).

Letter dated August 11, 1998, from the Chicago Cubs (re: verifying medical expenses for Alexis Quiroz's injury to be paid by Chicago Cubs).

Letter dated August 3, 1998, from Alexis Quiroz to the Chicago Cubs (re: mistreatment of Alexis Quiroz by Chicago Cubs).

Letter dated August 3, 1998, from Alexis Quiroz Sr. to the Chicago Cubs (re: mistreatment of Alexis Quiroz by Chicago Cubs).

Letter dated August 24, 1998, from Alexis Quiroz Sr. to the Chicago Cubs (re: mistreatment of Alexis Quiroz by Chicago Cubs).

Letter dated October 8, 1998, from David Wilder to Alexis Quiroz (re: terminating Alexis Quiroz's employment).

Letter dated March 29, 1999, from Roger A. Schwartz of Taylor & Associates to Alexis Quiroz (re: filing of claim with Industrial Commission of Arizona).

Letter dated April 1, 1999, from Roger A. Schwartz of Taylor & Associates to the Industrial Commission of Arizona (re: termination of Taylor & Associates representation of Alexis Quiroz).

Letter dated April 8, 1999, from the Industrial Commission of Arizona to Alexis Quiroz (re: workers' compensation claim).

Letter dated August 11, 1999, from Steven M. Gleason to Roy Krasik (re: Quiroz case).

Letter dated August 11, 1999, from Steven M. Gleason to SRISA (re: Quiroz case).

Letter dated August 17, 1999, from former SRISA officer to Steven M. Gleason (re: informing Gleason she no longer works for SRISA).

Letter dated August 18, 1999, from Steven M. Gleason to SRISA Officer (re: Quiroz case).

Letter dated September 9, 1999, from Steven M. Gleason to Alexis Quiroz (re: update on case).

Letter dated October 27, 1999, from Steven M. Gleason to Alexis Quiroz (re: status of case).

Letter dated January 31, 2000, from Roy Krasik to Jenifer Surma (re: Alexis Quiroz's medical expenses).

Letter dated February 11, 2000, from Jenifer Surma to Roy Krasik (re: Alexis Quiroz's medical expenses).

Letter dated February 22, 2000, from Roy Krasik to Alexis Quiroz (re: Cubs' response to January 31, 2000, letter from Krasik to Surma).

Letter dated April 11, 2000, from Alexis Quiroz to Steve Gleason (re: forwarding proposed letter to the Cubs for Gleason's and Stookal's review).

Letter dated April 11, 2000, from Alexis Quiroz to Jenifer Surma [mailed on April 19, 2000] (re: Cubs' mistreatment of Alexis Quiroz).

Letter dated April 25, 2000, from Marc B. Stookal to Alexis Quiroz (re: rescheduling appointment for shoulder examination by Cubs' doctor).

Letter dated April 27, 2000, from David P. Fidler to Sandy Alomar Sr. (re: requesting interview).

Letter dated April 27, 2000, from David P. Fidler to Rubén Amaro (re: requesting interview).

Letter dated April 27, 2000, from David P. Fidler to Oneri Fleita (re: requesting interview).

Letter dated April 27, 2000, from David P. Fidler to Juan Lara (re: requesting interview).

Letter dated April 27, 2000, from David P. Fidler to Patti Kargakis (re: requesting interview).

Letter dated April 27, 2000, from David P. Fidler to Roy Krasik (re: requesting interview).

Letter dated April 27, 2000, from David P. Fidler to Scott Nelson (re: requesting interview).

Letter dated April 27, 2000, from David P. Fidler to Alberto Rondón (re: requesting interview).

Letter dated April 27, 2000, from David P. Fidler to Jenifer Surma (re: requesting interview).

Letter dated April 27, 2000, from David P. Fidler to Julio Valdez (re: requesting interview).

Letter dated April 27, 2000, from David P. Fidler to David Wilder (re: requesting interview).

Letter dated May 9, 2000, from David P. Fidler to Marcelino Alcalá (re: requesting interview).

Letter dated May 9, 2000, from Arturo J. Marcano and David P. Fidler to Dr. José Luis Caicedo Yrumba (re: requesting interview).

Letter dated May 9, 2000, from David P. Fidler to Darryl Engle (re: requesting interview).

Letter dated May 9, 2000, from David P. Fidler to Drs. Dennis Goldberg and Barbara Powell (re: requesting interview).

Letter dated May 9, 2000, from David P. Fidler to Dr. Stuart Kozinn (re: requesting interview).

Letter dated May 9, 2000, from Arturo J. Marcano and David P. Fidler to Dr. Miranda (re: requesting interview).

Letter dated May 9, 2000, from David P. Fidler to Dr. Gilberto Ojeda Mirón (re: requesting interview).

Letter dated May 9, 2000, from David P. Fidler to SRISA (re: requesting interview).

Letter dated May 9, 2000, from David P. Fidler to Magdelena Schwartz (re: requesting interview).

Letter dated May 9, 2000, from David P. Fidler to Michelle Paz Soldan (re: requesting interview).

Letter dated May 18, 2000, from David P. Fidler to David Tumbas (re: requesting interview).

Letter dated May 18, 2000, from David P. Fidler to Drs. Michael Schafer and Stephen Adams (re: requesting interview).

Letter dated May 29, 2000, from David P. Fidler to Sandy Alomar Sr. (re: second interview request).

Letter dated May 29, 2000, from David P. Fidler to Rubén Amaro (re: second interview request).

Letter dated May 29, 2000, from David P. Fidler to Oneri Fleita (re: second interview request).

Letter dated May 29, 2000, from David P. Fidler to Dr. Dennis Goldberg (re: second interview request).

Letter dated May 29, 2000, from David P. Fidler to Juan Lara (re: second interview request).

Letter dated May 29, 2000, from David P. Fidler to Patti Kargakis (re: second interview request).

Letter dated May 29, 2000, from David P. Fidler to Roy Krasik (re: second interview request).

Letter dated May 29, 2000, from David P. Fidler to Scott Nelson (re: second interview request).

Letter dated May 29, 2000, from David P. Fidler to Alberto Rondón (re: second interview request).

Letter dated May 29, 2000, from David P. Fidler to Magdelena Schwartz (re: second interview request).

Letter dated May 29, 2000, from David P. Fidler to Jenifer Surma (re: second interview request).

Letter dated May 29, 2000, from David P. Fidler to Julio Valdez (re: second interview request).

Letter dated June 14, 2000, from David P. Fidler to David Wilder (re: second interview request).

Facsimile dated July 24, 2000, from Lou Melendez to David Fidler (re: requesting written interview questions).

Letter dated August 8, 2000, from Louis Melendez to Angel Vargas.

Memorandum dated September 29, 2000, from Arturo J. Marcano and David P. Fidler to Lou Melendez (re: enclosing written interview questions).

Letter [undated but sent in October 2000] from Jenifer Surma to Alexis Quiroz (re: enclosing $2,000 check).

Letter dated December 4, 2000, from Marc Stookal to Alexis Quiroz (re: forwarding medical report).

Letter dated December 20, 2000, from Arturo J. Marcano and David P. Fidler to Louis Melendez (re: Winston Acosta case).

Letter dated January 9, 2001, from Alexis Quiroz to Marc Stookal (re: responding to medical report).

Letter dated January 16, 2001, from Marc Stookal to Alexis Quiroz (re: responding to January 9th letter from Quiroz).

Facsimile dated January 19, 2001, from Kemper Insurance to Marc Stookal (re: forwarding check for medical expenses).

Letter dated January 22, 2001, from Louis Melendez to David P. Fidler (re: Winston Acosta case).

Letter dated January 23, 2001, from Marc Stookal to Alexis Quiroz (re: enclosing check for medical expenses).

Letter dated February 10, 2001, from David P. Fidler to Louis Melendez (re: Winston Acosta case).

Letter dated March 26, 2001, from Arturo J. Marcano and David P. Fidler to Louis Melendez (re: Winston Acosta case).

Letter dated March 26, 2001, from Arturo J. Marcano and David P. Fidler to Brian Cashman (re: Winston Acosta case).

Medical Reports, Receipts, etc. (in chronological order)

Prescriptions dated June 20, 1998, from Dr. William E. Mejía to Alexis Quiroz (re: bronchial pneumonia).

Receipt dated June 20, 1998, from Farmacia Ortíz Báez for prescriptions for Alexis Quiroz (re: bronchial pneumonia).

Note from the Hospital y Centro Sanitario Juan Pablo Piño dated July 25, 1998, to Alexis Quiroz (re: referring him to an orthopedic doctor for treatment of a luxation).

Receipts (#s 0081 and 0083) dated July 27, 1998, from Hospital Nuestra Señora de Regla, Baní to Alexis Quiroz (re: treatment of shoulder injury).

Receipts (#s 2243 and 2246) dated July 27, 1998, from Grupo Médico Baní, C. x A. Departamento de Rayos X to Alexis Quiroz (re: X-rays for shoulder injury).

Factura de Emergencia (#013939) dated July 27, 1998, from Dr. Miranda of the Centro Médico Regional to Alexis Quiroz (re: shoulder injury).

Receipt dated July 29, 1998, from Dr. José Luis Caicedo to Alexis Quiroz (re: medical consultation for shoulder injury).

Receipt (#10912) dated July 29, 1998, from Farmacia Granada to Alexis Quiroz (re: prescriptions for shoulder injury).

Receipt (#0214) dated July 29, 1998, from Farmacia "Vargas Maracay" C.A. to Alexis Quiroz (re: prescriptions for shoulder injury).

Medical Diagnosis dated July 31, 1998, from Dr. Marisela Torcat of the Instituto de Resonancia Magnética "La Florida" to Alexis Quiroz (re: MRI of shoulder).

Receipt (#59747) dated July 31, 1998, from Centro de Diagnóstico Biomagnetic, C.A. to Alexis Quiroz (re: shoulder injury).

Receipt (#25983) dated July 31, 1998, from Itriago, Torcat & Asociados to Alexis Quiroz (re: shoulder injury).

Medical Report dated August 3, 1998, from Dr. Gilberto Ojeda to Alexis Quiroz (re: treatment of shoulder injury).

Medical Report dated August 18, 1998 [English translation dated August 24, 1998], from Dr. Gilberto Ojeda (re: post-operative report on shoulder).

Receipt (#1165) dated August 24, 1998, from Dr. Mario Ricardo Páez Plazola to Alexis Quiroz (re: payment for rehabilitation services).

Medical Expenses List dated August 24, 1998, prepared by Alexis Quiroz and signed by Alberto Rondón.

Medical Report dated September 22, 1998, from Dr. Gilberto Ojeda to Alexis Quiroz (re: progress of recovery from surgery).

Medical Report dated November 17, 1998, from Dr. Gilberto Ojeda to Alexis Quiroz (re: progress of recovery from surgery).

Medical Report dated November 27, 1998, from Dr. José Luis Caicedo to Alexis Quiroz (re: shoulder injury).

Medical Report dated November 30, 1998, from Dr. Mario Ricardo Páez Plazola (re: rehabilitation of Alexis Quiroz).

Schedule of medical expenses dated August 24, 1998, incurred by Alexis Quiroz and signed by Alberto Rondón.

Medical Report dated March 18, 1999, from Dr. José Luis Caicedo to Alexis Quiroz (re: shoulder injury).

New Patient Visit Report dated May 3, 1999, for Alexis Quiroz by Stuart C. Kozinn, M.D. (re: examination of shoulder).

Medical Report dated October 15, 1999, from Dr. José Luis Caicedo to Alexis Quiroz (re: treatment of shoulder injury).

Medical Report dated October 24, 2000, from Dr. Michael Schafer to Oneri Fleita (re: examination of Quiroz).

Signing Bonus Checks and Pay Slips from Chicago Cubs to Alexis Quiroz (in chronological order)

Check receipt dated February 14, 1996, for $6,000 from the Chicago Cubs to Alexis Quiroz.

Paycheck stub dated June 14, 1996 ($237.50).

Paycheck stub dated June 28, 1996 ($237.50).
Paycheck stub dated July 18, 1996 ($237.50).
Paycheck stub dated August 12, 1996 ($237.50).
Paycheck stub dated August 16, 1996 ($237.50).
Paycheck stub dated September 10, 1996 ($174.17).
Paycheck stub dated July 10, 1998 ($660 for two pay periods).
Paycheck stub dated July 24, 1998 ($330.00).
Check dated October 16, 2000, for $2,000 from the Chicago Cubs to Alexis Quiroz.

Reimbursement Checks Issued by the Chicago Cubs/Kemper Insurance for Alexis Quiroz's Medical Expenses (in chronological order)

Check dated December 29, 1998, for $6,043.75.
Check dated May 13, 1999, for $1,650.91.
Check dated January 17, 2001, for $1,219.15

Miscellaneous Sources

Day, Kavanaugh & Blommel client questionnaire completed on March 24, 1999, by Alexis Quiroz.
Fact Sheet–Press Conference Alexis Quiroz issued by SRISA (undated).
FedEx receipt dated July 27, 1998, from Julio Valdez to Greg Keuter in Mesa, Arizona (re: X-rays of Alexis Quiroz's shoulder taken at hospital in San Cristóbal).
Fehr, Donald M. Comments at Symposium on Baseball in the Global Era: Economic, Legal, and Cultural Perspectives, Bloomington, Indiana, Feb. 27, 2000.
House Resolution 3288 — Fairness in Antitrust in National Sports (FANS) Act of 2001.
MLB Commissioner's Office, List of Administrator's Responsibilities, May 2000.
MLB Press Release, "MLB Honors Latin Impact in 2000 with 'Month of the Americas,'" Nov. 10, 1999.
Newspaper clippings and Internet sites of *Los Cardenales de Lara* 1997–1998 Winter League season.
NYLCare Health Plans PPO Member Identification Card for Alexis Quiroz, Group #10838.
Plummer, Rob. E-mail response dated June 18, 2001, to Steve Fainaru, "The Business of Building Ballplayers," *Washington Post*, June 17, 2001.
Pictures taken by Alexis Quiroz of the house serving as the living quarters for the Cubs' Summer League team in Santana, Dominican Republic, and of his time in Mesa, Arizona.
Prepared Statement of MLB Commissioner Allan H. (Bud) Selig, Hearing on *Baseball's Revenue Gap: Pennant for Sale?* Before the Subcommittee on Antitrust, Business Rights, and Competition of the Committee on the Judiciary, U.S. Senate, Nov. 21, 2000, S. Hrg. 106-1045, 23.
Press Release dated April 27, 1999, issued by SRISA.
Receipt dated May 19, 1999, from SRISA to Alexis Quiroz acknowledging receipt of $2,650.91 and promising return of $650.91.
Statement of Representative John Conyers Jr. (D-Ohio), Hearing on the Antitrust Exemption for Major League Baseball, Before the Committee on the Judiciary, U.S. House of Representatives, Dec. 6, 2001, 2001 WESTLAW 26188113.

Statement of Senator Mike DeWine (R-Ohio), Hearing on *Baseball's Revenue Gap: Pennant for Sale?* Before the Subcommittee on Antitrust, Business Rights, and Competition of the Committee on the Judiciary, U.S. Senate, Nov. 21, 2000, S. Hrg. 106-1045, 1.

Statement of Donald M. Fehr on Behalf of the Major League Baseball Players Association, Hearing on the Antitrust Exemption for Major League Baseball, Before the Committee of the Judiciary, U.S. House of Representatives, Dec. 6, 2001, 2001 WESTLAW 2618818.

Taylor & Associates, Firm Brochure.

Taxi cab receipt (#1141) dated July 28, 1998, from Vasopetaxis for transporting Alexis Quiroz from Nizao to Santo Domingo.

Testimony of Allan H. (Bud) Selig, Commissioner of Baseball, Hearing on the Antitrust Exemption for Major League Baseball, Before the Committee on the Judiciary, U.S. House of Representatives, Dec. 6, 2001, 2001 WESTLAW 26188117.

Tickets dated July 28, 1998, for Copa Airlines from Santo Domingo to Panama City, and for Antillean Airlines from Panama City to Caracas.

Ticket stub, Chicago Cubs v. Philadelphia Phillies, June 26, 1999.

Page numbers in italic type refer to illustrations.

ARTURO J. MARCANO GUEVARA is a lawyer from Venezuela who has worked extensively on baseball in Latin America. He is currently the International Legal Advisor to the Venezuelan Baseball Players Association and has appeared frequently in North American and Latin American media in connection with baseball issues.

DAVID P. FIDLER is an international lawyer and professor of law at Indiana University School of Law–Bloomington. He has served as an international legal consultant to the World Bank on Palestinian economic development, the World Health Organization and the U.S. Centers for Disease Control on global public health issues, the Federation of American Scientists on biological weapons, and the U.S. Department of Defense's Defense Science Board on bioterrorism.